24P: Make Your Digital Movies Look Like Hollywood

Pete Shaner and
Gerald Everett Jones

THOMSON
COURSE TECHNOLOGY
Professional ■ Trade ■ Reference

© 2005 by Pete Shaner and Gerald Everett Jones. All rights reserved. No part of this book may be reproduced or transmitted in any form or by any means, electronic or mechanical, including photocopying, recording, or by any information storage or retrieval system without written permission from Thomson Course Technology PTR, except for the inclusion of brief quotations in a review.

The Thomson Course Technology PTR logo and related trade dress are trademarks of Thomson Course Technology PTR and may not be used without written permission.

Publisher and General Manager of Course Technology PTR: Stacy L. Hiquet

Associate Director of Marketing: Sarah O'Donnell

Marketing Manager: Heather Hurley

Manager of Editorial Services: Heather Talbot

Senior Acquisitions Editor: Kevin Harreld

Senior Editor: Mark Garvey

Marketing Coordinator: Jordan Casey

Project Editor/Copy Editor: Marta Justak

Technical Reviewer: Michael Alberts

PTR Editorial Services Coordinator: Elizabeth Furbish

Interior Layout Tech: Bill Hartman

Cover Designer and Interior Illustrations: Mike Tanamachi

DVD Producer: Pete Shaner

Indexer: Kelly Talbot

Proofreader: Gene Redding

Cover Image: Courtesy of Jonathan Schwob (from a SOCAPA student production)

Canon is a registered trademark of Canon, Inc. Final Draft is a registered trademark of Final Draft, Inc. Sonicfire and SmartSound are registered trademarks of SmartSound Software, Inc. Vegas is a registered trademark of Sony Pictures Digital, Inc.

All other trademarks are the property of their respective owners.

Important: Thomson Course Technology PTR cannot provide software support. Please contact the appropriate software manufacturer's technical support line or Web site for assistance.

Thomson Course Technology PTR and the author have attempted throughout this book to distinguish proprietary trademarks from descriptive terms by following the capitalization style used by the manufacturer.

Information contained in this book has been obtained by Thomson Course Technology PTR from sources believed to be reliable. However, because of the possibility of human or mechanical error by our sources, Thomson Course Technology PTR, or others, the Publisher does not guarantee the accuracy, adequacy, or completeness of any information and is not responsible for any errors or omissions or the results obtained from use of such information. Readers should be particularly aware of the fact that the Internet is an ever-changing entity. Some facts may have changed since this book went to press.

Educational facilities, companies, and organizations interested in multiple copies or licensing of this book should contact the publisher for quantity discount information. Training manuals, CD-ROMs, and portions of this book are also available individually or can be tailored for specific needs.

ISBN: 1-59200-599-3

Library of Congress Catalog Card Number: 2004115266

Printed in Canada

05 06 07 08 09 WC 10 9 8 7 6 5 4 3 2 1

THOMSON
COURSE TECHNOLOGY
Professional ■ Trade ■ Reference

Thomson Course Technology PTR, a division of Thomson Course Technology
25 Thomson Place ■ Boston, MA 02210 ■ http://www.courseptr.com

This book is offered with a wish upon a movie star that the democratization of video will help people in every corner of our troubled world communicate better with one another and usher in an era of unprecedented accomplishment in public information and the arts.

Acknowledgments

It took a small army of dedicated professionals to make this book, including editorial, print production, and DVD production teams, as well as quite a few scrappy, tireless, and grossly underpaid movie crews. Peace, success, and happiness to you all!

The award for visionary fearlessness goes to Kevin Harreld, acquisitions editor, for seeing the value in our proposal for what seemed to others like an obscure topic in an already crowded marketplace. This was our second time around in a close, supportive relationship with editor Marta Justak, and despite our sometimes spirited discussions, we'd enthusiastically do it all over again. And the award for unstinting effort despite severe schedule compression goes to our expert print production staff: cover artist and illustrator, Michael Tanamachi, proofreader Gene Redding, layout artist Bill Hartman, and indexer Kelly Talbot.

We deeply value the support of editorial assistants Michelle Moore and Tom Page. Tom's encyclopedic knowledge of movie history is the basis for many of the anecdotes cited in the text.

We're giving the John Woo/Quentin Tarantino award for best book cover still photo by an emerging filmmaker to Jonathan Schwob and his mentor Christopher Llewellyn Reed at the School of Cinema and Performing Arts (SOCAPA, www.socapa.org). Thanks also to SOCAPA student Camila Fernandez for granting us permission to reproduce her work.

This book would be a less reliable source of information were it not for careful scrutiny by our technical editor Michael Alberts, himself an accomplished Hollywood pro (Ambidextrous Productions), whose hard-won real-world experience in this new medium includes editing Pete Shaner's HD 24p feature *Nicolas*. Michael, many thanks for taking time out from saving someone else's butt to save ours. We want to also recognize Bruce R. Cook, Ph.D., Professor of Cinema Studies, Los Angeles City College and CEO of New Millennium Productions for the many insights he shared with us. Sherwin Becker, John Cool, and Randall Peede, you will all see evidence of your mentorship in the text.

We want to especially acknowledge Richie Adams, who has assisted us with DVD menu design and contributed content for the special effects chapter. We greatly appreciate the contributions of experts Steven Douglas Smith and Sean Fairburn, whose on-camera interviews appear on the DVD. Heartfelt thanks to our redoubtable casts and crews, all the gang on the *Neo's Ring, Saturday Night,* Aqua Tan, Libby Lavella music video, and interview shoots, and especially Joshua Carter, Caleb Cindano, John C. Graas, Rick Haase, Elizabeth Hughes, Peter Meech, Bill Pitcher, Vesta Burmeister, Christine Clayburg, and Traci Shiraishi.

Thanks to our colleagues at software companies that provided demo applications for the DVD: Frank Colin, Final Draft, Inc.; Steve Foldvari, Sony Pictures Digital; and Brian Dickman and Richard Manfredi, SmartSound, Inc. We're also grateful to the manufacturers and vendors in this amazing industry that granted permission to display their products on our pages. Find their credits cited in the figure captions.

Personal thanks and praise for their virtuous attentions must go to Georja Umano, whose support is unconditional, as well as to longstanding friends and colleagues Matt Wagner and David Fugate.

About the Authors

Pete Shaner is a motion-picture writer and director who has written and directed two independent features: *Lover's Knot* and *Nicolas*, the first independent feature ever shot in 24p HD. He teaches digital video production and techniques at UCLA Extension. He has written for the TV series *JAG* and worked as the on-set technical advisor for *A Few Good Men*. Shaner has appeared several times as a guest on TechTV's *Call for Help*, where he explains digital video camcorder and production techniques.

Gerald Everett Jones has written more than 20 books on computer and business topics. His screenplay *Ballpoint* was accepted into the Screenwriter's Lab of the Independent Feature Project/West. He is a past director of the Independent Writers of Southern California and is a member of the Dramatists Guild and the Writers Guild of America. Jones has professional expertise in computer graphics, industrial video, and Web site development and served as writer and executive producer of the *InnRoom Shopping Network*.

You can contact the authors at www.lapuerta.tv.

Contents at a Glance

	Introduction	xv
chapter 1	Getting the 24P Mindset	1
chapter 2	The Essence of Film Look	9
chapter 3	Thinking Like a Producer	23
chapter 4	Thinking Like a Cinematographer	41
chapter 5	Thinking Like a Sound Designer	71
chapter 6	Thinking Like a Director	99
chapter 7	Thinking Like a Veteran Editor	129
chapter 8	Thinking Like a Special Effects Wizard	147
chapter 9	Thinking Like a Distributor	167
chapter 10	Thinking Ahead	195
	Index	205

Contents

Introduction xv

chapter 1
Getting the 24P Mindset 1
What's the Catch? 2
A Painterly Analogy 2
The Camcorder Revolution 2
Why Bother with 24P? 4
Old Mindsets: News Style and Film Style 5
What's Changed? 6
The New Mindset 6

chapter 2
The Essence of Film Look 9
What Makes Film Look Like Film? 9
    Excitement of Motion Blur 11
    Vividness of Contrast Range 13
    Rich Rendition of Color 14
    Depth of Field and Focus Control 14
    Shape of the Viewing Screen 15
    Sharpness and Detail 17
    Texture of Imagery 18
    The Theatrical Viewing Experience 18
What Are the Options? 19
    Shoot in 24P 19
    Shoot in 60i 19
    Shoot in 30P 20
    Shoot in PAL 20
Putting the 24P Mindset to Work 21

chapter 3
Thinking Like a Producer 23
Film Out or Film Look? 24
Thinking Through the Film-Look Factors 25
    Motion Blur 26
    Exposure Latitude 26
    Color Rendition 30
    Depth of Field 30
    Aspect Ratio 31
    Resolution 31
    Grain and Jitter 32
    Camera Movement 32

Producer's Checklist 33
1. You need a crew; you can't "run and gun" by yourself. 33
2. Turn off automatic camera controls. 34
3. Support the camera. 35
4. Paint with light. 35
5. Move the camera as you shoot. 35
6. Capture clean dialogue. 36
7. Build rich audio environments in post. 37
8. Don't overdo transitions and special effects. ... 38
9. Plan ahead for distribution. 38

Shoot Test Rolls 39

chapter 4
Thinking Like a Cinematographer 41
A DP's View of Camcorder Design and Operation .42
24P or Not? 43
Lenses 44
Viewfinder and LCD Screen 46
Automatic Controls and Ease of Use 47
Exposure Control 49
Monitor Support 51
Achieving White Balance 52
Focusing and Zooming 53
Shutter Controls 54

Other Auto Features 56
Semiautomatic Modes 56
Image Stabilization 56
Video Gain 56
Special Auto Modes 57
Tape Speed Selection 57
Digital Effects 57
Achieving Film-Look Lighting 58

The Ideal of Three-Point Lighting 58
Applying the Three-Point Principle 60

Motivating the Light Source 60
Achieving Acceptable Contrast Range 61
Establishing a Mood 61
Lighting Guidelines for Film-Look DPs 61
Favor Softer Light 62
Solve Lighting Problems by Reducing Rather Than Adding Light 62
Control Color Temperature 63
Using Filters and Gels 64
Watch Overhead Lights and Reflections 65
Reduce Light on the Background 66
Add Interest and Glamour with Extra Lighting Touches 66

Other Techniques for Leading the Eye 68
Color 69
Motion and Exceptional Objects 69

The Purpose of It All 69

chapter 5
Thinking Like a Sound Designer ... 71
DME: The Three Ingredients ... 72
The Hyperrealism of the Movies ... 72
- What Music Can Do ... 72
- Concentric Regions of Effects ... 74

Getting Good Production Sound ... 75
- Matching Microphones to the Setup ... 75
- Rigging and Using a Boom Mic ... 76
- Rigging and Using a Shortie ... 81
- Rigging and Using Lavs ... 82
- Rigging and Using Wireless Mics ... 83
- Using Dual-System Sound ... 84
- Eliminating Unwanted Production Noise ... 85
- Avoiding ADR ... 87

The Audio Postproduction Process ... 87
- Planning Layered Soundtracks ... 87
- Cleaning and Separating Dialogue Tracks ... 89
- Covering Audio Mistakes ... 90

Recording ADR ... 90
- Creating a Spotting Table ... 92
- Where to Get Music ... 93
- Music Editing Tips ... 94
- How to Get Sound Effects ... 95
- The Mix-Down Process ... 96
- Wizards of Audio Know This ... 97

chapter 6
Thinking Like a Director ... 99
Selecting Material ... 101
- Fewer Locations, Fewer Actors ... 101
- Less Talk, More Action ... 102

Production Planning and Scheduling ... 103
Planning Your Shots ... 106
- The Elements of Shot Design ... 109
- Blocking the Action ... 112
- How Much Structure? ... 112

Graphic Tools for Visualizing the Story ... 113
- Storyboard ... 113
- Shot Plan Drawing ... 114
- Deriving the Shot List ... 114

Preserving Continuity ... 115
- Stage Line ... 116
- Screen Direction ... 117
- Time Dependencies ... 118

What's Your Shooting Ratio? ... 119
Improvisation, Casting, and Rehearsal ... 120
Transportation, Setup, and Logistics ... 122
Controlling the Set ... 122
Slating and Timecode ... 124
Getting Elements for Digital Effects ... 125
It's All the Director's Fault ... 127

chapter 7
Thinking Like a Veteran Editor 129
An Overview of NLE 130
Technical Editing Issues in 24P 135
- Timecode 136
- Pulldown 137
- Pulldown Removal and Deinterlacing 138
- Interlacing and Tearing 138
- Rendering and Prerendering 139

Converting from 60I to 24P in Post 140
Using an Edit Decision List (EDL) 141
Editing Hollywood-Style 141
- Split Edits 142
- Jump Cuts 143
- Speed Ramping 144
- Match Cutting 144

When Is the Final Cut Final? 144

chapter 8
Thinking Like a Special Effects Wizard 147
Applying Film-Look Filters 148
Manipulating Time and Space 149
- 2D Images 150
- 2½D Imagery 151
- 3D Space 153
- Applying the Same Effect to a Sequence of Frames 154

The Art and Craft of Combining Imagery 155
- Improvising Effects with Luminance Keying 156

Using Analog Video and Film Sources 157
Color Correction 159
- Fine-Tuning Color for Broadcast Television 159
- Tweaking Color on Film 160

The Color Correction Process 160
- Primary Color Correction 161
- Secondary Color Correction 161
- Spot Color Correction 162

Achieving Smooth-Scrolling Titles 162
Cooking Up Some Eye Candy 163
- Time Bending 164

If They Asked Us, Could We Write the Book? 165

chapter 9
Thinking Like a Distributor 167
We Ask Once More: Do You Really Need Film Output? 167
The Economics of Commercial Theatrical Distribution 168
Using a Sales Agent to Approach Distributors 170
What Deliverables Do Distributors Require? 171
- Sample List of Deliverables 172
- Copyright: A Crucial Issue 174

Preparing Video Output for Different Distribution
    Media 175
Printing to Tape 175
    Copying a DV Cassette to VHS Tape 177
    Videotape Mastering for Duplication 178
Burning a CD 178
    Creating a VCD 179
Creating Video Files for the Internet 179
Authoring a DVD 181
    Levels of DVD Players 181
    DVD Structure 182
    Disc Manufacturing Considerations 184
Archiving Your Project 186
Submitting to Broadcast Television Networks 186
Producing for a Corporation 187
Working with a Film Recording Service 187
    Kinescope 188
    Flying Spot 189
    Laser 190
Summary of Film-Out Technical Requirements ...190
Welcome to Showbiz 194

chapter 10
Thinking Ahead 195
Seven Predictions About the Future of Digital
    Filmmaking 195
    Digital projection in theaters will eliminate the
        need for distribution of film release prints. 195
    Shooting on film will be around longer than
        film projectors. 198
    Camcorder and NLE technology will follow
        Moore's Law. 199
    When some precise requirements are met,
        controversy will end. 200
    The theatrical experience will be the same,
        yet different. 201
    Big studios and big networks will continue
        to exist. 202
    But no one has the faintest idea how the
        democratization of video will change
        the world. 203

Index...205

Introduction

Empowering a New Generation of Filmmakers

People in the movie business spend a lot of time waiting for their cell phones to ring.

They're waiting and hoping for some big-shot studio executive to commit millions of dollars of other people's money to "green light" a project that will employ them.

Relatively few of these talented folks will be lucky enough to get that call, and fewer still will find employment in their chosen profession on anything like a regular basis.

Eventually, many of them will decide to study for the real estate brokers' exam.

You Can Stop Waiting, Start Shooting

In 1995, the situation began to change.

That summer, Sony Corporation introduced the DCR-VX100 Mini DV camcorder. Three years later, Danish filmmaker Thomas Vinterberg and his Dogma 95 creative team used a DV camcorder to make *The Celebration* (aka *Festen*), a feature-length movie. Many industry pros publicly applauded Vinterberg and his colleague Lars Von Trier, but privately thought them eccentric experimenters. Then, in 2001, Alan Cumming and Jennifer Jason Leigh costarred in and co-directed *The Anniversary Party,* also shot with the VX100. Transferred to film, this movie played in worldwide theatrical release. When audiences didn't ask for their money back, some of those skeptical pros started to worry about where this was all going.

Meanwhile, hi-def (HD) video technology had been evolving, too. Director George Lucas informed Sony Corporation that if it would build an HD camcorder that captured imagery at the motion-picture frame rate (24fps), he would use it to shoot his next feature, *Star Wars Episode II: Attack of the Clones.*

Sony developed the camcorder, complete with cinema-style lenses engineered by Panavision, the maker of movie cameras. When the camcorder was in its final stages of development, coauthor Pete Shaner was in preproduction for his feature *Nicolas*. Through a contact at Panavision, Pete and his crew were able to obtain a test model of what eventually became known as the Sony CineAlta camcorder, the first HD unit to shoot 24p (24fps with progressive scanning), a mode that more nearly matches the way motion-picture cameras capture images on film.

Trained at USC film school, Pete could already be regarded as a Hollywood pro. He had previously written, directed, and produced a commercially successful feature, *Lover's Knot* (1996), shot on 35mm film. Using the CineAlta, he and cinematographer Steven Douglas Smith shot *Nicolas*, the world's first HD 24p feature in 2001. (You'll find clips from the movie and interviews with the crew on the DVD supplied with this book.) Not long after shooting on *Nicolas* wrapped, Lucas shot his movie (which we understand is also quite good).

On completing *Episode II*, Lucas told the press he figured he saved more than $2 million on film stock, processing, and transfers to video (for editing) by shooting digitally. That's *four times* what it cost Pete to make his feature. Clearly, the economics of moviemaking were changing.

Lucas went on to affirm that he would never again shoot a film, on film.

More recently, in 2004, another breakthrough occurred. Panasonic introduced the AG-DVX100 camcorder, a Mini DV unit featuring 24p mode. Whereas the CineAlta is priced around $100,000, the DVX100 sells for about $3,000.

Several other prosumer-level 24p camcorders are now on the market. Their picture quality is about one-fourth that of the CineAlta, which rivals 35mm film. So, it's fair to wonder, is DV good enough for a feature film?

Ask the filmmakers of *Open Water, Chuck & Buck,* and *Pieces of April*—to name just a few of many DV features that have been in commercial release.

Like their big-budget counterparts, some DV features have been released on film, while others have gone straight to tape and DVD. And also like studio pictures, some have made money, and some haven't.

The point is that the cost of entry has dropped dramatically, and low-budget productions are very much in the game. *Open Water* is not *Star Wars II* or even *Nicolas* in the scope of its budget or production values, but it was all the rage at the Sundance Film Festival, and filmmaker Chris Kentis didn't have to ask a studio's permission to make it.

To be blunt: You don't have to wait for the phone to ring or for someone else to provide you with financing. If you can afford to buy or rent a camcorder, a computer, and some other inexpensive gear, you can make a movie.

Sure, There Are Lots of Books on DV...
What's so different about this book?

Some Hollywood pros regard DV as little more than a toy. When DV was first introduced, there was a lot of media hype about how easy it is for non-pros to get results. You don't need lights, they said. You don't need a crew, and you can just run and gun until you drop.

24P: Make Your Digital Movies Look Like Hollywood

Not so fast, hotshot. If you use a camcorder carelessly, as if it were little more than a toy, you'll get results that look like home movies.

And some of the DV features we mentioned, while they were no doubt shot more carefully, don't have that Hollywood look. Why? Is it just that DV is inherently crummy?

We say, emphatically no.

What the Hollywood veterans are in no hurry to tell you is that, if you know what they know, if you shoot the way they do, and if you care passionately for the craft of moviemaking, your digital movie product could be pretty enough to truly make them sweat.

The maker of *Nicolas* and a guy who writes tech books for people who don't talk tech will tell you how.

Or pop the companion DVD in a player, and we'll *show* you how.

But you'll still need your cell phone…

…so you can order pizza for your crew.

How to Use the DVD

The DVD that accompanies this book provides examples of the kinds of projects you can produce using 24p technology to create film-look video. You'll find examples of footage originated in-camera at 24p, as well as 60i footage converted to 24p in postproduction. Most of it was shot and edited in DV format, but you'll also find some clips from *Nicolas,* which was shot and finished in HD 24p. (Playback from the DVD is limited to standard TV resolution, however.) With the exception of *Nicolas,* which was edited on Avid, the editing was done using Apple Final Cut Pro, and the DVD was authored using Adobe After Effects and Apple Motion and DVD Studio Pro. We used Red Giant Magic Bullet Suite for the postproduction 24p conversions, and the music for all clips except those from *Nicolas* was scored using SmartSound Sonicfire Pro.

To watch the movies, insert the DVD into a computer that has a DVD-R or -RW drive (such as a Mac SuperDrive), or into a set-top DVD player. Mac computers require DVD Player or comparable software. Windows machines must have Windows Media Player or a comparable application. You can access all clips through the on-screen menus.

You can pick up a lot just by watching the shorts and interviews. If you want to delve deeper, you'll probably find a more detailed explanation in the book. If you still have questions, send the authors an email at info@lapuerta.tv or check the Reader Support section of our Web site at www.lapuerta.tv.

The disc also contains demonstration software. You can only access these files on a computer equipped with a DVD-R or –RW drive. On a Mac, use the Finder application to explore the disc and open the files. On a PC, use Windows Explorer. The applications are provided in both Mac and PC versions, with the exception of Sony Vegas, which is available only for computers that run Windows.

chapter 1
Getting the 24P Mindset

What if the tools for making a high-quality commercial movie could fit into the trunk of your car? Into a backpack, even? And what if all the camera and editing gear you needed cost less than, say, $10,000 (and far less to rent for a shoot or edit)?

Perhaps you'd dig that unsold screenplay out of the drawer and get serious about shooting it—your way.

Perhaps you'd stop begging for big bucks from indifferent studio moguls and overcautious network executives and just get your story made—your way.

Perhaps you'd make a classier product for your budget-strapped commercial client, shoot it her way, and invest the profits—your way.

Perhaps you'd stop paying attention to the naysayers who advise that digital video is "not quite good enough," and you'd resolve to pioneer a new medium, in ways you don't yet dream possible—your way, of course.

Those magic tools exist today, right here, right now. Media industry pundits have been saying for years that DV would mean the "Democratization of Video." But most of them don't have a clue how immense and far-reaching its impact will be on the world.

Think about it: If you don't need their money, they can't tell you what to say.

What's the Catch?

Producing a digital movie isn't just about learning how to use cheap tools of production. Not only must you get your movie made, you have to get distribution.

And there's the rub.

Simply put, your product must look as slick as anything the studios or networks can produce. Audiences will expect it to have a "film look." If it does, and if your story is compelling, the mega distributors won't care what tools you used.

They will be too busy calculating their margins from a hit movie they acquired for peanuts.

> **WHAT *IS* 24P?**
>
> The relatively new digital video mode called 24p delivers two important qualities of film-look video: 1) A rate of capturing images that matches the 24 frames per second (fps) of motion pictures, and 2) progressive scanning (p), which grabs an entire frame in a single pass, more nearly the way film cameras do.
>
> However, to make 24p look not only like film but also like a commercial-quality motion picture takes considerable artistry and skill.

A Painterly Analogy

To use an analogy with fine-art painting, think of 24p as one type of brush. Let's say your goal is to create a gorgeous oil painting (film look), worthy of the old masters. But, primarily for economic reasons, you can't use the medium of oil paint (film). You want to find a way to achieve much the same look with water-based acrylics (video).

Why, you might ask, wouldn't I prefer instead to use acrylics as a medium unto itself? Why try so hard to make video look like something it's not?

That's a very good question. And the simple answer is that buyers of paintings equate meticulous oil-based techniques with quality. Not only will they pay more for the product, they might not even consider anything done in the acrylic medium worthy of their attention, much less their money.

To dispense with the analogy, if you want to make a movie worthy of commercial theatrical distribution—or even slick enough to turn heads on the festival circuit—you'd better make it look like film.

The Camcorder Revolution

First and foremost, 24p is a switch on some new camcorders. The first cameras to offer it were high-definition (HD) models, ranging in price from about $50,000 to $100,000 (see Figures 1.1 and 1.2). Then several prosumer digital video (DV) models followed, ranging from $3,000 to $5,000 (see Figures 1.3 and 1.4). Then came a hybrid format, HDV, which records compressed high-def images on a MiniDV cassette, along with camcorders in the prosumer price range (see Figures 1.5 and 1.6).

> Technically, DV is a specific video recording format, as are VHS, Betacam, and Digital-8. The generic term *digital video* can refer to any aspect of the technology, including the recording formats DV, HD, and HDV, as well as proprietary variants such as DVCAM and HDCAM (Sony), Digital-S (JVC), and DVCPRO (Panasonic). In this book, when we're referring to the recording format, we'll write it as DV. When we spell it out as digital video, you'll know we're talking about the technology.

24P: Make Your Digital Movies Look Like Hollywood

Figure 1.1
The Sony CineAlta camcorder (HDW series) was developed at the request of George Lucas, who used it to shoot *Star Wars Episode II: Attack of the Clones* in 24p HD. However, before the camera was delivered to Lucas, coauthor Pete Shaner and his crew used it to make the first 24p HD feature film, *Nicolas*. (Photo courtesy Sony Electronics, Inc.)

Figure 1.2
The Panasonic AJ-HDC27F is an HD camcorder that is marketed as the VariCam because it lets the operator vary the frame rate, permitting special effects such as in-camera slow motion, as well as 24p. (Photo courtesy Matsushita Corporation of America)

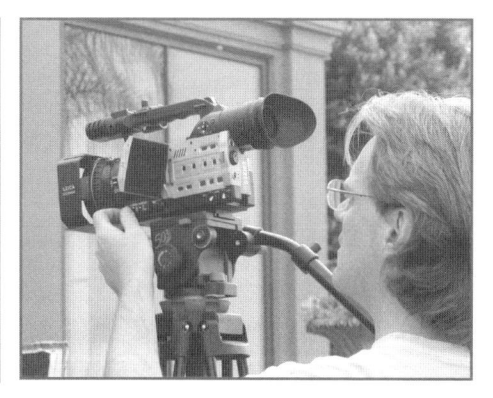

Figure 1.3
The first prosumer 24p DV camcorder was the Panasonic AG-DVX100. It features a Leica zoom lens that is not removable, so it's the only choice you have with this camera.

Figure 1.4
The Canon XL1 DV camcorder has become the mainstay of indie filmmakers. It accepts interchangeable lenses that use the standard Canon mount. More recently, the company introduced the XL2 model, which added 24p mode to its extensive list of features.

Figure 1.5
The JVC JY-HD10U was the first HDV camcorder on the market. It captures high-definition imagery and then compresses it in MPEG2 format for recording on a DV cassette. It does not have a 24p mode and records HDV in a 720-line format. (Photo courtesy JVC Professional Products Company)

Figure 1.6
The Sony HVR-Z1U shoots HDV, and among its mode selections is a 24fps mode called CineFrame. (Photo courtesy Sony Electronics, Inc.)

1. Getting the 24P Mindset

> Coauthor Pete Shaner wrote, produced, and directed his feature movie *Nicolas* (2002) with an early production model of the Sony CineAlta camcorder. Months later, George Lucas began shooting *Episode II*. So Shaner's movie was the first feature shot in 24p. Stills from *Nicolas* are included in the "Color Plates" section of this book, and clips can be found (in letterbox DV format) on the accompanying DVD.

In this book, we'll discuss all these formats, but we'll concentrate on DV because it's the most affordable and yet can deliver remarkably stunning results. Along the way, we'll also discuss some of the implications of 24p technology for HD and for HDV.

> An example of an early DV feature was *Anniversary Party* (2001), directed by Alan Cumming and Jennifer Jason Leigh. Although no DV camcorders were available in the DV format at the time, the frame rate of the movie has a decidedly filmed look. That's because it was shot in British PAL television broadcast format, which has a frame rate of 25fps. For years afterwards, indie filmmakers in North America created a strong demand at movie equipment rental houses for PAL cameras so they could experiment with film-look video.

Why Bother with 24P?

Making video look like film is one reason, and a good one, to consider 24p equipment and techniques. But that's not the only reason. The others include:

Film out. The 24p process can simplify the technicalities and expense involved in achieving film out, or transfer of digital video production to film for theatrical distribution. Although commercial theaters are expected to convert to digital projection eventually, a film-less distribution system isn't yet a reality. Digital projection is currently limited to some theaters in major U.S. cities. And for foreign theatrical markets, distribution on film is the rule and will likely remain so for years to come. So producing for the film medium—even though you may be using all-digital production methods—is still an important consideration for the serious filmmaker.

Independent theatrical marketing. Film festivals have become the primary way for indie filmmakers without studio backing to break into the commercial market. These days, all film festivals accept submissions in digital format, making costly transfers to film unnecessary as a condition of submission. Although some people in the movie industry contend that a filmmaker will stand a better chance of securing a distribution deal with a film negative already in the can, going to the expense of film transfer without the underwriting of a distributor is an expensive gamble. A more practical approach is to make the product look as much like film as possible for purposes of festival and exhibition and private screenings for potential buyers. Ideally, and we admit that it doesn't always work out this way, it may be possible to defer the hassle and expense of film transfer until a distribution deal is in place. It stands to reason that the closer you get to a film look in your video product, the less nervous your potential buyers are likely to be about how good the film-out product will look.

Archival purposes. For technical reasons that have to do with the legacy of film-to-video conversion for television, a 24fps video format is the best all-around choice for later conversion to any of the other formats, whether film or video.

DVD release. As a common practice, DVD manufacturers convert commercial filmed movies to 24p video. Saving just six frames per second from a video's usual 30 can significantly increase the running time that can be fitted on the disc. And it also gives the mastering technicians the option of increasing the variable bit rate (data bits per second) to improve the quality of selected sequences. In particular, action sequences and scenes with complex backgrounds can benefit from an increase in bit rate (whereas encoding the entire movie at the higher rate would exceed the capacity of the disc). The DVD player takes care of converting the video back to the 60i standard that NTSC television requires.

Old Mindsets: News Style and Film Style

Video and film have evolved not only as separate technologies but also as separate cultures, each with its own standards, practices, and trade jargon. The following descriptions might be oversimplified and extreme, but they encapsulate the traditions and mindsets of these two distinct cultures.

News-style camera operators have traditionally been lone-gun soldiers of fortune. Carrying camcorders equipped with onboard microphone and photoflood spotlight, they venture out to capture breaking news in the street. The crucial objective is to get the story on tape. It's preferable to get any shot at all than to miss the event because you're waiting for the light to be just right or fine-tuning the camera settings. And the deadlines are short. There's little or no time for postproduction artistry. No sooner does the news videographer return to the station than the footage must be quickly reviewed and edited for that evening's broadcast. Or it might simply be beamed up from a location truck to a microwave tower or satellite so that it can be relayed to the network and around the world instantaneously.

Inside the television studio, the setups for broadcast have evolved from the traditional practices of live television. Multiple cameras (typically, three or more) are trained on the newscasters (or game show participants or soap actors), all of them feeding simultaneously into a control booth, where the director makes on-the-fly decisions about switching "the feed" (or the recording) from one camera to another. On the set, lighting is not so much aesthetic as practical: Lighting levels must be flat, working equally well from any camera angle.

Film-style method is totally different. The scenes of a movie are shot single camera and out of sequence, depending on the availability of movie stars, locations, special equipment, and prevailing weather. The crew is the size of a small army. Following the meticulous instructions of a cinematographer, they set up each shot so that the light is nearly perfect from just one vantage point, the camera's. Even modest-sized productions take about six weeks to shoot. And postproduction, often including elaborate soundtracks and special visual effects, can take many, many months.

In Chapter 2, we'll explore some of the technical reasons why video and film imagery look so different, as well as how audiences have come to expect a distinctly different type of experience from each of these media.

What's Changed?

With the advent of computer-based work methods over the last two decades or so, video and film technologies have begun to converge. Today, it's unheard of to produce a motion picture without employing a great deal of video technology. Videotape recording and monitors are used on the film set to support instant playback so the director can critique takes with the cast and crew. After shooting, film dailies are converted to digital video computer files so that the editor can do his assembly on a computer-based nonlinear editing (NLE) system. The editing and postproduction are done entirely in the digital realm, just short of the final step of creating a film negative and striking release prints. In fact, it's become increasingly rare for the original camera negative to be physically cut at all. Instead, the lab transfers the footage, according to a log of the editor's decisions, to a high-resolution computer file called a *digital intermediate (DI)*. So-called opticals (once done photographically), such as titles and special effects are added to the DI as computer-generated imagery (CGI).

So, you see, most of the film process is already gone—except for the shooting and the releasing.

However, the two cultures, video and film, remain. And their mindsets persist. From time to time in this book, we'll refer to news style or film style as we give examples of traditional approaches and work practices and how they relate to the 24p mindset.

The New Mindset

So different is the mindset of 24p and film-look video from traditional video and film practices that the authors will boldly state:

Making a movie in 24p is as different from DV as DV is from 35mm film.

And don't forget HD and HDV.

With all the creative and technical choices involved in these digital media, you can't keep doing things the way you learned them in film school, in the field with the video news crew or on the film set.

In effect, to choose 24p and all the choices that inevitably follow, you must go back to film school, thinking through the entire production and post-production process with a new mindset. Some of the tried and true techniques from a century of filmmaking and a half-century of television production still work and work well.

Others are about as useful today as a slide rule, a steno machine, or a typewriter.

Now, you may be a working producer, cinematographer, director, or editor. And you know your role. Or you may be a student or aspiring filmmaker, and you don't yet know how you'll make your mark. But no matter what your role has been, to be effective in the new media, you should understand the mindset from the perspectives of all the key people in the process.

For example, if you're the director, you'll do a better job if you know what the editor needs and expects you to deliver. If you're the producer, you won't get very far if you don't know what equipment the cinematographer will want you to provide.

That's why we've organized this book according to the chronological sequence of production, each chapter examining the film-look digital process from the point of view of the professional who is most involved in or most responsible for each stage of production.

When we're done, you'll know how to do it the new way, from start to finish.

Then you can set about finding *your* way.

chapter 2
The Essence of Film Look

Some filmmakers who have turned to shooting digital video simply don't bother with film look at all. Apparently they reason that video is its own medium, with its own creative aesthetic and technical constraints. (See the accompanying sidebar "The Vow of Chastity.")

The authors respect the integrity and efforts of any artist who seeks to define his own style. But, as we pointed out in Chapter 1, the commercial reality of worldwide cinema distribution is that both distributors and audiences expect movies to have a certain polished look.

In this chapter, we'll describe the distinct technical factors that comprise film look, and we'll point out how well or how badly these can be simulated in the realm of digital video.

What Makes Film Look Like Film?

An important decision before you do any shooting is whether you are producing for film or simply want to achieve a film look. Here are the key factors that give a filmed motion picture its characteristic look:

- Excitement of motion blur
- Vividness of contrast range
- Rich rendition of color
- Depth of field and focus control
- Shape of the viewing screen
- Sharpness and detail
- Texture of imagery
- The theatrical viewing experience

Founded in Copenhagen in 1995, DOGMA 95 (aka Dogme95) is an artistic movement among director-videographers who want nothing to do with traditional Hollywood film look. The first DV feature produced according to this manifesto was *The Celebration* (aka *Festen,* 1998), directed by Thomas Vinterberg. If you're enticed by this style of production, read this chapter, then rent this movie on DVD and note how it does or doesn't meet your own expectations as a movie fan.

The Vow of Chastity

I swear to submit to the following set of rules drawn up and confirmed by DOGMA 95:

1. Shooting must be done on location. Props and sets must not be brought in (if a particular prop is necessary for the story, a location must be chosen where this prop is to be found).
2. The sound must never be produced apart from the images or vice versa. (Music must not be used unless it occurs where the scene is being shot.)
3. The camera must be hand held. Any movement or immobility attainable in the hand is permitted. (The film must not take place where the camera is standing; shooting must take place where the film takes place.)
4. The film must be in color. Special lighting is not acceptable. (If there is too little light for exposure, the scene must be cut or a single lamp attached to the camera.)
5. Optical work and filters are forbidden.
6. The film must not contain superficial action. (Murders, weapons, etc. must not occur.)
7. Temporal and geographical alienation is forbidden. (That is to say that the film takes place here and now.)
8. Genre movies are not acceptable.
9. The film format must be Academy 35mm.
10. The director must not be credited.

Furthermore, I swear as a director to refrain from personal taste! I am no longer an artist. I swear to refrain from creating a "work," as I regard the instant as more important than the whole. My supreme goal is to force the truth out of my characters and settings. I swear to do so by all the means available and at the cost of any good taste and any aesthetic considerations.

Thus I make my VOW OF CHASTITY.

Copenhagen, Monday 13 March 1995

On behalf of DOGMA 95, Lars von Trier, Thomas Vinterberg

Copyright © 1995 by Lars von Trier and Thomas Vinterberg www.dogme95.com.

Excitement of Motion Blur

In general, fast-moving subjects leave a blur on film that video lacks. The reasons, and the effect on viewers, are rooted in the histories of each medium.

A video camera, whether analog or digital, takes 60 still pictures every second. While its frame rate is 30fps, it captures each frame in two passes. Each pass, or field, samples an alternating set of scan lines (see Figure 2.1). In televisions and video displays, the two sets of scan lines are interlaced to produce a single frame. This scanning mode is designated 60i.

> Remember that 60i means 60 *fields* per second, not frames. In some publications you'll see conventional video referred to as 30i. In such cases, the 30 refers to *frames*, not fields. To simplify matters in this book, we use 60i consistently to refer to the NTSC scanning mode.

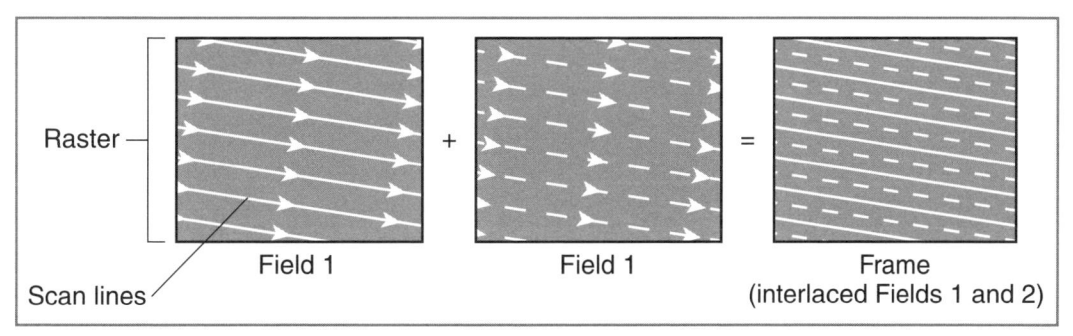

Figure 2.1
The scheme of interlaced scanning is a holdover from early television broadcasting. The scanning electron beam in a television picture tube switches on during a left-to-right trace that causes photosensitive phosphors coating the inside of the tube to glow as visible scan lines. The beam is switched off during the right-to-left trace (called *horizontal flyback*) and during the bottom-to-top trace (called *vertical flyback*). A camcorder's CCD circuitry must generate the same scanning pattern to capture each video frame. By contrast, 24p and all progressive scanning modes capture every scan line in an entire frame in a single pass.

This scheme of interlacing was developed in the early television era because the phosphors in picture tubes couldn't hold an image long enough for a full frame to be scanned in a single pass. By refreshing the screen twice as often, interlacing made the picture flicker less. (The first sets still flickered badly.)

> The television standards of 50i in Britain and 60i in North America don't have anything to do with aesthetic choices. They're the direct result of earlier decisions by governments and utility companies on the frequency of electrical power. Alternating current in Britain is 50Hz, and it's 60Hz in North America. The developers of the first television sets used the cycling in the power line to synchronize scanning in the picture tube.

Although current display technologies don't require interlacing to produce flicker-free pictures, the scheme hasn't changed. Partly in response to strong federal regulation of broadcasting, the television industry chose not to make any changes that would render older television receivers obsolete.

Because video captures moving subjects fast enough to greatly reduce motion blurring, it conveys a feeling of passivity and stillness, even when its subjects are moving. Audiences perceive video as a "live" medium, an electronic eyewitness.

> Polish émigré novelist Jerzy Kosinki coined a phrase for the eyewitness effect of video— *Being There,* the title of his novel about the culture of electronic mass media (later made into a feature film starring Peter Sellars).

Early film captured motion at 18fps, as slowly as it was possible to do so without being unacceptably jerky. The objective was to minimize consumption of expensive film footage. When talkies were developed in the 1920s, motion-picture engineers discovered that 18fps was too slow for acceptable audio reproduction from the new soundtracks. So the speed of 24fps was adopted, the minimum at which dialogue and music wouldn't sound tremulous.

Today, computer technologists speak in terms of the sampling rate at which digital circuits take readings of analog waveforms, such as light or sound. The higher the sampling rate, the more realistic and true-to-life the translation to digital will be.

So, in terms of sampling rate, the video rate of 60 fields per second is more than twice as faithful to reality as film's 24 frames per second.

When it comes to motion capture, video is more realistic than film. In artistic terms, the filmed imagery is more of an abstraction because it samples reality much less often. Viewers therefore perceive film more as a historical record than a current event, more as contrived art than as unvarnished news.

IS THERE A CORRELATION BETWEEN FRAME RATE AND BRAIN WAVES?

The 24fps motion-picture rate and the 30fps video rate evolved for technical reasons, apparently unrelated to the debate that rages today about aesthetic differences between these media. However, bloggers at some filmmaking Web sites have speculated that there may be some deeper correlation with human perception and brain waves. (We don't know of any scientific studies as yet.)

Humans can perceive an animated sequence of still images as continuous motion because images persist briefly in the brain even after the signals from the retina of the eye have ceased. This phenomenon is called "persistence of vision" or "flicker fusion." Some people have theorized that viewers begin to sense flicker, although perhaps not consciously, at about 28fps. If that were true, then it would explain why viewers might perceive film as somehow "artificial" because its flicker is perceptible at a subliminal level. And they perceive video as "real" because the frame rate is just high enough for flicker to disappear completely.

The way film captures motion is particularly apparent in the fight scenes of action-adventure movies. As the sword comes down, it leaves a telltale blur in its path.

Audiences have come to associate this blurring with a sense of artificially heightened reality. In a word, motion blur is exciting.

Vividness of Contrast Range

The difference in brightness between the lightest and the darkest areas of an image is its contrast range. Limited contrast range is probably the biggest limitation of present-day video technology as compared to film. Controlling contrast—and using the limited range effectively—is probably the biggest challenge in achieving film-look video.

Contrast range is expressed as a ratio, about 100:1 in the case of film. That is, the white areas in a single frame of film can be as much as 100 times brighter than the black areas. Even the best video cameras can record only about 30:1.

> You'll see widely different published numbers for the contrast ranges of film and video. Adherents of film may toss around numbers like 1,000:1, for example, to emphasize the difference. The ratios don't necessarily make good common-sense comparisons because the brightness scale is logarithmic, marked off in inverse powers of 10. So, the difference between 1,000:1 and 100:1 is just one tick on that scale. Contrast range expressed this way as a ratio of brightness is important mainly for learning the concept. In practice, it's easier to think of it as a range of possible exposure settings on a camera. In general, film allows a range of about eight f-stops. Video lets you use about five. In the terminology of cinematography, this range is called *exposure latitude*. In practice, exposure latitude varies by particular film stock or CCD. Technical improvements are being made all the time, so our five f-stop rule isn't hard and fast.

On an even more practical level, the difference comes down to how much detail you can see in an image. In particular, it's much more difficult to overexpose film. Even the brightest areas of an image can retain some detail and shading. It's not that whites look whiter and blacks look blacker on film. Pure white is white and pure black is black in both media. An overexposed white area on film is clear, permitting virtually all of the projector's light to pass through. A totally black area is opaque, blocking the projection beam. In video, an overexposed white area is said to be *blown out*, or 100 percent saturated. A totally black area contains no picture data and is effectively zero percent saturated.

In video, blowing out the whites happens all too easily (see Color Plate 1). And if you *stop down* (decrease the exposure) to retain more detail in the bright areas, the shadows will lose all detail and become "muddy" or just pitch black.

Dealing with contrast range is largely a matter of artistic and technically skillful lighting. We'll have a lot more to say about it in Chapter 4.

Rich Rendition of Color

A video term that describes the range of colors a camera can see is its *color space*, which has to do with encoding schemes developed decades ago for color television broadcasts. In digital cameras, it describes how many bits are used to encode three components of color. The technical theory behind this is a bit complex, so for now think of video color space as a pair of labels. Professional video cameras record 4:2:2 (the "best-quality" label), and some prosumer and all consumer DV cameras give 4:1:1 (the "good-quality" label). Practically, professional cameras can capture a richer variety of colors than the consumer models can. There is no color-space equivalent for film, which captures color by a completely different scheme. But if there were, it would be something like 4:4:4, which you can think of as "premium-quality" color.

> Another less often used term for color space is *chromatic resolution*.

In achieving film-look video, the inherent color capabilities of video aren't the main issue. Lighting for acceptable contrast range remains the biggest challenge, and achieving pleasing color is a related issue that can sometimes be improved by good art direction. However, if you're after garish effects, digital postproduction makes it possible to manipulate color very easily.

Where color is concerned, the filmmaker's biggest problem is scene-to-scene variation in color rendition. Due mainly to differences in the light sources, skin tones might look reddish and warm in one shot, cool and bluish in others. The solution lies in careful lighting techniques and correct camcorder settings. (For more information on the cinematographer's approach to shooting and lighting DV, see Chapter 4.)

Depth of Field and Focus Control

The range of distances that can be in sharp focus within an image is the depth of field. It's a characteristic of lens design (lens length, aperture, and film size). Wide-angle lenses have greater depth of field—everything in the shot is in focus. Telephoto lenses (also called *long lenses*) have shallower depth of field—the subject can be in focus and the background will look blurred, or soft (see Figure 2.2).

Film permits a shallower depth of field than video does. So you can be much more selective about which subjects, or which parts of the subject in a closeup, are in focus. The viewer's eye and attention will be drawn to the focused area. Shallow depth of field, like artistic lighting, gives you a tool for showing the audience where to look.

Figure 2.2
Using a telephoto lens to shoot closeups is a time-honored Hollywood technique that exploits shallow depth of field so that the subject is sharp and the background is pleasingly soft. This both separates the subject from the background and draws the viewer's eye to the sharpest area—the subject's face.

In fact, a hallmark of artful Hollywood cinematography is the focus pull, in which the focus changes abruptly during a shot, shifting the attention of the audience from foreground to background or vice versa and from one subject in the frame to another. However, when shooting fast-breaking news or sports on video, focusing by such fine degrees isn't desirable. The operator has just one chance—not several takes—to get the shot, and continually adjusting focus needlessly complicates the job and may make you miss the shot.

The technical reason for the marked difference in depth-of-field capability isn't simply a matter of picking the right lens. It's rooted in camera target size (see Figure 2.3). Infinite depth of field—everything near and far in focus—occurs when the target size is a pinpoint. The CCD, or photosensitive chip, in a video camera measures about ⅔ inch across in the best professional video cameras and is as small as ¼ inch in cheaper consumer models. By contrast, a frame of 35mm film is about 1.5 inches across. That's about three times larger in area than the largest video CCD chip. Because of the principles of optics, the larger the target size, the shallower the depth of field, and the more selective the focus.

Along with lighting and contrast range, we'll discuss ways to control depth of field in Chapter 4.

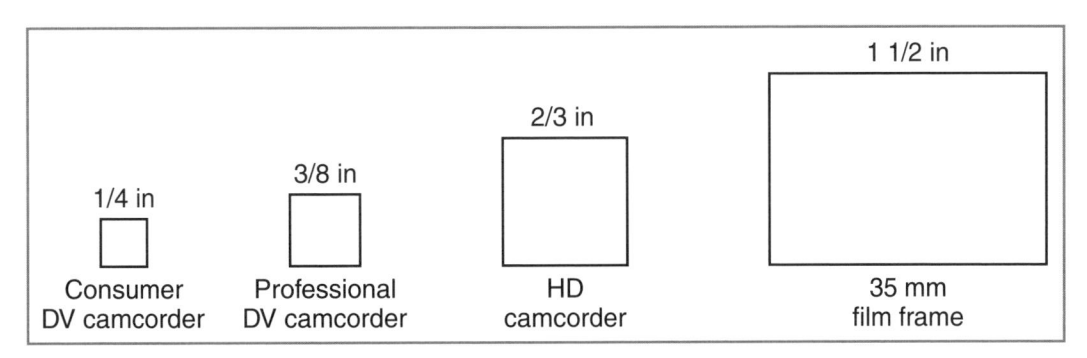

Figure 2.3
The larger the optical target size in the camera, the shallower the depth of field and the greater control you have over focusing. Note that a 35mm frame has fully three times the surface area of the largest CCD chips used in HD camcorders.

Shape of the Viewing Screen

The ratio of the width of the frame to its height is the aspect ratio. DV and standard broadcast television sets have an aspect ratio of 4:3. HD and wide-screen sets are 16:9 (see Figure 2.4). A 16:9 image shown within a 4:3 screen, which creates a broad black border top and bottom, is called *letterbox format*.

Theatrical film is offered in a variety of wide-screen formats, which are all based on use of anamorphic camera lenses that distort the image to fit the 35mm or 70mm film frame and projector lenses that do the reverse. The most widely used aspect ratio for movie production today is the Panavision

1.85:1 format, which is much the same as HD's 16:9. Other film release formats include Cinemascope (2.55:1 and 2.35:1), VistaVision (1.96:1, 1.85:1, 1.66:1), Todd-AO (2.25:1 and 2.20:1), and Ultra Panavision 70 (2.76:1).

As a rule, digital cameras designed for HD have chips with pixels arranged in 16:9 format, and DV cameras are arranged in 4:3. All of them, except for some consumer camcorder models, permit you to switch from one aspect ratio to the other when shooting. That is, you can choose to shoot 4:3 on an HD camera or 16:9 on a DV camera. In general, you shouldn't do this unless you know that your camcorder achieves this without sacrificing resolution. Some cheaper models with 4:3 chips simply discard the top and bottom rows of pixels. Others perform an anamorphic squeeze electronically, which doesn't discard pixels or cause loss of resolution.

However, whether you shoot in 4:3 or 16:9, you can easily change aspect ratio in postproduction, also without a loss of resolution.

If you are shooting a theatrical movie in HD or HDV, the correct aspect ratio when shooting would be 16:9. If you know you'll be releasing in a wide-screen format other than Panavision 1.85:1, you'll have to investigate whether anamorphic lenses for the format are available for the camera.

As an alternative, with the aid of a lens adapter, you can use cinema lenses, including anamorphic types, with some DV camcorders (see Figure 2.5). The adapter has the added benefit of giving you greater control over depth of field. It increases the target size by focusing the beam from the lens onto the face of a prism that's the same size as the 35mm frame; then it redirects the light to the camera's CCD.

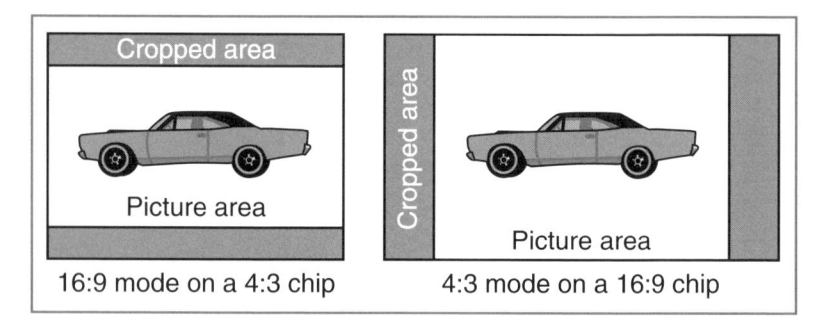

Figure 2.4
With some exceptions, the CCDs of DV camcorders are designed for 4:3 aspect ratio (standard TV), HD camcorders for 16:9 (wide-screen). However, prosumer DV models such as the Canon XL2 are beginning to feature 16:9 chips.

Figure 2.5
This lens adapter from P+S Technik makes it possible to use lenses designed for motion picture cameras with a Canon XL series camcorder. It corrects for differences in image size by focusing on the face of a prism that's the same size as a 35mm frame. (Photo courtesy P+S Technik GmbH)

Sharpness and Detail

The sharpness and detail captured in a film or video image are its spatial resolution. The other aspect of resolution is chromatic.

Digital video resolution is expressed as the number of pixels, or picture elements, used to describe each frame (see Figure 2.6). DV has a resolution of 720×480 pixels, which fits the requirements of standard definition television (SDTV). There are several HD formats now being broadcast as high-definition television (HDTV), and the most filmlike is 1920×1080.

Producing in HD shouldn't cause concern about acceptable resolution. If anything, HD images can appear too sharp.

But when producing low-budget DV, the concern for the filmmaker is that showing it on a wide-screen TV, projecting it onto a theatrical-sized screen, or transferring it to 35mm film should, in theory, show scan lines that will be visible to the audience. In practice, that's not a problem. Present-day wide-screen televisions, digital projectors, and film-transfer techniques use various line-doubling schemes and other image-enhancement techniques that virtually eliminate scan lines.

The net result is that DV viewed on the wide screen does not appear as sharp overall as HD or 35mm film. The best way for a filmmaker to overcome this lack of resolution is to regard it as a creative quality of the medium, favoring technical choices that make best use of the relatively softer DV imagery.

> When you see the term *resolution* by itself in this book, in magazine articles, or in product literature, the reference is usually to spatial resolution.

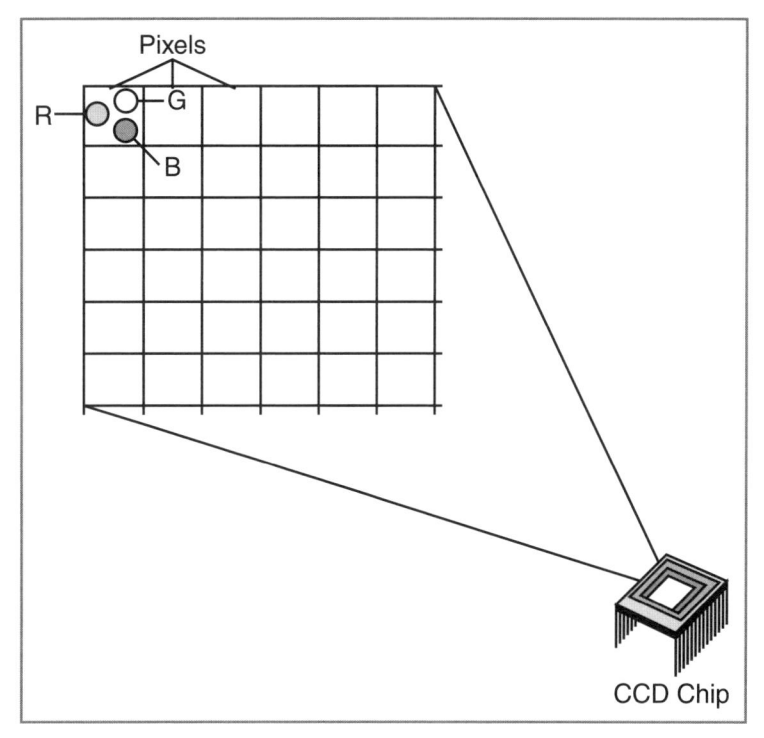

Figure 2.6
The surface of a camcorder CCD is a grid of tiny picture elements, or pixels. Some camcorders, including the JVC HDV model, use a single-chip design in which red (R), green (G), and blue (B) light-sensing elements are arranged adjacent to one another on the chip's surface. Other camcorders, such as the Canon XL series, use a three-chip design, designated 3CCD. A prism in the camcorder splits the light beam into the three primary colors, which are captured on separate chips.

Texture of Imagery

Film contains layers of photosensitive chemicals deposited as microscopically tiny crystals. The crystals aren't deposited regularly as the pixels on a CCD are, but are laid down in a random pattern, or grain. Particularly in underexposed areas of an image, the grain can be apparent to the viewer. It can lend an artistic texture that audiences have come to associate with a film look, much as the glossy, varnished finish and raised brush strokes of an original oil painting distinguish it from the lackluster surface of a print reproduction.

Achieving a grainy look in digital video is easy. The effect can be added in postproduction, and you have a great deal of control over its subtlety. Interestingly, the grain effect is a type of video noise, or random signal. As with reducing the frame rate, adding grain to video to make it look more like film actually involves reducing its technical quality.

Aged film also shows scratches and dust when projected. These are also easily replicated in postproduction as types of video noise. You obviously don't want to overdo these effects, since presumably a good commercial product should look as good as a clean film print fresh from the lab. But for artistic purposes, especially when you're trying to make a sequence look like archival film footage, adding scratch and dust effects can be very useful.

The Theatrical Viewing Experience

There's one more characteristic of film that occurs when you project it in a theater. Like scratches and dust, jitter is a telltale characteristic of aged film. It shows up as a slight but continuous unstable jumpy motion on the projection screen. It's caused by an imperfect fit between the sprocket holes on the edges of the film and the registration pins in the projector. When the film is new, the pins engage the sprocket holes with precision, pulling each film frame into position in the gate. As the sprocket holes become worn from repeated projection, they enlarge, and the registration is increasingly less precise.

Technically, jitter has two components of motion: up-and-down, called *bob,* and side-to-side, called *weave* (see Figure 2.7).

Jitter is shamefully easy to add in postproduction. As with scratches and dust, overdoing it is usually a bad idea. But adding it subtly can be a nice finishing touch to making film look convincing.

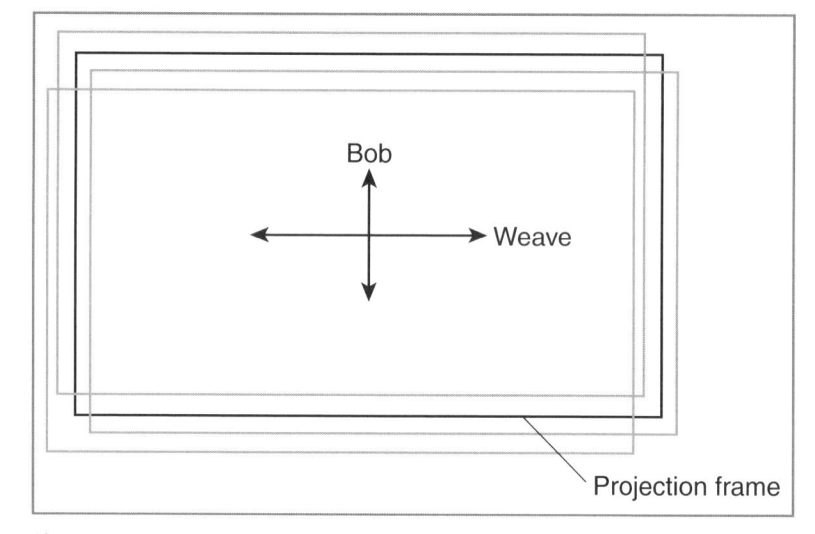

Figure 2.7
Jitter in film projection is caused by worn sprocket holes, which cause the image to bob and weave within the projection frame on the screen.

What Are the Options?

There are several different approaches to achieving film look, film out, or both. Your first choice is shooting mode, and it will affect all the choices you make afterward. Your options are:

- Shoot in 24p.
- Shoot in 60i.
- Shoot in 30p.
- Shoot in PAL (50i or 25p).

Shoot in 24P

If you buy, rent, or borrow a camcorder that can shoot in 24p, you're off to a good start. But remember that choosing this mode is an irreversible decision, creatively speaking. Although making the choice doesn't guarantee a quality film look, it does eliminate the possibility of your show looking like plain-vanilla NTSC video (the standard broadcast TV format in North America).

But, if film look is so superior aesthetically, why not shoot 24p all the time? As with film look itself, the answer lies in audience expectations. Traditionally, viewers associate 60i video with live broadcasting and immediacy. Video as it appears when shot in 60i mode delivers the expected look for sports, news, and "reality" shows.

If you're shooting HD, yours will be a simpler world because that format can store and play back video at 24fps. So you can shoot, edit, and release in 24p. End of story.

If yours is a DV production, life and your range of choices will be considerably more complicated. DV is strictly 60i NTSC (unless you're producing in Europe or Asia). So even though the camcorder records images in 24p, it converts them to 60i before recording them on tape. You can therefore choose to edit and release in 60i. However, your edits will be easier and cleaner—and you'll be that much closer to achieving a film look—if you use an editing system that's capable of converting the video stream back to 24p. We'll discuss the benefits and technicalities of 24p editing in Chapter 7.

Shoot in 60i

Shooting in conventional NTSC (60i) is not as boring a choice as you'd think. In many ways, it leaves all your options open. That's because you can convert from 60i to 24p in postproduction. One tool among several for doing this is Magic Bullet from Red Giant Software, a plug-in for Adobe After Effects. If you go this route, you'll shoot and edit in 60i and then finish by converting to 24p.

Shooting in 60i rather than 24p has the advantage of helping you defer many technical decisions until postproduction. And it certainly opens up your options in selecting a camcorder.

In theory, shooting in 60i and converting to 24p later should produce less striking results than going all the way in 24p. Motion blur, in particular, will be minimized in your original camera footage, which will seem still and dull before you convert. However, Magic Bullet not only deinterlaces the imagery and converts the frame rate, but it also does some interpolation to emphasize motion blur. The results can be remarkably similar to shooting in 24p.

Shoot in 30P

A tempting choice when shooting DV that will probably cost you dearly later is simply to choose 30p mode when shooting. Many DV camcorders that don't offer 24p do have this feature, which preserves the conventional NTSC frame rate, turns off interlacing, and captures each frame in a single pass.

> There are perfectly valid reasons to shoot in 30p. For example, if there's a lot of action in a scene and you know you're not releasing on film, 30p will make the motions appear smoother (if that's the effect you want).

Like 24p, 30p gets converted to 60i inside the camcorder in DV recording. Depending on the camcorder, this can be accomplished in either of two ways, one of which results in a serious loss of quality. The better approach is a true progressive mode in which all scan lines in the frame are captured in a single pass. The less desirable way is to grab two fields in 60i mode, discard one field, and then perform line doubling on the first to generate a full set of scan lines. This effectively sacrifices half of the picture detail.

If your goal is video output that simply shows more motion blur, shooting in progressive mode might do the trick. The problem is, that's as far as you can go. Magic Bullet will not convert 30p to 24p. To use Magic Bullet, you have to start with 60i.

A further disappointment will be that transfer labs won't accept 30p for film out.

Shoot in PAL

The Phase Alternating Line (PAL) system is the broadcast television standard in the UK and Japan. It records and plays back at 25fps, with 50 interlaced fields per second, or 50i. Progressive mode in a PAL camcorder is therefore 25p, just one frame off from movie rate. Converting PAL to film has always been much more straightforward than doing so for NTSC. The lab simply speeds up the playback rate of the original PAL footage by four percent and lowers the pitch of the audio track slightly so that voices sound natural.

DV editing systems can convert readily between 50i PAL and 60i NTSC. You can even intermix the formats when editing and then output in either.

Until 24p NTSC camcorders appeared, some indie filmmakers swore by the practice of using PAL camcorders for film out. Camera rental houses in the United States stocked them, but charged a premium. Now that 24p is on the scene, you can expect PAL camcorders to become even more rare in this country, since the advantage of using them for film production has largely disappeared.

PAL DV camcorders do still have a slight edge on 24p DV models. Their spatial resolution is somewhat better—displaying 625 scan lines instead of 480. However, their color space is a more restrictive 4:1:0 (the zero doesn't mean nothing, but that's another story!).

> When director Michael Mann set out to shoot the feature *Collateral*, he wanted to capture the special aura of Los Angeles at night. In certain weather conditions, a marine layer rolls in after sunset, blanketing the city in low-hanging clouds. Lit by reflections from street lights, the entire sky has a soft glow that looks like unending twilight. At such times, the human eye can look down the street and see for several blocks.
>
> Film can't capture those scenes, but the low-light sensitivity of video CCDs can. Mann's crew shot the night scenes of *Collateral* with the Grass Valley Viper FilmStream, an HD camera from Thomson.

Putting the 24P Mindset to Work

The following chapters will explore the finer points of the creative and technical choices that go into producing a digital movie. We'll help you cultivate a mindset that applies the expertise and craftsmanship of Hollywood to the new electronic media. And we'll give you some guidelines for making choices that achieve the results you want—and that audiences and film buyers expect.

But, remember, you won't find hard and fast rules here. Like film, the medium of digital video has its own unique capabilities and its limitations.

Although film stock manufacturers and camera companies continue to innovate, film is reaching its maturity. Its heritage is rich, and its rules are well understood.

Digital video is a whole new world, most of it unexplored. Its rules have yet to be written, and it's up to pioneering artists like you to write them.

In view of the sophistication of cinema art today, you might wonder whether there's really anything new to discover. But we can point to at least one example of the digital medium being chosen not for its ability to emulate film but for its own unique qualities.

chapter 3
Thinking Like a Producer

No matter what your eventual creative or technical role, you should start each new movie project thinking like a producer. By "producer," we don't mean a money mogul or a studio executive or the agent who booked the star. We mean an experienced hands-on *line producer*, who is responsible for hiring cast and crew, buying or renting equipment, and developing a production schedule.

> We don't necessarily recommend him as a role model, but if you want to learn more about the notorious life of a big-time Hollywood producer who has seen good times and bad, screen *The Kid Stays in the Picture* (2002), based on the life of Robert Evans.

Even if you're an experienced line producer, you'll probably have to change some of your most trusted rules of thumb if you want to be successful shooting and finishing in 24p.

You need the new mindset.

If you hire people who don't understand the digital medium, or if you procure the wrong equipment, or if you allow too much or too little time to get things done, it will be difficult if not impossible to achieve the results you want.

By appreciating new techniques and work methods, you can plan for success. You can build a team that has the 24p mindset, you can shoot tests to see what works, and you can give your cast and crew the tools they need to achieve the stunning Hollywood look you're seeking.

> You might think it's something of a joke that the star's assistant or agent might get a screen credit as a movie producer, but it happens, and all too often. There is no formal definition of what a professional producer does. Someone who obtains a big chunk of the financing of a picture certainly deserves an executive producer credit. A writer who sought out an interesting true life story and then did all the legwork to get the underlying rights can deservedly be called a co-producer. But sometimes the credit is given in lieu of other compensation, other times simply as a high-class favor. The Producers Guild of America (PGA, see www.producersguild.org) is trying to discourage the use of such virtually meaningless producer credits. The PGA is a professional society of line producers, those folks who work hard for a living. Oh, and an "independent producer," or indie, is any entrepreneurial filmmaker who is not associated with a studio. A professional organization that supports the indies is Independent Feature Project (see www.ifp.org).

Film Out or Film Look?

An important overall question at the outset—perhaps *the* most important technical question—is whether the project is aiming for *film out* or simply for *film look*. In general, deciding on film out will restrict your choices to more professional and expensive gear, requiring you to shoot with a camcorder that can deliver 24p and finish with a nonlinear editing (NLE) system that will let you cut at 24fps.

If you're fortunate enough to have a so-called negative pickup deal with a studio or distributor, you must go for film out, no question about it. Under such a deal, if you deliver a completed film negative, the potential buyer has the option of distributing the movie and picking up your production expenses. (Nice work if you can get it!)

Or, if you know you're producing primarily for television, the choice should also be obvious. For example, making a glossy commercial on video is one type of project that shouldn't require film out at all. You can shoot in 60i, preserving all your options, and apply the 24p look in postproduction.

However, making a movie for a cable network is a tougher call. The network contract for a two-hour movie is generally just enough to cover production costs, typically $1–3 million, sometimes less. The deal grants the producer the right to seek foreign distribution rights, including theatrical exhibition. That's the main source of the producer's profit, if there is any. If that's your deal, planning for film out will be crucial to gaining the interest of foreign distributors. (For more information on seeking distribution deals and how they can affect your production planning, see Chapter 9.)

> Need hands-on advice on movie scheduling and budgeting? The bible on the subject is Ralph Singleton's *Film Scheduling: Or, How Long Will It Take to Shoot Your Movie?* The budget "falls out" of the schedule. You simply need to know who and what you need to hire, and for how many days.

If, instead, you're making a student film or your first low-budget indie movie, it's a considerable long shot that film out will ever be necessary. You can do your festival submissions on DVD or digital tape (depending on the festival guidelines), and you can shop your project to potential buyers on disc or on tape. Even if you go so far as to book private screenings in commercial theaters for buyers in Los Angeles or New York, you can probably find a venue that has digital projection. If perchance you're lucky enough to enter negotiations with a distributor, you can haggle over who will pick up the expense of converting your video to film.

> Indie producer Gary Winick has shot quite a few theatrical features on DV that have been in commercial release. He and his colleagues pursue an aesthetic much like the Dogma 95 "Vow of Chastity" cited in Chapter 2. That is, he's not particularly concerned about achieving film look. We'd encourage you to rent a couple of these movies to see what we mean. Watch *Tadpole* (2002) with the commentary turned on. There's a scene in a New York living room where Winick talks about having to move fast, shooting dialogue with two camcorders at the same time. More careful lighting was abandoned in favor of simply getting the shots before the crew had to leave the apartment. *Tadpole* was a hot ticket at the Sundance Film Festival, but its commercial release was disappointing. Some critics blamed the DV medium, but we suspect that the subject matter wasn't, ah, mainstream (you'll have to see what we mean for yourself). Also watch *Pieces of April* (2003), a particularly soulful story. When the family's car emerges from a tunnel into the Manhattan daylight, the video blows out blindingly. A film-look director probably would not keep that shot.

In such circumstances, getting your movie made at all and then getting attention should be your goals. Particularly if you're strapped for cash (and who isn't?), it would be wiser to beg or borrow equipment (from a school cinema department, for example), use the editing system in a media lab, and do your best with the tools at hand. And, as we pointed out in Chapter 1, delivering a masterful film-look video should take you a very long way toward showing opinion-makers and buyers that your work deserves serious consideration.

Thinking Through the Film-Look Factors

Anyone who makes any creative or technical decisions about your project should have a core understanding of the factors they need to control to make video look like film. In particular, the producer, the director, and the DP must come to an agreement about the importance of each factor to achieving the desired look.

To recap from Chapter 2, these crucial factors are:

- Motion blur
- Exposure latitude
- Color rendition
- Depth of field

- Aspect ratio
- Resolution
- Grain
- Jitter

Reviewing this list with a producer's eye reveals which production talents and equipment choices must be hired for the job. This is a team consultation, and it starts off primarily as a creative discussion, which then leads to technical choices. The key questions are the following:

1. What is the director's vision for realizing the material? Is the interpretation of the script and its characters bright and comedic or dark and brooding? How much does the story rely on action? How much on emotion and closeups?

2. How does the DP intend to implement the director's vision? What's the overall look you're going for? What choices will make the movie's imagery distinctive, and how do they follow through on the director's creative vision?

3. Coming back to the producer's role: What creative and technical talent, and which pieces of production gear, will be required to deliver those results?

We won't pretend to provide rules for every type of production, but here's how a digital-savvy producer might think through the list of film-look factors.

Motion Blur

The more the movie's story relies on action—chases and fights—the more crucial motion blur will be toward achieving a Hollywood look. Certain types of special effects, such as time bending, also call for blurring.

A need to emphasize motion blur affects decisions about camcorder selection and postproduction methods. Particularly if you're going for film out, you'll need a camcorder that shoots in true progressive mode (capturing full-frame resolution on each scanning pass, not by simply throwing away the second field). As a further consideration, consult with the director and DP to find out whether they might want to vary the camera's shutter speed, shutter angle, or both. Some camcorders don't have these features, which can heighten the visual effect of action and special effects. In particular, a camcorder that offers shutter speeds slower than $1/30$ can produce the exaggerated blurring you might want for certain bizarre effects. (If you don't want blurring, shoot at a shutter speed as close as possible to the field rate, or Shutter=Off, if you have that option.)

Exposure Latitude

As we stated in Chapter 2, dealing with video's contrast range is probably the biggest technical challenge in achieving film-look video. From a practical standpoint, this comes down to how many people, as well as how much and what type of gear you pick to do your lighting.

Veteran film producers have cherished rules of thumb about the size of lighting crews and what kind of gear they will need. For example, consider the situation of a producer scheduling and budgeting an indie feature. Judging by experience, this producer might assume the interior shooting days will require two light kits and a gaffer/grip crew of three or four.

In film, painting with light can tolerate some areas of deep shadow in the image. For example, film noir movies exploit this technique in the extreme in order to create gloomy urban settings. But because of video's relatively narrow exposure latitude, shadow areas tend to go entirely black, losing all detail. Traditionally, video shot in studio has been lit high-key, with very bright light from all angles, to keep contrast range narrow by minimizing shadows. This approach gives TV sitcoms and soap operas their characteristic over-bright look.

A better strategy—both technically and economically—is to use available light as much as possible. The DP should be extraordinarily conservative about adding light to a scene. And it's best to solve lighting problems by *taking light away* rather than by adding more illumination. Reducing illumination can be done by moving light sources away from the subject or by rigging the set with materials that diffuse (soften) or mask (block) the light (see Figures 3.2 and 3.3).

The main challenge when using available light indoors is color balance. It's therefore more important to equip the crew with a variety of color-correcting gels and filters than to load them up with lights. Where additional lighting is needed indoors, soft fluorescent movie lights may be much more useful than conventional halogen lights.

> A typical light kit contains three mini-sized halogen-quartz movie lights and stands. It's a standard rental item for low-budget film crews (see Figure 3.1).

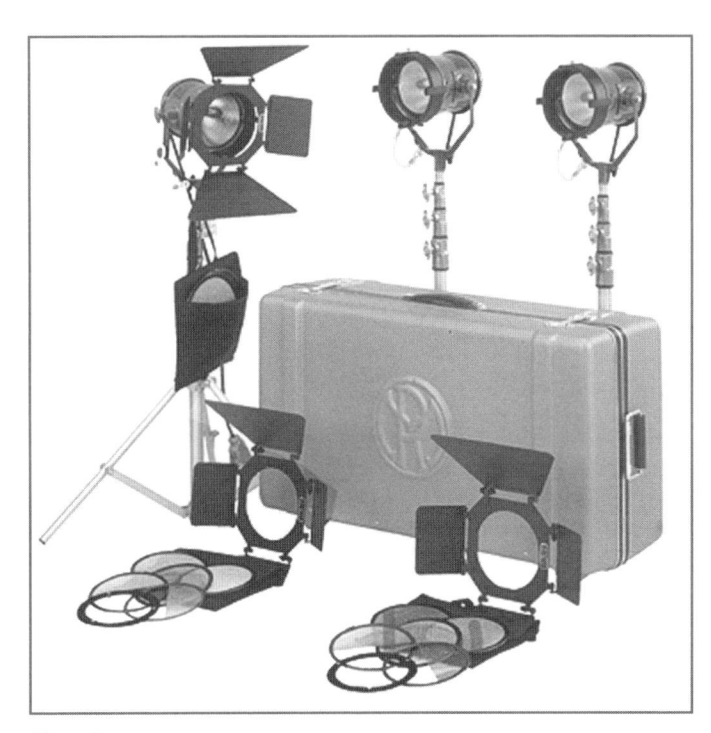

Figure 3.1
If you follow a strategy of using less and softer lighting than you would with film, a video crew can use relatively lightweight gear. This light kit contains three "teenie-weenie" size, open-face tungsten halogen-quartz lights (suitable for shooting interiors), barn doors (for masking the beam), scrims (for diffusing the beam), and gel holders (color-correcting film). A kit like this rents for about $50 per day. (Photo courtesy Mole-Richardson Co.)

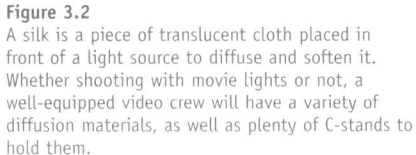

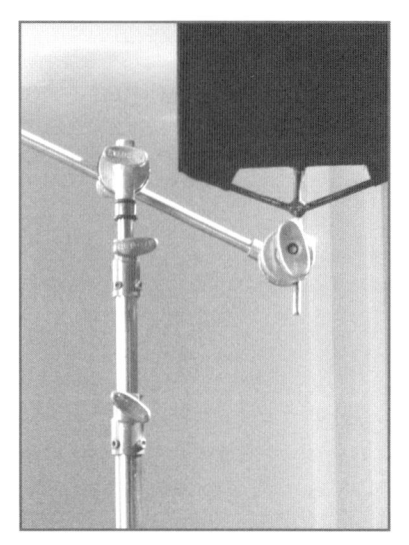

Figure 3.2
A silk is a piece of translucent cloth placed in front of a light source to diffuse and soften it. Whether shooting with movie lights or not, a well-equipped video crew will have a variety of diffusion materials, as well as plenty of C-stands to hold them.

Figure 3.3
A flag (left) is constructed much like a silk but is made of opaque material. A roll of black felt can be used to mask larger areas, such as windows (right).

When shooting exteriors, the trick is to shoot on overcast days or move into the shade, using reflectors and diffusion to redirect and control sunlight (see Figure 3.4). On an overcast day, the available light is highly diffuse. There are hardly any shadows at all, and you may need to add some key light to the subject to create a shadow. On hazy days, there will be shadows, but the contrast between the bright and shadow areas will be narrower, and the overall look will be softer, than if you shot on a sunny day. And even these softer shadow areas will look darker on video than they would on film.

The bottom line for the production planner is that a modified approach to lighting is called for. Think in terms of fewer lights, which translates to fewer people and trucks to transport and rig them. But also think of a variety of relatively portable gear that the crew can use to control the amount, quality, and color of available light. These include such inexpensive but handy items as gels and filters, as well as silks, flags, and shiny boards.

All this translates to less expense for equipment, transportation, and rigging. But it places extra emphasis on the skill and resourcefulness of the DP and the lighting crew and probably calls for more production assistants (PAs) to assist with the rigging.

Figure 3.4
On the Aqua Tan set, the authors used large silks and reflectors to control the bright sunlight at a California beach house. The actors played in the shaded area of the back porch, and key light was created by reflected sunlight. (You can view 24p Aqua Tan footage on the DVD.)

There are good technical and economic reasons to prefer a softer look when shooting video.

If, instead, the director insists on a brighter, high-key look, be prepared to rent lots of trucks and hire lots of skilled grips and gaffers. And don't forget permits and parking for your fleet of trucks on location and a small fortune in catering to feed all those hungry folks on the set.

And by the way, every experienced producer also knows that the less gear used in a setup, the easier and quicker it will be for the crew to strike the set and move on to the next one.

So, if you light video intelligently, making best use of the medium with less gear, your crew can probably shoot more setups in a day.

Food for thought, eh? Maybe that high-key lighting isn't so essential after all.

This brief discussion by no means tells the whole story. There's much more detailed information in Chapter 4 about cinematography for film-look video. (Budgeters and schedulers need to know this stuff, too.)

Color Rendition

Choices involving color space are straightforward and primarily affect your DP's choice of camcorder. If you're producing for broadcast television, the color-space requirement is 4:2:2, which is a feature of all professional camcorders. Most prosumer models don't have it.

The 4:1:1 color space that's typical of prosumer and consumer DV camcorders and all HDV models can look perfectly fine. Most of the picture detail—the edges and textures—is in the "4" component of the signal, which is literally every bit as good as broadcast color. The difference lies in the subtlety of colors. (You can think of 4:1:1 and 4:2:2 color as two sets of crayons, the first with a selection of 16 colors, say, and the other with 64.) In fact, broadcast color can look duller by comparison, precisely because it is more lifelike. The 4:1:1 scheme shifts colors toward the primaries. Reds look redder, greens greener, blues bluer than the human eye or the 4:2:2 cameras see them. Audiences might even like the look. Unnatural color doesn't necessarily mean displeasing color.

> Consider that Kodak engineered its old snapshot film Kodachrome to exaggerate the reds—because consumers preferred the artificially vibrant color.

It's possible (and actually quite easy) to convert from 4:1:1 to 4:2:2 broadcast color in postproduction. The problem is this heightening of color we just noted, and it shows up when you take the conversion one step further. To be broadcast-legal, colors can't be oversaturated, or too intense. To return to the crayon analogy, broadcast-legal colors are a set of pastels. (This limitation prevents interference between television channels that are adjacent to one another in broadcast frequency.) When desaturating imagery to make it suitable for broadcast, not only will some colors become less intense, but they can also shift that much farther away from the original colors. Bright green trees can take on a brownish cast. Warm skin tones can become sickly.

Remember that we're talking about subtleties here, and color correction in postproduction can help repair the damage wrought by conversion. But the most reliable and least expensive approach is to shoot 4:2:2 to start with if the broadcast industry is your intended marketplace. Shooting 4:2:2 won't guarantee broadcast-legal color, but it can reduce the extent of color correction you have to do to achieve it.

If you're headed for film out, color space can be much less of an issue—as long as the color of your footage is pleasing to the eye. Film can record whatever you get on video, whether it's 4:2:2, 4:1:1, or PAL's 4:1:0. DV color might not be as intense, but that's not always true. Like the consumer shutterbug's preference for Kodachrome, making it pretty doesn't necessarily mean rendering it accurately.

Depth of Field

Selective focus, made possible by shallow depth of field, is a creative technique, rather like brushwork in an oil painting. Some directors and DPs will want to do it, others won't. In general, keeping the background soft while holding the subject in focus helps separate the subject from the background and adds depth to the image. Separation and depth can also be achieved by artful lighting, but keep in mind that lighting choices are more limited in video, so you need all the help you can get.

To preserve the camera crew's options regarding focus, choose a camcorder that accepts interchangeable cinema-style lenses (see "Lenses" in Chapter 4). Selective focus will be possible with the longer lenses and with telephoto zoom.

One of the reasons for the popularity of the Canon XL series camcorders is that they accept all Canon cinema lenses. Because of differences in target size between this camcorder's relatively tiny CCDs and the 35mm frame, the distance markings on the lenses won't be accurate, but the lenses are otherwise fully usable. A lens adapter (refer back to Figure 2.5) not only increases target size and improves ability to pull focus during a shot, but it also makes the lens markings correct. Budgeting for and renting such an adapter might be important if selective focus is a hallmark of your director's style. (These adapters aren't cheap. A typical rental rate is $300 per day, somewhat less expensive by the week.)

Aspect Ratio

Standard definition television (SDTV) uses 4:3 format, and HDTV is 16:9. To shoot in other wide-screen formats, such as Cinemascope, requires cinema-style anamorphic lenses, and possibly also a lens adapter. The producer needs to be concerned about this because the camcorder, lenses, and adapter are significant budget items.

However, you probably won't know enough to fret about this unless you have a production contract. If you're aiming for wide-screen theatrical distribution, the safest bet is to choose a camcorder that has a true 16:9 chip. Its output will be very close to Panavision wide-screen (1.85:1), and that's a fairly safe bet.

> There's actually at least one advantage to shooting 4:3 over 16:9: If you convert to letterbox in post, you'll have more room for adjustment if you want to reposition (repo) the shot. For example, you can adjust the headroom over an actor.

As we advised in Chapter 2, if you intend to shoot with a camcorder that has the 4:3 chip format, don't plan on shooting in 16:9 mode if the camcorder achieves it by lopping off the top and bottom rows of pixels. You'll get better imagery by converting to 16:9 in post.

Resolution

Shooting in the aspect ratio that's native to the camcorder chip assures the highest possible resolution from the camera. The idea is to always use as much of the chip's surface area as possible and then handle any format conversions in postproduction.

Remember that DV resolution is 720×480 pixels, and the best HD resolution is 1920×1080.

There are actually several HDTV broadcast standards in use, but the two main ones use either 1080 lines interlaced (1080i) or 720 lines progressive (720p), which has a resolution of 1280×720. If you know you're producing for a network that broadcasts in 720p, you might be tempted to shoot in 720-line HDV, but remember that the broadcast color space is 4:2:2, and HDV recording can be 4:1:0. That's not a showstopper, but it's something to think about. Then, too, Hollywood deals have a tendency to come and go during production, so you might start out producing for one network and end up releasing on another.

Some camcorders, such as the HDV models, shoot in a lower resolution and give you the option of selecting a higher resolution on output. For example, the JVC JY-HD10U shoots in 720-line mode but gives you the option of selecting 1080-line output. The camera achieves the higher resolution the same way you can in postproduction, by applying an interpolation process that generates the missing scan lines. In general, you'll have better control over results if you do the conversion in postproduction and simply use the camcorder footage just the way it was recorded.

Grain and Jitter

Effects like grain and jitter aren't applied until the very late stages of postproduction, usually at the same time you're doing color correction. The same can be said of other filter effects, such as scratches and dust, black-and-white, and sepia. In general, even if the camcorder offers these effects as in-camera recording options, don't use them, and make all such decisions later in post. (Don't add these effects for film out.)

Camera Movement

Although not included in our original list of film-look factors, moving the camera during a shot is a characteristic of high-budget Hollywood style. Designing camera moves requires additional time and effort in preproduction, typically when the director is developing storyboards and discussing them with the art director and DP.

Equipping and rigging camera moves can be expensive. A full-blown studio production will have access to dollies and cranes, and will provide skilled technicians to set up and operate them.

For the low-budget filmmaker, we can suggest a variety of less expensive ways to move the camera during a shot. Instead of a dolly, you can use just about anything that rolls, including shopping carts, skateboards, and wheelchairs—or simply sit the camera operator on a blanket and drag him along a slick interior floor.

The main problem with such improvised dolly techniques is that they aren't necessarily stable or repeatable. What you save on equipment might be eaten up by more time on the set as the cast and crew do take after take to get it just right.

A modest-priced alternative is the doorway dolly (see Figure 3.5), a standard rental item at many movie equipment houses. The dolly comes with interlocking sections of tubular-steel track, either straight or curved. You'll need to plan for the staff and setup time required to lay the track, as well as hire an experienced dolly grip to push the dolly platform during shots.

A low-budget alternative to using a crane is to find a high vantage point on location and use a zoom lens to follow the action (see Figure 3.6).

> Renting a doorway dolly and track can cost less than $100 per day, about $30 for the dolly, $12 for each eight-foot section of track, and $20–25 for the wheels (you need special curved wheels for curved track). All rentals are less expensive when you negotiate a weekly rate with the rental house.

Figure 3.5
On the Aqua Tan shoot, we used a doorway dolly in just about every setup at the location. The goal was to keep the camera moving so that the edited sequences would seem more buoyant and fluid. Note that the tripod is chained to the dolly to prevent its tipping over and possibly injuring a crewmember or damaging the camera.

Figure 3.6
Although not exactly the same action as a crane shot, you can give the impression of swooping down or soaring up on the action by shooting from a high vantage point and zooming in or out during the take. This technique is both much less expensive and much safer than using a crane.

Producer's Checklist

As you, the producer, begin to develop a budget and schedule for your project, here are some important things to think about to be sure you have all the bases covered.

1. You need a crew; you can't "run and gun" by yourself.

Make a distinction in your mind between news-style and film-style shooting. Veteran videographers call news style *running and gunning*: A crew of one hits the street with a camcorder slung over her shoulder and chases a breaking story. She's shooting with available light or with a camera-mounted spotlight. She may be assisted by a sound technician or, more often, a newscaster who operates an interview mic.

Save news-style shooting for documentaries. Getting the Hollywood look is all about shooting film style. That means single-camera, meticulous setups, three-point lighting, and several takes for each shot.

We don't mean that Hollywood features can't contain some news-style sequences. They can and do. Just make sure that any documentary-style footage serves the story and doesn't just look like sloppy camerawork.

The choice of camcorder and the size and functions of the camera crew will depend on the DP's preferred shooting styles and will, of course, affect your budget. If the director and DP expect to pull focus during shots or follow fast action with long lenses, the camera operator shouldn't have to do it. There will be too much going on during a take. You'll therefore not only need the lenses and equipment for achieving shallow depth of field, but also a focus puller, known more commonly as the *first assistant camera operator*.

And if you'll be doing camera movement as well, you'll need a dolly grip, who may also serve as second assistant camera operator, with responsibility for keeping camera and sound logs.

So that's a minimum camera crew of three—camera operator, first assistant (focus puller), and dolly grip. But if the dolly grip will be too busy to prepare logs, you'll need four.

2. Turn off automatic camera controls.

Most consumer and some prosumer camcorders are designed for fully automatic operation. Built-in features, such as automatic focus (AF), automatic exposure (AE), and automatic white balance (AWB), are switched on by default. That default setting occurs so that an operator with minimum skill can simply point and shoot and get recognizable (but not great) results.

Remember that turning off automatic camcorder controls is a necessary first step toward achieving professional-quality imagery.

Professional camcorders are designed for manual operation, with most-used controls positioned where they can be reached easily, and their readouts and settings are easy to inspect. Although it's tempting to use lower-cost camcorders, understand that they are actually more difficult to operate in manual mode than pro cameras are. That fact can mean time wasted on the set or, worse, unusable shots.

3. Support the camera.

Bouncy handheld camerawork is a sure sign of an inexperienced amateur. And besides, it's downright annoying to watch for any length of time.

As a budget item, include a professional-quality tripod. Specs provided by the camera store or rental house should tell you how much weight it's designed to support. That must be enough to hold camera, long or zoom lenses, adapters, and accessories.

Since camera movement is so crucial to the look you're seeking, the tripod should also permit smooth panning and tilting. The more expensive tripods have fluid heads that dampen vibration.

We're not ruling out carefully executed handheld camera movement. A skilled operator can do nice work by cradling the camera in his hands and holding it away from his body (see Figure 3.7). But this approach works best for the occasional short take. If the camera must follow actors around, consider providing the crew with a mobile camera mount, such as a Glidecam (see www.glidecam.com). These mounts work best with lightweight camcorders.

Figure 3.7
The correct position for handheld shots is to cradle the camcorder in the hands, held away from the body. The operator's arms will act as shock absorbers, minimizing jarring as you walk to follow the action. Watch the flip-out LCD screen to monitor the action, not the viewfinder. Shown here is a consumer DV camcorder (the Canon ZR40) with a wide-angle lens adapter, employed as a second-unit camera in a "making of" video.

4. Paint with light.

The whole production should be designed with the intention of getting gorgeous imagery, allowing for the narrow contrast range of video and making use of its low-light sensitivity. Maximize the use of available light wherever possible, which will help you keep down the amount of lighting gear and size of the crew. And remember, the lighter they travel, the faster they can work.

5. Move the camera as you shoot.

Providing the camera operator with a professional-style fluid-head tripod will go a long way toward assuring smooth camera movement. In preproduction, the creative team should consider which scenes would benefit from dolly or crane effects. Then build your shooting schedule accordingly, grouping days together that will require any specialized rental gear, such as the dolly and track. To the extent that the DP is confident that the camera department can improvise dolly shots with inexpensive gear such as a wheelchair, so much the better.

6. Capture clean dialogue.

As a basic working rule, the mission of the sound technicians on the set is to capture clean dialogue. All sound effects and music will be added in postproduction.

As with any other department, the producer's support comes down to procuring the right gear and the right people to operate it. The essential piece of gear in this case is a good boom microphone and boom pole (see Figure 3.8). Examples of studio-quality shotgun mics are the Sennheiser ME66 and the Audio-Technica AT815b.

Holding the boom pole take after take is a tedious job. It's therefore an all-too-common practice on low-budget shoots to assign this task to a green production assistant. That's usually a mistake. An experienced boom operator knows how to keep the mic pointed at whichever actor is speaking and will also take care that the mic doesn't dip down into the shot. Another good practice that entails some expense is to equip the boom operator with a portable mixer (see Figure 3.9). The mixer gives the operator better control over sound levels.

Figure 3.8
The shotgun mic on this boom pole is shrouded in a foam-rubber windscreen. The boom operator must find a stance where he can hold the mic aloft, just outside the top of the frame, throughout each take.

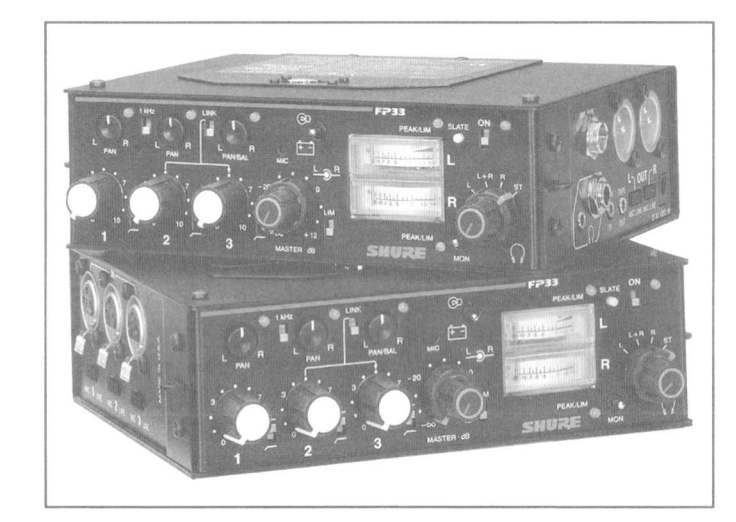

Figure 3.9
The Shure FP33 is a portable, battery-powered mixer popular with digital video crews. It's light and compact enough to be worn on the boom operator's belt. Two units are stacked here to show the jacks and controls on either side. (Photo © 2005 Shure Incorporated)

An even better, although more expensive, approach is to record dual-system sound, capturing the mic output to an auxiliary digital audio tape (DAT) recorder as well as to the audio input of the camcorder (see Figure 3.10). Such a setup can improve both the quality and the crew's control over the soundtrack, and the in-camera recording serves as a backup.

A mixer is a necessary equipment item for dual-system audio recording. You'll need a sound recordist to operate and monitor the DAT machine. And give control of the mixer to that person instead of to the boom operator.

We'll have much more to say about the details of capturing sound on the set in Chapter 6.

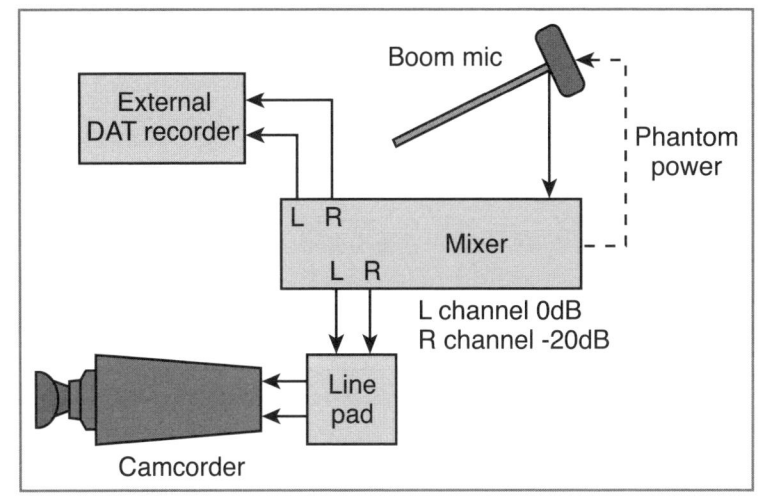

Figure 3.10
In dual-system audio recording for digital video, twin outputs from a mixer go to an auxiliary DAT recorder, as well to the camcorder's audio input. The sound recordist can adjust the DAT audio input level to peak and set a lower level for the camcorder. By recording at different levels, the camcorder track serves as a backup in case the production sound during the scene peaks so high on the DAT that it's distorted.

7. Build rich audio environments in post.

Perhaps surprisingly, one of the essential features of the Hollywood "look" is a rich soundtrack. Here's where many low-budget productions fall far short of audience expectations.

In a Hollywood movie, sound editors build a rich audio environment for each scene, adding layer after layer, audio track after audio track, containing subtle sound effects. The goal is to enhance the illusion for the audience of being in a particular place. The sounds of cutlery and plates tinkling and conversations buzzing help convince us that we're in a busy restaurant and not on a sound stage. Sounds of birds and a babbling brook tell us we're in a lovely garden and not on the back lot next to a freeway.

And, contrary to conventional wisdom, music doesn't create emotion in the audience, but the right music selection can amplify the emotional content of a scene.

Audio postproduction to clean up dialogue and add sound effects and music can take months. Do as much as you can afford. And if you don't hire a separate sound editor to do this work, at least make sure that your editor has a flair for meticulous audio work.

Make sure that you allow sufficient time in your schedule and money in your budget to deliver a quality audio product. It could really make a difference in the salability of your project.

We'll advise you how to think like a sound designer in Chapter 5.

8. Don't overdo transitions and special effects.

Elaborate transition effects, such as wipes and radials, are another sign of a rookie. On narrative projects, the experienced editor sticks to straight cuts, inserting the occasional dissolve to indicate a time lapse. What does this advice mean to a producer? It extends to all types of "eye candy" you might plan—use them sparingly. Budget and plan for the effects you need to tell the story. That is, if the weaponry in the story is lasers, you'll know to plan for adding the light traces and blast effects in post.

Now, this advice doesn't hold for all types of projects. If you're producing a music video or a television commercial, all bets are off. To dazzle your audience and astound your competitors, you'll need every trick in the book, and then some. We'll offer some suggestions on creating special effects in Chapter 8.

9. Plan ahead for distribution.

It doesn't make sense to hire a DP—or even to choose a camcorder—before you consider the requirements of the distribution medium. And if you don't know how your movie will be distributed, you need to make choices that preserve your options.

If broadcasting is your goal, shooting must keep significant action within the safe action area, and titles must not extend beyond the safe title area (see Figure 3.11).

If you'll be distributing on DVD, remember that this format requires your material to be organized into chapters. (Even movies that appear to play back continuously are actually organized by chapter on the disc.) The task of breaking your movie into chapters is much the same as providing commercial breaks in a

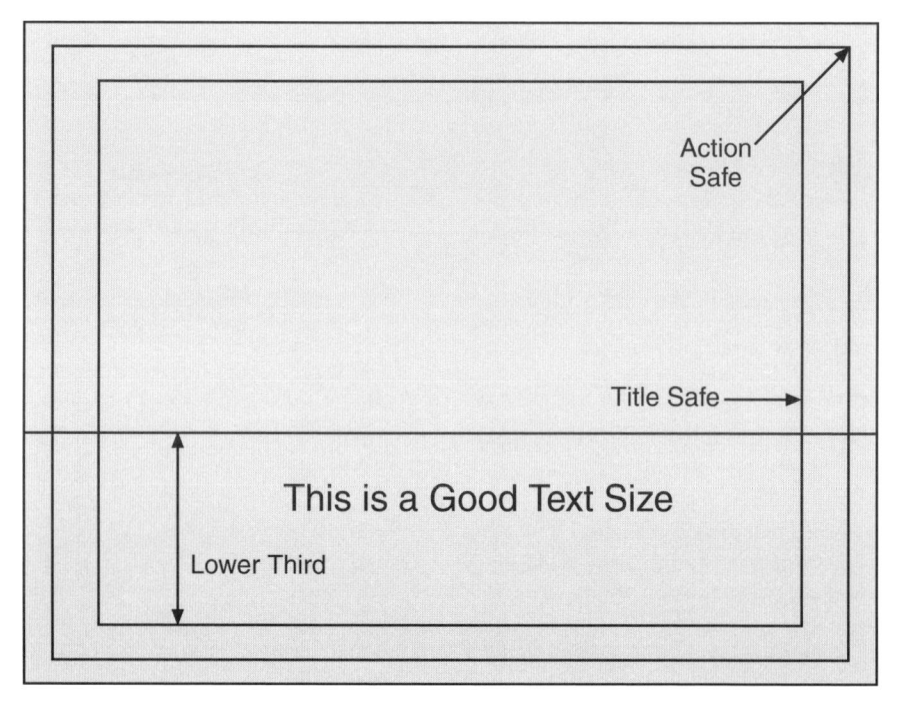

Figure 3.11
Broadcast television standards specify a safe action area and a safe title area. These restrictions allowed for variations in television displays, which used to be much more noticeable than they are in today's sets.

television movie. In either case, you must find logical break points that end on rising action, leaving the audience eager to find out what happens next. And although the breaks aren't visible to a theater audience, film productions must be broken into reel changes. (We'll give you detailed distribution requirements in Chapter 9.)

> Although modern projection systems mount the entire movie on a single platter, a movie is still shipped as a set of separate reels. In foreign markets, older multiple-reel projection systems are still in use.

As we've said, plan for film out only if you have high confidence in your ability to secure a theatrical distribution deal. If that's your plan, study Chapter 9 and make sure that you understand the technical requirements for submitting video footage to a film-transfer house.

If, mainly for economic reasons, you plan to shoot DV, you have the options of shooting in 24p or in 60i. (We don't recommend 30p, for reasons given in Chapter 2.)

If you shoot 24p, you should think about using an NLE such as Final Cut Pro or Sony Vegas that permits you to edit at 24fps. Then you can convert to 60i as a final step for output to video.

If you shoot in 60i, you can edit in 60i and then convert to 24p as a final postproduction step, using the Magic Bullet application, for example. It does have this advantage: You may have more flexibility in moving your project from one editing system to another by keeping both your camera original footage and master recording in standard video.

We'll have much more to say about editing in 60i or at 24fps in Chapter 7.

Shoot Test Rolls

Our best advice to the producer in preproduction is to set some time and money aside for shooting sample footage, or test rolls, before making final decisions about what gear and special production talent you'll need.

Test rolls should simulate available light conditions at your intended locations and should aim to capture the overall look and mood you're seeking. If you don't own a camcorder, don't buy one yet. Rent the model you intend to use, shoot your tests, and evaluate the results. (Even then, it might be more cost effective to rent a better model for the duration of shooting than to buy a less expensive one.)

Put the test footage through any of the conversion steps you plan for postproduction. For example, try shooting in 24p and editing at 24fps, output to standard video, then study the results for motion effects, color balance, depth of field, and sharpness.

If you're planning on film out, select a transfer-house partner and have them work with you to take your test footage through the conversion process so that you can inspect the film result.

All this testing will inform every creative and technical decision that follows. Admittedly, it's a trial-and-error approach. Rest assured, during production you'll meet technical challenges—and you know there will be some when you try anything new.

Our advice: Just make as many mistakes as you can *before* you assemble cast and crew on the first day of shooting.

> Writer-producer Larry Wilson (*Beetlejuice, The Addams Family*) has a theory that there are only two kinds of producers in the movie business. Some are "attackers," and others are "attractors." He advises that you can't be both; you have to make a choice and live the role. The attackers are top-dog aggressors. They win through intimidation. But attractors draw creative talent to their projects because of their talent and even, yes, their generosity. We won't commit career suicide by naming any living attackers here, but suffice it to say that in the old studio days, Columbia's Harry Cohn was a standout example. Two of the most renowned and beloved Hollywood attractors of all time are married to each other—Joanne Woodward and Paul Newman. Fortunately for the sake of our souls, indie filmmakers tend to be attractors because it's about the only way people will work with you when you've got no money to pay them.

chapter 4
Thinking Like a Cinematographer

Of all the people on a movie set, the cinematographer (also called the *director of photography,* or DP, even when the medium is video) has the most direct control over the imagery and whether it achieves anything approaching a polished, Hollywood look. Later, in postproduction, the editor will have an influence in her selection of takes and choice of transitions, and technicians such as colorists will add finishing touches. And the sound editor and composer will create a rich audio environment that transports the audience the rest of the way into a world of highly convincing make-believe.

But it's the DP who commands the camera and the lights. These are the fundamental image-capturing tools, and if you don't know how to use them to exploit the qualities of digital video, you'll never get the look you want, whether it's sensuous or garish.

Any technical or creative decision you make on the set will affect all the decisions that follow—and will limit your options in postproduction. For example, the mood of the shots will affect the editorial pacing and music selection. Admittedly, it's the director's interpretation of the script that suggests a mood initially, but setting and rigging the lighting to deliver that result will largely be left to the DP.

As we've said, the 24p mindset changes the approach to shooting video, requiring it to be both more filmic and more in line with traditional studio discipline. It also adds new constraints and challenges, including coping with video's relatively narrow contrast range and, in general, learning to work in softer, lower light.

Because the DP is so involved in these types of decisions, everyone on the project should appreciate how he thinks and should understand and value the results he's trying to achieve. So when new work methods call for him to ask for different ways of doing things, the cast and crew shouldn't lose time fretting about it and can just go about the job of getting it done.

> Shot in black-and-white, film noir movies of the mid-twentieth century, such as Jacques Tourneur's *Out of the Past* (1947), set a gloomy, ominous mood with shadowy lighting and sharp contrasts. The genre has been cited by film critics as epitomizing the cinematographer's ideal of painting with light. In fact, film noir is an excellent example of the filmmaker's dual mindset of matching creative decisions to technical constraints. These films were most popular in the post–World War II era, playing to audiences of returning veterans and their dates. Predominantly male, many of these soldiers were raised in rural communities but flocked to the urban areas after the war, seeking jobs. Their sense of alienation from the horror of war combined with the disappointment of having to scrape for work and the reality of adjusting to life in the crime-ridden cities perfectly suited the mood of dark thrillers about cynical private investigators going up against mobsters and corrupt politicians. From the technical standpoint, most film noir movies were low-budget studio projects (so-called "B movies") actually shot at night to reuse existing big-budget sets, using minimal lights to conserve on both crew size and electrical power, and employing European émigré directors and stars who didn't command big salaries.

A DP's View of Camcorder Design and Operation

As we discussed from the producer's viewpoint in Chapter 3, on a fully crewed Hollywood set, the DP might not operate the camera. However, on low-budget DV productions, the DP may also be the camera operator, or the director may double as DP. And in a guerilla-style production, the director, the DP, and the camera operator may all be the same person.

Selecting tools is a major part of the DP's job. So, regardless of the DP's role in camera operations, she should have hands-on experience with a variety of camcorders. Picking the camcorder that suits both the director's style and the technical requirements of the production is a crucial decision that should be weighed carefully early in the project.

A logical preliminary step is to evaluate camcorders, particularly from the standpoint of their ability to deliver film-look results that fit the director's style. Camcorder design will impose some technical constraints. It will also determine how the operator will actually use the camera on the set, as well as the lighting plan that is developed to capture the imagery.

Here are some factors to consider when evaluating a camcorder's ability to deliver film-look footage:

- 24p or not?
- Lenses
- Viewfinder and LCD screen
- Automatic controls and ease of use
- Exposure control

- Monitor support
- White balance
- Focusing and zooming
- Shutter controls
- Other auto features

24P or Not?

If you're going for film-look video, an early decision must be made whether or not you need a camcorder that can shoot in 24p mode. Shooting "plain-vanilla" NTSC (60i mode) has its benefits, and it certainly gives you a much wider selection of camcorders.

Remember that deciding on film look involves much more than simply shooting at 24fps. It invites all the expectations that audiences normally have of a Hollywood product—careful artistic lighting, a musical score that enhances the emotional dimension, layered sound effects that create a rich, realistic audio environment, and even otherworldly special effects.

Adding any or all of these elements will take time and money.

So, if you don't have adequate time or money, perhaps film look shouldn't be your goal, after all. If, for example, you're covering a live event, if the subject is somehow current and newsworthy, or if you're shooting the CEO's speech and you won't get lots of takes, striving for a film look might be a needless complication and might even be the wrong impression to give the audience.

Here's an encouraging thought: Since it's possible to convert 60i to 24p footage in postproduction, shooting in 60i will rarely be a mistake. Just be aware of its disadvantages:

- If you shoot in 60i, the creative team won't be able to judge the dailies for motion aspects of film look. They'll have to wait until postproduction to see how the action is rendered in 24p.
- Long after shooting is done, the conversion process will take time. Depending on the speed of the computer you are using, the rendering process could take several hours, even days. If you're on a tight deadline, you might not have the time to spare.

If, on the other hand, you shoot in 24p, what you see in the camcorder footage is pretty much what you'll get on the theater screen. But the decision is irreversible. If you later convert to the 60i broadcast standard, the conversion will do nothing to "correct" the blurred motion effects you captured at the movie frame rate.

> Some camcorders have an additional option for shooting 24p called *24p Advanced,* or 24pa. To use this mode, you must have an editing system that can also operate in this mode, recovering 24fps from the 60i data. For more information on shooting and editing in 24pa, see Chapter 7.

Lenses

At this point in the evolution of DV camcorders, the main practical impact of deciding to shoot in 24p mode will be to restrict your choice of lenses. When this book went to press, the Canon XL2 was the only prosumer DV camcorder that offered both 24p mode and a selection of interchangeable, cinema-style lenses. Granted, the built-in Leica telephoto zoom on the Panasonic AG-DVX100 is an excellent all-purpose lens, but it might not be ideal for the occasional shot that must be extremely long or extremely wide.

If, for example, the director relies heavily on telephoto closeups, a built-in zoom lens won't permit as much variation as you could get with a full complement of interchangeable lenses. The same will be true for a director who favors wide-angle closeups that add comedic distortion to the actors' faces (see Figure 4.1).

Note also a significant difference between lenses, meaning whether or not they're interchangeable. Cinema-style lenses (see Figure 4.2) operate by mechanical movement, which is precise and repeatable. For example, the focus rings on these lenses have distance markings on the barrel. So, a focus-puller could mark the desired setting on the barrel with a grease pencil and be assured of being able to hit that setting on the next take.

Figure 4.1
Shooting an actor's closeups with a wide-angle lens tends to distort the face, enlarging the nose and lips in unflattering ways that some directors feel adds a comic flair. This is a favorite technique, for example, of director Terry Gilliam (whose films include *The Life of Brian, Brazil,* and *Monty Python and the Quest for the Holy Grail*). (Photo courtesy Camila Fernandez, SOCAPA)

Figure 4.2
In a cinema-style lens, focusing and zooming are controlled by mechanical sets of gears that move the optics by precise and repeatable increments. If you see distance markings on the lens, it's probably cinema style. (Photo courtesy JVC Professional Products Company)

Most video-style lenses (see Figure 4.3) operate by electromechanical movement. Twisting the focus ring sends electrical signals to a servomotor that actuates distance adjustment. Their action is not easily repeatable from one take to the next, and there are no distance markings on the lens. Returning the focus ring to a grease-pencil marking will not necessarily match the previous setting.

The difference between cinema-style and video-style lenses isn't primarily a matter of manufacturing expense or selling price. It actually reflects a difference in traditional work styles between television and film. In news-style videography, being able to inspect the distance scale on the lens is not particularly important—if the operator is concentrating on sighting through the viewfinder, he can't see the markings on the lens. (But he's not clueless. A readout of the current setting is overlaid on the viewfinder display.)

Some video camera veterans also have a different attitude about electromechanical lens operation, which lets them vary the zoom rate in proportion to the speed of their twisting of the zoom ring. The circuit actually applies acceleration so that a sudden and dramatic zoom can be achieved with just a quick, short twisting action. Once the camera operator is familiar with the "feel" of this feature on a particular camera, it's easier to follow fast action.

Figure 4.3
Video-style lenses have nonrepeatable electromechanical movements that are popular with run-and-gun news-style camera operators. There are no distance markings on the lens because settings aren't exactly repeatable. But when you're in a hurry, a slight, sudden twist of the wrist can cause a marked shift in focus or zoom, possibly making it easier to follow the action.

Current HDV camcorder models typically have built-in zoom lenses, so stepping up to the higher-resolution format won't buy you any more sophistication in your choice of lenses. Yes, it's possible to use cinema lenses on the DVX100 and some other models with a P+S Technik adapter, but doing so will increase the bulk and weight of the camera considerably, and it will approximately double your camera rental expenses.

An important reason to shoot on long lenses is to gain greater control over depth of field, as we've emphasized in previous chapters. The shallow depth of field characteristic of telephoto shots lets the DP be selective about focus. It's another way to control where the audience is looking, because the eye will always go to the sharpest area of the picture.

Viewfinder and LCD Screen

Camcorders generally offer two basic methods to help you frame your shot: viewfinder or flip-out LCD screen. Film-style DPs tend to prefer viewfinders, News-style videographers find the flip-out screens allow them to hold the camera more steadily when they're making handheld shots, especially with smaller cameras. LCD screens are also handy for checking menu settings when it's not convenient for you to be looking through the eyepiece of the viewfinder.

Most prosumer and professional cameras have both a viewfinder and a flip-out LCD screen. The choice here isn't so much whether the feature exists, but how the camera operator prefers to use it and whether the camera design suits that purpose.

You'll recognize the viewfinder by its eyepiece, a small lens surrounded by a rubber shield called an *eye cup* (see Figure 4.4). The eyepiece shields the image from the surrounding glare.

The viewfinder focuses on a tiny screen inside the camera body that displays the video picture. The image is a miniature of the shot you'll capture if you press the Record Start/Stop button. The viewfinder status display also shows alphanumeric text and symbol overlays that tell the operator about camera settings, lighting conditions, and the charge level of the battery.

Depending on the camera, the viewfinder display will be black-and-white or color. Here's another important decision: The high-end camcorders tend to have black-and-white viewfinders, since it is easier to judge focus and other picture details with a black-and-white display. You will seldom, if ever, find this feature on a prosumer camera.

You should also look for camcorders with viewfinders that can be set to overscan, showing an area that's slightly larger than the final recorded picture—a standard motion-picture camera feature you'll now find on some prosumer and professional camcorders. The extra area surrounding the picture will help you spot moving subjects before they enter the frame. The fraction-of-a-second warning you gain might give you just enough time to pan or change focus. An overscan viewfinder is particularly useful for anticipating an actor's entrance.

Figure 4.4
A camcorder viewfinder has a rubber eyepiece to shield the operator's eye from the surrounding glare. The viewfinder shows the video display on a small internal LCD within the camera, overlaid with camera menu settings and status indicators. With the possible exception of its being black-and-white for better focusing, it's the same display you'll see on a flip-out LCD or an external video monitor.

> When sighting through a viewfinder that doesn't have the overscan feature, you can get much the same effect by not pressing your eye up hard against the eyepiece—that way you can see things in your peripheral vision. However, veteran camera operators learn to keep *both* eyes open, sighting through the viewfinder with one eye and watching the periphery with the other. It's a trick that requires some practice.

An external LCD screen flips out from the body of the camera like a car door (refer back to Figures 1.3 and 3.7). Compared to the viewfinder image, the LCD display is relatively large—one or two inches across—and it's usually in color. However, the LCD is a poor tool for judging focus by eye. For this, camera operators rely on lens distance settings and the viewfinder display.

The flip-out LCD screen lets you shoot handheld with the camcorder in front of you rather than pressed to your head. This technique makes for a steadier picture. For example, when you press the eyecup of a viewfinder to your face and then walk and shoot, physical contact with the bobbing of your head jars the camcorder. If you use the flip-out screen, you can cradle the camcorder in your hands away from your face. The muscles at your elbows are natural shock absorbers, smoothing the camcorder's ride and steadying the image. It's handy for run-and-gun newsgathering, especially if you're using a small camera.

> Most flip-out screens are mounted on a swivel so that you can rotate them for viewing as you stand facing the camera lens. This feature can be useful if you don't have a crew and you're standing in for a closeup, or if you're shooting your own presentation. Rotating the screen can cause the image to be presented not only upright but also mirrored. This might seem odd, but clever camcorder designers realized that subjects are more used to seeing themselves in a mirror. In fact, it can be quite difficult to keep yourself in frame if you turn mirroring off (which you can do through the menu), in which case you'll see yourself the way others see you—with your hair parted on the other side.

Automatic Controls and Ease of Use

Any camera store window-shopper knows that professional camcorders have lots of switches and dials that consumer models don't have. Prosumer camcorders fall somewhere in between. The designers of consumer camcorders obviously don't want home movie buffs to fret with the details of operation. They want you to be able to take the camera out of the box at your birthday party, turn on the power, load a cassette, and then just point and shoot. This ease of use is achieved by making most camcorder functions automatic, relying on sensors and digital circuitry to make decisions about focus, exposure, white balance, and so on.

And as any experienced camcorder operator knows, automatic controls are a sucker's bet. The results will be acceptable occasionally and at other times will range from mediocre to awful. Autofocus (AF) can't keep subjects truly sharp unless they're standing absolutely still. Auto exposure (AE) can't react fast enough to changing light levels if you pan from sunlight to shadow or vice versa. Auto white balance (AWB) assumes the brightest area in the shot is pure white, when it might instead be bright orange or hot pink. And it will compensate by giving all the other colors in the shot an unnatural tint.

So the lesson for every serious videographer is to turn off automatic controls and learn to focus, expose, and white-balance manually.

However, on a consumer camcorder, that's actually rather difficult. Because there may be no handy switches or knobs for these settings, you must adjust them by making selections from the menu display, much as you would on a computer screen (except this one on the camera is tinier and harder to see). Even after you've had some practice doing this, you might not be able to make adjustments quickly enough to keep up with fast-breaking action.

Short and sweet: Using most consumer camcorders in manual mode, the way a pro would, is a pain.

Although pro cameras also have much the same automatic features as their low-priced cousins, auto modes are typically turned off by default. The camera designers assume you want to be in manual mode most of the time. And you have the option of turning any combination of the auto modes back on. All the knobs and switches for manual operation are there, and these are located on the camera body in places where you can access them easily, even if you're running and gunning.

On most, if not all, video cameras, you'll find whatever knobs and switches they have located on the *left* side of the camera body, as you point the lens at the subject. This design is a legacy from the days when cameras were so large and bulky that the only way to use them without a tripod was to cradle them on the operator's shoulder. Camera designers have always assumed it's the *right* shoulder (see Figure 4.5). The controls are laid out so that operators of shoulder-slung cameras can use the left hand to alternately twist the exposure and focus rings on the lens and adjust the knobs. The right hand supports and steadies the camera by grasping a strap or handle on the right or top side. The fingers of the right hand may also operate the Record Start/Stop push button and possibly also a rocker switch (located on the handle) for motorized zoom. On a camera with a cinema-style lens, an alternative to pressing the zoom rocker switch would be to twist the zoom ring on the lens with the left hand.

The exact location and layout of these controls on the camera body is by no means standard, varying considerably among makes and models. Ergonomic designs—as well as how well a particular operator adapts to the layout of the controls—are obviously major factors in deciding which camcorder will do the

Figure 4.5
Camcorder controls on prosumer and pro models are typically found on the left side of the camera body where you can operate them with your left hand as you hold the unit on your right shoulder, steadying it with your right hand.

job for you. Besides its selection of cinema-style lenses, another reason for the popularity of the Canon XL series has been its unique ergonomic design, which features, among other controls, a large circular dial for switching camcorder modes and functions (see Figure 4.6).

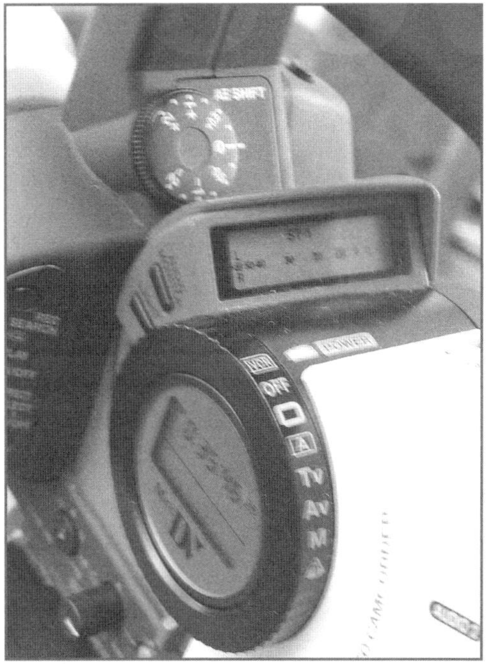

When you're shooting film-style with the camcorder mounted on a tripod or boom arm, presumably you have more time to set up each shot, and the layout of controls is less critical. Still, you want the controls you use most often to be where you expect to find them. And, perhaps more importantly, you'll want their indicators or status displays to be readable at a glance so that you can easily check the settings before you roll tape.

Pay particular attention to ergonomics when you're evaluating prosumer camcorders. Because these products represent trade-offs, or compromises, between functionality and price, the designers' choices might not necessarily be to your liking. At minimum, you must be able to turn off any automatic feature and control it manually. And if the default setting for an auto feature is "on," be aware that you could easily overlook turning it off in your haste to get a shot. Yes, the camcorder will probably have a manual-override setting. But will the setting persist after you turn the unit off and then back on? Or will it default back to auto mode?

In general, the more cumbersome it is to engage the camera's manual modes, the less desirable and the more troublesome it will be on the set.

Here's an example of such a design trade-off, albeit on relatively cheap cameras: Many consumer camcorders load and eject the tape cassette from the bottom. This design helps make the body as compact as possible. It can also be convenient for reloading quickly, inserting the tape with your left hand when you're holding the camera with your right. However, when you screw the camera down on the head of a tripod, you'll find that you must then unscrew and lift it off to change tapes. Although annoying, the bottom-loading feature might not be a problem—unless you're recording a live event such as an executive speech that goes longer than the tape's 60-minute running time.

Figure 4.6
The large, circular multifunction switch is a popular ergonomic feature of the Canon XL series.

Exposure Control

As a rule, if a camcorder doesn't have a zebra function, you don't want it. Zebra is a reliable tool for monitoring your exposure level for both news-style and film-style videography. It's found on all professional cameras and most prosumer cameras. Used correctly, it's the best way to ensure you don't overexpose parts of your shot.

Zebra stripes are a black-and-white optical effect that appears in the viewfinder to highlight overexposed portions of the image (see Figure 4.7 and Color Plate 1). To adjust for proper exposure, rotate the exposure (f-stop) ring or dial to reduce the aperture size until the stripes disappear. Once you've done this, as long as the actors' faces in the scene appear well lit, you're ready to shoot. If the faces don't look right, leave the exposure alone, adjust the lighting, check the zebra stripes again, and then reset the exposure, if necessary.

> Camcorder models differ in their default settings for the level at which zebra stripes appear. Many use 80IRE, which is about where highlights in skin tones become overbright. However, Hollywood-style videographers may prefer to change the level to 100IRE so that they know exactly when blow-out occurs. This permits you to use every bit of the upper end of the contrast range, but it's risky unless you're experienced at judging how highlights work in closeups.

Figure 4.7
On a camcorder with zebra function, stripes appear in overexposed areas on the display. In this case, the overhead light and the performer's white shirt will blow out unless you reduce the exposure level. As you adjust the exposure control to stop down, the stripes will disappear at the correct setting, although the overhead light is so intense that it'll blow out no matter what.

Any decision to ignore zebra stripes should be deliberate. You might choose to do this if everything else in the scene looks great and the overexposed area is a small portion of the screen. It's an artistic decision. You can simply permit the overexposure, letting the highlight blow out. The result will be a white area that contains absolutely no image detail. In effect, it's a hole in the picture information. Therefore, no matter how much you might adjust brightness or contrast in postproduction, you will recover no edges or colors—that area of the image will be blank. At risk of overstating the obvious, remember that permitting blown-out highlights is an irreversible decision.

Monitor Support

Again, if the camcorder has a black-and-white viewfinder, that's the most accurate way for you to evaluate focus. However, it's easier to judge composition and framing on the relatively larger screen of a color monitor. (Filmmakers have been using field monitors for years to look at instant video replay on the set.)

> Technically, a B&W viewfinder uses the signal from the green CCD, which has more edge information than the other two colors (red and blue).

Don't use a conventional TV as your monitor if you can avoid it. Televisions sets have built-in color-correction circuits that won't show exactly what you're getting. Use a real field monitor, designed for this purpose, and connect it to the camcorder's Video Out (or Monitor) jack (see Figure 4.8). A desirable feature in a camcorder is an S-Video output jack (possibly labeled Y/C), which will give a better-quality picture.

The most accurate way to judge picture quality is to use a waveform monitor, a type of oscilloscope that shows voltages of various video parameters on a graphic display (see Figure 4.9). If you're skilled at reading it, a waveform monitor can be a very precise way of measuring and monitoring exposure levels and RGB color. Although it's rare for a traditional filmmaker to know how to use one, waveform monitors will become increasingly prevalent on the set as digital video tools replace film.

Figure 4.8
A field monitor is a must-have for judging image quality and framing. It can become a crowded area on the set as chairs are placed in front of it for director and client. And, if outdoors, there will be rigging like a small hut to shade the screen from the sun. The crew's slang term for such a tricked-out field monitor is "Video Village." Here on the Aqua Tan set, we've positioned the monitor for the director to watch as the camera shoots the actor descending the spiral staircase.

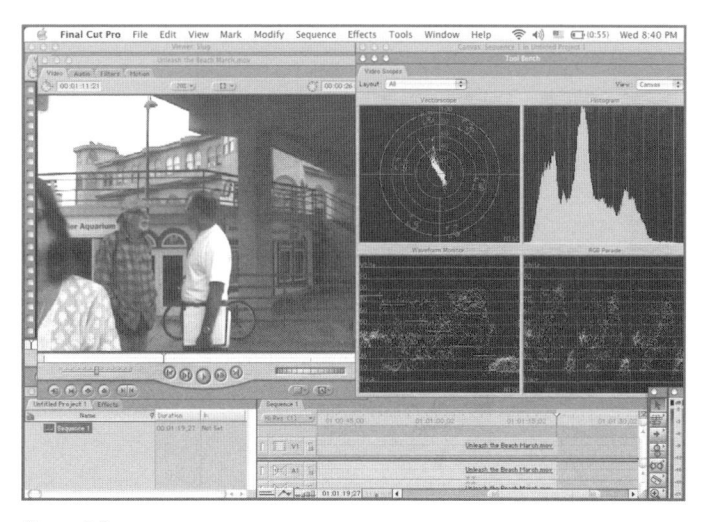

Figure 4.9
Pro-level editing applications, such as Final Cut Pro, contain a Waveform Monitor display screen, which has the same readings as the hardware you can use on the set to check measurements of the camcorder's video signals. Also shown are Vectorscope, Histogram, and RGB Level displays, which emulate other studio test instruments.

Achieving White Balance

If your camcorder's white balance is set improperly, the whole scene can take on an undesirable tint. You may be able to fix this in post, which is one of the areas in which video has advantages over film. But life will be simpler and less expensive if you get the scene in the can properly in the first place. (Grips can rig some color temperature adjustments, as we'll explain shortly in this chapter.)

> It's increasingly common for film productions to use a digital intermediate, or DI, from which a film negative will be created by tape-to-film transfer. Since the DI is essentially a high-resolution digital video computer file, most of the required color correction, transitions, and special effects can be done on the realm of computer generated imagery (CGI) before the negative is created. In this respect, a production shot on film these days uses film only for the shooting and the releasing. The steps in-between are digital. For more information on digital intermediates, see Chapter 9.

As a matter of practice, use the manual white-balance control every time you change camera setups or move or adjust the lights. It's a straightforward procedure. Place a white object, such as a bounce board, in the scene. Zoom into it until it fills the frame and set the white balance. On many camcorders it is as easy as pressing a button (see Figure 4.10 and Color Plate 5).

> There isn't always time to adjust white balance when you're in a hurry. In such cases, there's still a good way to avoid the fully automatic mode. Most camcorders permit you to select one of two semiautomatic white-balance modes: indoor (tungsten) or outdoor (daylight). These settings can appear in the camcorder display as either a light bulb or a sunburst symbol.

Figure 4.10
Press the camcorder's manual white-balance button each time you change setups or lighting. Focus on a white card or bounce board that entirely fills the frame.

Focusing and Zooming

Focusing is what makes the picture sharp (or fuzzy, if you do it incorrectly). On all professional and most prosumer cameras, you can adjust focus by rotating a focus ring, a circular fitting that wraps around the barrel of the lens. On consumer cameras that don't have a focus ring, you must typically disable autofocus and turn a dial on the camera body.

Manual focus can be done by eye, judging the sharpness simply by inspecting the image in the viewfinder, LCD, or (less reliably) the monitor. However, focusing by eye isn't always accurate. Edges can be difficult to see in small, low-resolution displays. And fine focus adjustments may not be noticeable, given the inherent depth of field of video.

With any video camcorder, focusing will be most critical when you are using a telephoto lens or the telephoto setting on a zoom lens. The best way to make sure you're in focus when using a telephoto zoom is actually to engage autofocus, briefly:

1. Make sure autofocus is off.
2. Zoom in on the subject all the way.
3. Engage autofocus momentarily (typically, by pressing the AF button). As long as the distance to the subject doesn't change, the camcorder will now stay in focus anywhere within the zoom range.

This procedure won't work all that well on moving subjects, though, since the AF circuit probably won't be able to respond fast enough to find an edge on which to focus.

Speaking of zooming, twisting the zoom ring isn't the only way to control it. Most camcorders have a semiautomatic continuous zoom control. It's usually a rocker switch (see Figure 4.11) or a pair of push buttons labeled In and Out or + and − or T (telephoto) and W (wide). For example, to zoom in, you press and hold the rocker switch (or the In or + button), and the camcorder increases the magnification until you let go of the switch.

Figure 4.11
Pressing and holding down this rocker switch on the Canon XL series is an alternative to twisting the zoom ring for actuating a continuous transition from wide to telephoto or vice versa. (This camcorder also has another zoom switch on top of the unit, next to the Record button.)

Getting a smooth, controlled zoom can be tricky. On camcorders that use unmarked, electromechanical lenses, zoom is subject to all manner of imprecision. The zooming action of most cameras isn't linear. The speed of the zoom may vary, depending on how hard or how fast you press the switch. More pressure or a quicker action can cause a faster zoom. It's very important for you to practice with your camcorder to achieve the rate of speed and smoothness you want without visual jerks or jarring effects that will annoy the audience.

Take time to experiment with the zoom: Camcorder zoom controls vary in layout and sensitivity among the different models. There can even be more than one option on a given camera. For instance, the Canon XL series has two zoom controls. There's a larger zoom rocker switch near the lens barrel and a smaller switch on the handle. Both switches can vary the zoom speed according to touch, and the larger switch also applies acceleration, depending on how hard you press it.

> Even if the camcorder is on a tripod, you risk jiggling it by putting your finger on the zoom control, especially if you're using a shake-sensitive telephoto setting to begin with. Try using the zoom switch on the camcorder's remote control, if it has one. The remote lets you operate the zoom without touching the camcorder.

Shutter Controls

When you're trying to follow fast action, selection of shutter speed can be a key decision. You'll find a shutter speed control on all but some low-end consumer camcorders.

For motion-picture camera operators making the transition to video, the notion of shutter speed requires another shift in mindset. In a motion-picture camera, shutter speed is the same as frame rate. For example, increasing the number of frames per second creates a slow-motion effect. Because the projection rate is a constant 24fps, capturing more frames each second will create the illusion that time is passing more slowly than normal.

In a motion-picture camera, a related but different setting—shutter angle—controls how long the frame is exposed to light, but it doesn't affect the frame rate. Increasing the shutter angle reduces blurring and, at just the right setting, can have the effect of freezing action.

In a video camera, shutter speed is analogous to film shutter angle. This setting controls the length of time the CCD is exposed to light during each frame. The frame rate doesn't change. That is, if you're shooting in 60i mode, the frame rate remains 30fps, regardless of how you vary the shutter speed. And if you're shooting in 24p mode, the frame rate is 24fps, regardless of shutter speed.

> To see the effect of varying film shutter angle, study the combat sequences in the opening minutes of *Saving Private Ryan* (1998). The result is a feeling of unreality and an altered experience of time.

> Some video cameras, such as the Panasonic Varicam series, do let you vary the frame rate to shoot fast- or slow-motion sequences. These cameras also have a shutter-speed control, which varies the exposure time for each frame. As with other video cameras, varying the shutter speed doesn't affect the frame rate.

For action shots, increasing the shutter speed (thereby *reducing* the duration of exposure per frame) tends to reduce or eliminate blurring, which might make the action seem cleaner, crisper, more realistic, and less film-like.

Most video cameras permit shutter speed settings from about 1/60–1/8000. The correct setting is largely an aesthetic decision. Remember, though, that increasing the shutter speed, reducing the exposure time per frame, will require opening up the f-stop and probably also increasing lighting levels. For example, capturing a foot race at 1/2500 would probably require breaking our rule about not shooting in the bright sun.

A few prosumer and many professional cameras permit shutter speeds that are actually slower than the frame rate—1/20, for example. A shutter speed that's slightly slower than the frame rate will increase blurring. It it's even slower, then actors seem to take on magical abilities, seeming to jump through space as they move (see Figure 4.12 and Color Plate 8).

Figure 4.12
In this action scene that's an homage to the "bullet time" sequence from *Nero's Ring,* shutter speed is set slower than the frame rate in order to exaggerate blurring and make the suited agent character appear to have the ability to move at superhuman speed as he circles around the embattled hero.

Varying shutter speed from the normal setting can make action seem smoother or more erratic, depending on the other camera settings, the speed of the action, and the lighting conditions. It's an unpredictable effect, best experimented with.

Some movie lights, especially fluorescents, pulsate slightly, varying in intensity with the alternating current in the electrical power line (60Hz). At some video shutter-speed settings, these lights will appear to flicker noticeably. But the effect might not be apparent on the monitor during shooting. You might have to play back the tape to check for it. (Be careful about playing back takes on the set. You can create a timecode break, an error in the timecode and a problem for the editor, and you also risk accidentally taping over a good take.)

Other Auto Features

Camcorders have a variety of other features. Many of these, apparently designed mostly for their marketing appeal, are only occasionally useful for the serious professional.

Semiautomatic Modes

Some camcorders have a pair of shooting modes called shutter priority and aperture priority. When you switch from manual or full auto to shutter priority, you select the shutter speed manually, and the camcorder controls the exposure automatically. In aperture priority, you set the aperture (exposure), and the camcorder controls the shutter speed. (Don't use aperture priority if you're seeking film out.)

Although we usually advise against using auto modes, shutter priority can come in handy when you're trying to follow fast-moving subjects. Aperture priority works best in low-light conditions.

Image Stabilization

Like other auto modes, automatic image stabilization is another case of the camcorder trying to correct a bad situation, and often not succeeding. In all but the most expensive cameras, it's an electronic function that sacrifices resolution. The camera leaves a border around the active pixel area and then moves the framing around within it to compensate for your slight jiggling of the camera. But there aren't enough pixels in the border area to compensate for big bumps, and the camera's circuit couldn't react fast enough if there were. Best advice: Put the camera on a tripod or other steadying mount and turn automatic image stabilization off.

Some high-end cameras have optical image stabilization, typically based on a shock-absorbing mechanism that cushions the prism. That feature is much more reliable than the electronic kind, but it's still usable only if the jiggling is fairly subtle.

> If you plan to zoom during a shot, turn electronic image stabilization off. Otherwise, you'll confuse the poor camera's "intelligent" circuits, resulting in a jumpy zoom as it keeps trying to hold your framing.

Video Gain

In general, the CCDs of video cameras respond to lower light levels than all but the fastest film stocks. With even a low-cost camcorder, it's quite feasible to shoot when the scene is lit only by street lights, car headlights, or even candlelight. Most video cameras offer the ability to push this capability as far as possible. Typically called *low-light mode*, it supplies extra voltage (called *bias*) to the CCDs. The bias voltage increases the sensitivity of the pixels to light, but it shows up in the video signal as noise. The resulting imagery has a grainy quality, not unlike the grainy quality of low-light film exposure.

On some cameras, low-light mode kicks in automatically when the manual exposure setting isn't wide enough to get a minimum-strength output from the CCDs. On other camcorders, you have to select the mode manually.

Images captured in low-light mode can look arty or crummy, depending on your artistic sensibility. If you get stuck shooting in low-light mode just so you can get any shot at all, you may be able to enhance the grainy effect in postproduction—and make it look all the more deliberate.

Special Auto Modes

Although no automatic modes are good alternatives when you could control the camera more competently manually, some will be lifesavers when conditions are less than ideal.

For example, spotlight mode reduces video gain in the center of the picture to compensate for the glare of a camera-mounted spotlight. If you're the lone camera operator and you're using a spotlight either at night or as fill in bright sunlight, this mode can help even out the overall exposure and reduce contrast.

Sand-and-snow mode reduces video gain in overbright areas of the picture. As with spotlight mode, its goal is to even out overall exposure and reduce contrast between foreground subjects and bright backgrounds.

Sports mode attempts to increase shutter speed in combination with increasing the aperture as you follow fast action. If being in manual mode might mean you'd miss the shot, shutter priority could give you more reliable control.

Tape Speed Selection

While not an auto mode, per se, all DV camcorders use the Standard Play (SP) automatically unless you change it. We don't recommend switching to Long Play (LP) or using thinner LP tape. Tape is so cheap you needn't worry about wasting it, and with slower speed and thinner tape, you'll just increase the possibility of data loss during a crucial take.

The rare exception might be that situation when you absolutely, positively must capture a live event in a single take that will go longer than the 60-minute capacity of a standard MiniDV cassette.

> If you're covering a live event and it's a mission-critical shoot, rent a camcorder that will accept pro-style DVC cassettes, a larger format that can record up to three hours in SP mode.

Digital Effects

Marketers of consumer camcorders love to hype digital effects features, such as transition effects and sepia tone, that can be performed in-camera as you shoot. Pros know to stay away from applying any digital effects in-camera that can be done just as easily—and with greater control and flexibility—in postproduction.

Achieving Film-Look Lighting

Film-look lighting is both a craft and an art. The practical purpose of lighting is simply to make sure the subject and its surroundings will be visible on the screen by achieving the correct exposure of the CCDs. At the same time, the cinematographer's art of painting with light is a visual storytelling tool: It shows the audience where to look or what to think about a character or an environment. Lighting technicians achieve these goals by selecting, placing, and rigging lights, reflectors, and other light sources on a location or set.

From a narrative standpoint, the main purpose of lighting is to set a mood. TV sitcoms are always lit brightly and cheerily, priming the audience for laughter. Horror films usually transpire in dark interiors with mysterious shadows carefully designed to inspire anxiety and reinforce a scary story.

Both analog and digital video have a bad reputation for flat, boring lighting. Part of that reputation is deserved and based on historical necessity. Live broadcasts on early TV used multicamera setups, which required the subjects to be lit more or less equally from all directions. In fact, many types of TV shows are still lit that way, including newscasts, game shows, and soap operas.

When video ventured outdoors to cover news and sports, artful lighting was rarely possible. It was hard enough to follow the fast-breaking action.

But that's ancient history. Today's DV camcorders are small and portable with excellent low-light sensitivity. You therefore have an opportunity to tell your story or convey your message by painting with light just as the Hollywood cinematographers always have. And we're not talking about art for art's sake. Creative lighting not only adds aesthetic interest to your production, but it also allows you to direct the viewers' attention to elements within the image you want to emphasize. Good lighting technique requires you to make deliberate creative and technical decisions, decisions that ultimately will determine how the audience responds to your imagery—and to your story.

The Ideal of Three-Point Lighting

Classic Hollywood lighting technique has a century-long evolution, but it's all rooted in a basic three-point plan (see Figure 4.15). The classic shot is a full frontal closeup worthy of a star:

Key light highlights the subject, showing the viewer where to look. In a classic lighting plan, the key light is a bright, hard light, coming from above and to one side of the subject's face. Purists say that the key light should be aimed so that the shadow of the nose touches the corner of the mouth (Figure 4.13).

Fill light is located in front of the subject, on the side opposite the key. It's a soft light that fills in the harsh shadows cast by the key, thereby reducing contrast overall, particularly on the face. (Harsh facial shadows are thought desirable only when the subject is supposed to look gruesome, menacing, or horrific.)

Backlight is typically hard, aimed at the subject from the back, giving depth to the picture by separating the subject from the background. Because its shadows are thrown forward, falling behind the camera, you don't usually have to be concerned about them. A backlight may be the brightest light on the set.

Lit properly according to a three-point plan, a shot is lit and viewed best from just one camera angle. Besides the expense of using multiple cameras and operators, this lighting technique went along with the traditional Hollywood practice of shooting a succession of single-camera setups rather than getting them all at once, the way it was done in television.

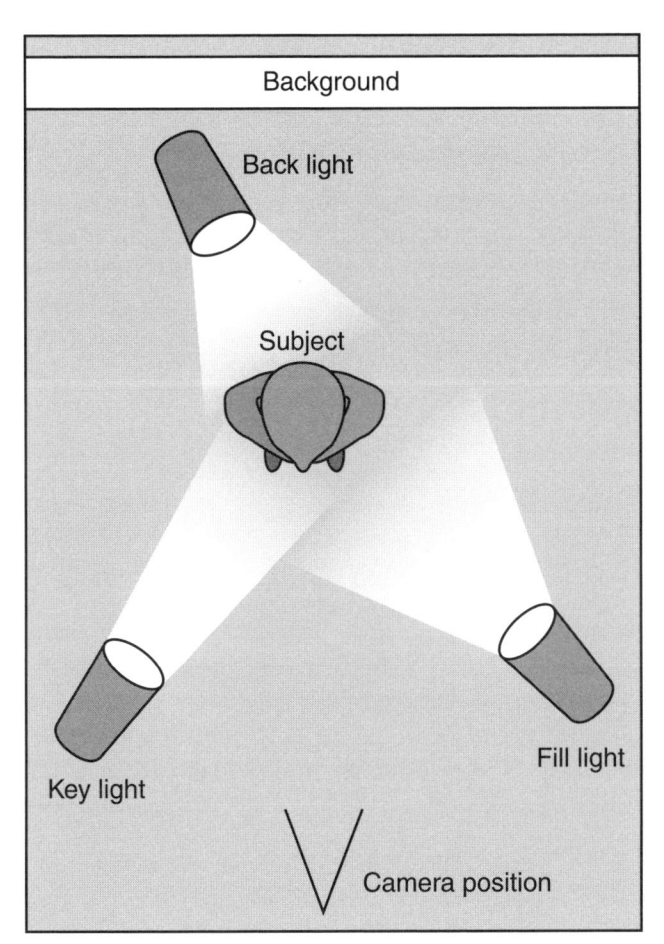

Figure 4.13
Classic three-point lighting is a long-standing Hollywood practice that draws attention to the subject, reduces harsh contrasts, and separates the subject from the background.

Figure 4.14
Veteran DPs will tell you to aim a key light so that the shadow of the tip of the actor's nose touches the corner of the mouth.

Applying the Three-Point Principle

Perhaps the single most important practice in achieving film-look video is to always look for opportunities to create three-point lighting, regardless of the situation.

It's easy enough, though time consuming, to do this when you have truckfuls of movie lights and an army of grips and gaffers. But the artful DP must learn how to light from three points with available light and minimal crew. Consider the worst case—when you're shooting by yourself in bright sun. Here's one solution that adheres to the three points:

1. Position the camera so the sun is *behind* your subject.
2a. Bounce sunlight into the subject's face as the key light. You can soften it somewhat by bouncing off a white board rather than a shiny reflector. Such a soft key may require no fill.

or

2b. Use one single daylight-type source as your key light. If you're shooting alone, it can be a camera-mounted spotlight. (And, if it has this feature, try switching the camcorder's spotlight mode on to reduce contrast.)
3. If you use a hard key, bounce the sun back toward the subject from the opposite angle to create fill.

Again, this is a worst case scenario. You'll improve the odds of getting good exterior shots by doing whatever you can to reduce overall contrast range of the scene—moving into the shade or shooting mornings, evenings, or on overcast days.

Motivating the Light Source

Convincing the audience that your primary light source mimics real-world lighting is called *motivating* the key light. Even if the key light is artificial (a movie light aimed to flatter a face), your audience should believe it's coming from a natural source such as a window, table lamp, or bright reflection from an overhead object, such as a light-colored wall or mirror.

Usually the DP will approach lighting by determining the motivation and therefore the source and location of the key light. Then she will consider the other two points of the three-point plan. Occasional exceptions involve strong sources of available light that must be dealt with before you can set the key. For example, if you're shooting indoors, you must mask or color-correct the bright light from a window before setting other lights. If you use sunlight in the plan, even if complemented with a movie light, it should motivate the key because for the audience the window will be the obvious natural source.

Achieving Acceptable Contrast Range

Balancing the intensity of each of your three primary light sources to achieve an acceptable contrast range is the main technical challenge of getting each setup to look and record just right. As a rule, you should allow a variation of just five f-stops in a video shot, as opposed to the typical eight you'd have with film.

Film blacks look blacker and the whites look whiter than they do in video, and more detail is visible in both shaded and sunny areas. In video, if you expose for a dark or darkened face in the shade of a tree, the brightly lit areas will be washed out. If you stop down to soften the highlight on the actor's brow, the rest of the face will turn to mud. So to give your video a film look, pay special attention to keeping your lighting levels more even than you would on film. You can handle some contrast-range problems in post, but it is far better to light the scene carefully in the first place.

Establishing a Mood

When you're limited to five f-stops in a given frame, you must rely more on the overall lighting level to convey emotional overtones and subtexts (unspoken thoughts and feelings) than a film DP might.

If you want brilliant highlights or deep blacks, you have the creative option of permitting them to be blown out or totally black. In other words, you *can* break the five f-stop guideline as long as you do it on purpose. However, it's best to make sure those out-of-range areas are relatively small in relation to the other objects in the frame—both so the shot won't look like a mistake and so the audience won't miss any important visual details.

Lighting Guidelines for Film-Look DPs

To keep you in the mindset as you set up each shot, here are some rules of thumb for achieving the Hollywood look on video:

1. Favor softer light.
2. Try to solve lighting problems by reducing rather than adding light.
3. Control color temperature.
4. Watch overhead lights and reflections.
5. Reduce light on the background.
6. Add interest and glamour with extra lighting touches.

Favor Softer Light

Video responds beautifully to soft, diffuse light, the kind you get outdoors on an overcast day. DPs love soft light because it "wraps around" the subject in a pleasing way, softening or eliminating shadows. Soft light requires less fill to achieve correct exposure, neatly fitting the requirements of video's relatively narrow contrast range.

But there are other ways to achieve a softer look besides waiting for the sky to cloud over.

Indoors, the quickest and easiest way to soften a movie light is to bounce it off the ceiling or a light-colored wall. The ceiling is a particularly good choice because light coming from above usually appears motivated, as if it's coming from overhead lighting. Another way to motivate a bounced light source is to angle it so it appears to be coming from an open window or doorway.

> If a wall you need to use as a reflector is too dark for good reflection, you can tape a bounce board to it or mount the board on a C-stand.

If you want a more directed beam, once the lights are set, grips can fit lights with silks, which diffuse the light, or flags, which mask a portion of the beam.

A particularly effective technique for working outdoors on a sunny day is to move the setup into the shadow of a building and then use bounce boards or reflectors to redirect the sun into that area (see Figure 4.15). Fill light can be created by placing diffusion in front of a reflector, and the harder key light might also be reflected, but with little or no diffusion.

Figure 4.15
A three-point lighting plan can be done outdoors on a bright day using a combination of reflectors, bounce boards, and silks. In this setup on the Aqua Tan set, a production assistant aims a reflector at the actor's face to provide the key light.

Solve Lighting Problems by Reducing Rather Than Adding Light

If your f-stop range exceeds five stops, you have two options: You can either remove it from the light areas or add light to the dark areas. As a rule, start by taking light away.

It will almost always be cheaper and easier to take light away from the hot area in a scene—and probably also open the aperture—rather than to add light to dark areas. Since the contrast range of video is so narrow, you won't see much benefit from adding light unless you add it almost everywhere. The exception is when you shoot in bright sunlight. Then your options are either to use big fill lights or reflectors or not to add fill and thus to permit deep shadows.

The quickest way to lower the intensity of a light is simply to move it back away from the subject. Intensity of light falling on a single subject from a single source follows the inverse square law: Moving a light twice as far from a subject will make its intensity four times less.

Some other techniques for reducing light include:

◆ Turn off or mask available light, including windows and overhead light.
◆ Add scrims, flags, or diffusion to reduce the output of movie lights.
◆ Use dimmers on practicals and tungsten lights that cannot be diffused or on any light that must fade up or down during a scene.

Control Color Temperature

White light sources aren't actually pure white. They have a range of tints, which cinematographers and lighting technicians call *color temperature*. The temperature, or color of the light, is measured in degrees on the Kelvin scale (°K). For example, sunlight is at the blue end of the spectrum, and incandescent lights such as table lamps tend to be orange. Color tints from different light sources, or mixed lighting, in a shot must be balanced in relation to one another so they look more natural or pleasing to the eye when recorded on film or on video. The result is a color-balanced lighting setup.

In everyday life, we ignore minor differences of color temperature because the human brain compensates for them. But film and CCDs don't compensate the way our vision does, and recorded results can be noticeable and unattractive. If you're shooting in a room with sunlight coming through a window, you must use movie lights with daylight color temperature (about 5500°K) or tint the windows to match tungsten lights, which have a color temperature of about 3200°K.

Besides mixed lighting, another way to deal with color temperature is to adjust the overall color response of the camera itself. In photography, you can choose between film stocks that have emulsions balanced for outdoors (daylight) or for indoor incandescent (tungsten) lighting. Since camcorders don't use film, you can't adjust for color temperature by using different film stocks. Instead, camcorders rely on the continuously variable white-balance feature.

> White balance should *always* be set manually, shooting a white card or bounce board so it fills the frame. Automatic white balance can make ugly choices, even on expensive camcorders. The white-balance function samples an area in the scene as a reference for setting maximum RGB pixel values. Technically, when R, G, and B signals are all at peak voltage, the white level is at 100 percent, or 100IRE.

Using Filters and Gels

Filters and gels are made of colored, transparent optical material that changes the tint of the light passing through them. Filters attach to camera lenses, thereby changing the overall tint of the image, while gels (colored gelatin sheets) fit into holders that mount in front of light fixtures and control the temperature of that particular source. Larger sheets of gel can be applied directly to windows to change the color temperature of incoming sunlight (see Figure 4.16 and Color Plate 3).

In video, since placing a filter on the camera will affect everything in the shot, its primary use usually isn't for color correction. (In film, filters can be used to adjust overall color for different film stocks.) DPs use lens filters more often for creative effects: enhancing a sunny or gloomy mood or making a daylight scene look like it was shot at night (called shooting *day-for-night*).

Gels come in sheets and rolls, which must be cut by hand and sandwiched in metal frames for insertion in the light fixture. Types of colored gel and their uses are listed in Table 4.1. The gels deteriorate rapidly from the heat of the light and must be replaced several times a day. Grips can also cover windows with large sheets of gel to balance daylight with indoor tungsten lighting. Rolls of color-corrective gels are available from equipment rental houses and photo supply stores.

Figure 4.16
If you're shooting indoors and you white balance a camcorder in tungsten movie lights, any sunlight coming through a window will cast an undesirable cold blue tint. To prevent this, cover the window area with a sheet of CTO gel. The gel's orange color compensates for its opposite primary color, blue. An alternative in the setup shown above (indicated by the arrows) would be to shut off the movie lights completely (or gel them blue) and reflect the bright, diffuse daylight back into the faces of your subjects.

> Another use of diffusion filters is to hide large pores and blemishes in star closeups. DPs call any particularly dense diffusion a *linoleum filter*. Of course, there is no filter made of linoleum. The term was originated by the actress and notorious celebrity Tallulah Bankhead. She had not shot a film in 15 years when she reported to the set in London to film *Die! Die! My Darling!* in the 1960s (released as *Fanatic* in 1965). She had aged, and it showed. She reportedly quipped, "They shot Shirley Temple through a gauze filter. For me they had to use linoleum."

Table 4.1 Types of Photographic Gels and Their Uses

Type of Photographic Gel	Purpose
ND (neutral density)	Reduce overall light intensity
CTO (color temperature orange)	Change daylight to tungsten
CTB (color temperature blue)	Change tungsten to daylight
Plus green	Change daylight or tungsten to fluorescent
Minus green	Change fluorescent to daylight or tungsten

It's tricky to mix artificial sources, such as a combination of movie lights and practical table lamps. Even though all of these are types of tungsten (indoor) lighting, their color temperatures will probably be quite different. For example, the incandescent bulb in an ordinary table lamp will be considerably cooler and yellower in color than a hot halogen movie light. You can gel one set of lights selectively to match the other, possibly using multiple layers of gel to increase the effect. When shooting indoors, use *one* of the following strategies for best color balance:

- Gel the window shades with CTO, or mask them entirely. Use tungsten lights all of the same type, and mask or turn off overhead lights.
- Leave the windows uncovered. Use artificial sources color-balanced for daylight and mask or turn off overhead lights.

Watch Overhead Lights and Reflections

Despite our advice to the contrary, it might look unnatural in your scene if you shut off all the overhead lights in an office. But if you decide to leave them on, be prepared to cover them with sheets of gel. Or gel your movie lights individually to compensate for the overhead color temperature. Also, keep the overheads out of the frame, if at all possible.

Ordinary fluorescent lights—the kind you'll find in building fixtures—can vary widely in color temperature, depending on the type of tube. It is best to identify their type when scouting locations. If you know whether they're closer to daylight or tungsten, you can choose your movie lights accordingly.

Another complication that's difficult to assess when you're scouting locations is reflections in windows and pictures on walls. One way to eliminate reflections is to apply dulling spray, available from photo supply houses. The spray won't damage surfaces and dries off. (In a pinch you can use hair spray, but it can damage surfaces, and you'll need soap and water or household cleaner to get it off.)

Reduce Light on the Background

Recall that, in a three-point lighting plan, the backlight literally shines on the subject's back and helps separate it from the background. A potentially confusing and different term is *background light*—an additional, optional source—directed away from the subject to illuminate the background, such as a wall. Background light is desirable to increase the overall brightness of the set and perhaps elevate the mood of a scene. It's also useful for showing the audience details of the set, such as a picture hung on the wall.

> When shooting moving objects such as vehicles or athletes on video, the safest choice is to light the scene as flat as possible, even at the sacrifice of visual interest. Flat lighting minimizes the contrast range within the frame and makes it possible to shoot the subject from multiple angles at the same time or for the subject to move around in unpredictable ways, while still maintaining acceptable exposure.

If you choose to light the background, avoid making it too bright. Reducing light on background areas is usually a good place to start if you need to reduce the contrast range in a shot. Dimming the background light can lower the overall lighting level in a scene and will make it possible to use what lights you have to better advantage. Otherwise, you may need most of your fill lights simply to compensate for the bright background.

Add Interest and Glamour with Extra Lighting Touches

At a minimum, it's the DP's job to light a scene in a way that features (and possibly flatters) the subject while avoiding highlights that are too bright and shadows that are too deep for correct exposure. But for the director, lighting is not a technical issue at all. It's about creating an impression in the minds of the audience, and there are no technical rules for that.

Whatever look the director wants to see in the imagery, the DP must find a way to deliver it. To add creative touches, filmmakers have built up an arsenal of lighting tricks, honed over the last century to help them achieve a particular look for their subjects:

- Rim light
- Spotlights
- Eyelight
- Kickers

Rim light is a kind of backlight that adds a pleasing glow to an object's outline and emphasizes its edges (see Figure 4.17). It's particularly useful for beauty shots of products in commercials, as well as for bestowing a saintly look on a star. (Some lighting technicians use the terms rim light and backlight to mean the same thing. In practice, a rim light is more intense.)

Film-look videographers should be especially interested in finding opportunities for using rim light because it's another technique for adding depth to otherwise inherently shallow video imagery. Combined with backlight and selective depth of field, rim light is another way to separate a subject in the foreground from the details in the background.

Spotlights, or spots, are intense beams trained on objects or areas in a scene that aren't illuminated sufficiently by the key light. Spots can give the impression of light spilling from another room, bright reflections, or accents. For example, light spilling from a doorway into a darkened hallway can impart suspense as an actor emerges from the room or approaches the doorway cautiously (see Figure 4.18).

Figure 4.17
A rim light is a particularly intense backlight that casts a glow around the subject. It's another technique for separating the subject from the background and thereby adding depth to the image. The effect can be glamorous or downright threatening.

Figure 4.18
A spotlight located behind a doorway can create spill, a bright light emanating from an off-camera location into a darker area. It can be a spooky effect.

You can also use a spotlight the way it's employed on the theatrical stage—to highlight a featured subject. But be careful. A gaffer can keep a movable spotlight (or follow-spot) trained on the subject, but the effect will look phony to the audience unless there is a motivating source in the scene, such as car headlights.

Eyelight is a small, narrowly focused spotlight aimed at an actor's eyes (see Figures 4.19). It's almost always used in the stars' movie closeups. DPs typically mount an eyelight on the camera itself, directly above the lens, so the reflection will be centered in the subject's eyes. The effect adds sparkle, interest, and personality. The difference is striking in a closeup with no eyelight. Villains are usually lit without eyelight, giving them a dead, soulless look that emphasizes their evil nature. Even without a black hat, the audience knows right away that this stranger is not to be trusted.

Kickers are spotlights placed on the fill side of a subject to emphasize its contours. Often a backlight can double as a kicker if you move it slightly to the left or right while keeping it aimed at your subject. Kickers can add emphasis to jawlines or cheekbones or luster to the hair. They are traditionally used to make a leading character appear more heroic or more glamorous.

Other Techniques for Leading the Eye

Lighting isn't the DP's only tool for dazzling the audience in contrived ways. Given the constraints of video as compared to film, videographers who are going for a film look should pay particular attention to ways they can design shots without resorting to expensive lighting solutions.

Here are some other Hollywood tricks, besides lighting, to lead the viewer's eye. Going beyond the discipline of cinematography, they are topics for collaborative discussion, especially with the director, the art director, and the editor.

- Color
- Motion and exceptional objects

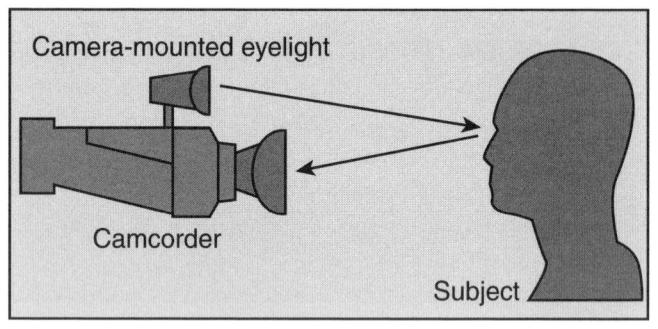

Figure 4.19
An eyelight is typically a small spotlight mounted on the camera directly above the lens. It creates a reflection in the actor's eyes that adds appeal. As a rule, the bad guys don't get eyelight.

Color

All things being equal, viewers will focus on the brightest (or most unusual) color in the shot. For instance, you could put your main character in red and dress everyone else in shades of gray. Similarly, among an army of white hats, the audience will watch the black one. Panning across a cluttered desktop, the important clue might be bright yellow.

> In *Star Wars Episode II: Attack of the Clones*, some of the wardrobe choices indicate careful attention to limiting the contrast range for HD videography. Notice that, in the early scenes involving the Jedi Council, all of the characters' robes are in different muted shades, and all have about the same grayscale value. However, the leading characters are wearing the warmer colors.

Color is a particularly good way to draw attention, especially since the alternative of adding a hot highlight might blow out the shot.

Motion and Exceptional Objects

The audience will follow whomever or whatever happens to be moving in a shot. If several objects are moving at the same time, the eye will follow the one moving the fastest. Some of your best editing choices join two disparate actions that seem to blend into one continuous movement across the cut. In effect, by following the action, the viewer's interest is being "pulled" into the new scene.

Unique physical characteristics of objects, such as size, shape, or texture, can make them stand out, especially when everything in a shot is moving. The audience will quickly spot a jackal in a herd of gazelles, for example, even if it isn't in the center of the frame.

The Purpose of It All

More than any other movie professional—with the possible exception of the editor—the cinematographer's job requires both in-depth technical expertise and creative imagination. The camera and lighting techniques we've described in this chapter are tried and true methods, used in thousands of movies for decades. And, with some careful modification, they're just as applicable to DV.

But their ultimate purpose is not so much technical as it is to elicit emotional response. Showbiz technology changes and evolves from stage to screen to digital cinema, but human emotions remain the same, and so does the way the eye reacts to stimuli.

A master of visual trickery of all kinds to dazzle the eye, the accomplished film-look videographer is a true magician.

Our friend and colleague Charles Koppelman has written a marvelous book, *Behind the Seen: How Walter Murch Edited Cold Mountain Using Apple's Final Cut Pro and What This Means for Cinema*. Why do we mention it in a chapter on cinematography? Because the cinematographer and the editor must literally see eye to eye. If the DP and the director don't deliver the shots the editor needs to build the story as it's described in the script, a movie might still result, but it could come as a surprise. To find out how editing can save a movie, read Koppelman's enlightening sidebar "Nothing Ever Changes, or Does It?" on page 271 of his book, which you should own (since, like us, you must be more than a bit interested in the future of cinema).

chapter 5
Thinking Like a Sound Designer

Without the dimension of audio realism, your most masterful efforts at creating a Hollywood look will fail. Gorgeous or thrilling as the imagery might be, without a rich soundtrack, the viewers' imaginations will be stuck in their theater seats.

And, of course, a sound designer can do much more, not only transporting the audience to a different and specific place and time, but also manipulating their perceptions and their emotions as they watch the screen story unfold.

Sound designers are acutely aware of the human tendency to ignore much of the soundtrack of our everyday lives. For example, city dwellers learn to tune out routine noises such as the rumble of a bus, the roar of a motorcycle, the whoosh of traffic, and the occasional car horn or siren. But put these noises in a scene where they don't belong, and the disconnect will be obvious to anyone. Conversely, leave street sounds out of a scene where they'd normally be heard, and the illusion also fails.

> In the feature film biography *Ray* (2004), blind singer-songwriter Ray Charles takes his future wife Della Bea to a restaurant. Realizing she's becoming emotionally involved with this man, she poses an obvious question, wondering how he manages to get around by himself. He replies that he has to pay more attention to sounds—like the hummingbird outside the window. At first, she's incredulous, perhaps thinking he's teasing her. But when she and the audience concentrate and listen closely, they, too, hear the hummingbird. Charles' hearing wasn't necessarily more acute than the average person's, but he had to train himself to focus his attention on the slightest noise to give him clues about his surroundings.

Like many other creative choices in filmmaking, sound design involves careful selection of what belongs and what doesn't in a scene to achieve the illusion of realism. You don't necessarily need to bring every possible sound from a particular environment into a scene, and there's no magical number of required effects or rules for combining them. An experienced sound technician simply gets a feel for what works in each case.

71

DME: The Three Ingredients

To build a rich audio environment, sound designers blend three ingredients: dialogue, music, and effects (*DME*, they call it). However, the designer doesn't necessarily have full control of them. Consider that:

- The quality of the dialogue depends on the diligence and skill of the sound crew on the set, including the boom mic operator, the sound mixer, and the sound recordist. Removing or reducing extraneous noise is the major postproduction challenge when working with dialogue.
- Music is the contribution of composer, arranger, and performers, but the designer works closely with them, as we'll describe.
- The designer can really show off in the realm of effects, building layer after layer of individual sounds to create a synthetic audio environment that is more real than reality.

Wait a minute—what's more real than reality?

The Hyperrealism of the Movies

In the everyday world, when a person moves from one environment to another, recognizing and becoming aware of a new place involves all the senses: sight, sound, touch, smell, taste, kinesthesia (the feeling of moving through space), and even the sense of the passage of time.

Film is limited to just two of these: sight and sound. If you lose one of your senses, as Ray Charles did, you must rely more on the others. Because of its sensory limitations, movies must control and manipulate—and often, exaggerate—what the audience sees and hears to overcome the missing sensory stimulations and deliver the illusion of being an eyewitness to unfolding events.

What Music Can Do

Music is especially important for creating this sense of hyperreality. Everyday life doesn't come with a musical soundtrack (a condition, some say, the iPod was invented to correct). But audiences expect to be carried along by music, even in low-budget movies.

> Music has always been an essential element of the movies. Live piano accompaniment in the theater was a very early innovation in the silent-movie era, inherited from the traditions of the vaudeville stage. Sometimes, movie studios shipped sheet music along with the film reels, but more often exhibitors relied on the improvisational talents of the pianists, who changed melodies, varied tempo, and punctuated scenes with suspenseful trills and dramatic crescendos to fit the action on the screen. They even had a variety of noisemakers, such as cowbells and slide whistles, to create reinforcing sound effects.

Movie music serves two main purposes:

- **Amplifies emotion.** When it's used most effectively, music doesn't introduce a feeling that's not already in the scene. Rather, it builds on the viewers' feelings as they begin to stir and "feel" the movie, intensifying the experience.
- **Provides continuity.** It's a miracle that an audience can perceive a spliced-together jumble of discrete shots as anything like a continuous experience or coherent story. Music helps link shots to form scenes and scenes to form sequences. Also, you might recall that one of the sensory experiences movies lack is the realistic flow of time. Most, if not all, movies compress time so that stories that take place over days or even years pass by in the interval of a two-hour sitting. As we'll emphasize in Chapter 7, one of the editor's main concerns is pacing, which relates to the artificial experience of the flow of time. By its rhythms and tempos, music is a very effective tool for reinforcing the pacing of a movie and altering the perceived flow of time.

> A classic example of a movie that doesn't purport to compress time is Louis Malle's, *My Dinner with André* (1981). It's a 110-minute conversation in a restaurant that presumably takes just that long. However, even in a literal sense, the flow of time in the movie isn't necessarily realistic. A real-life experience might contain more conversational pauses, longer transactions with the waiter, and some restroom breaks. Another example is Alfred Hitchcock's 80-minute *Rope* (1948), which he shot in a succession of continuous takes, stopping only to change film magazines. Or there's the famous Western showdown saga *High Noon* (1952), directed by Fred Zinnemann. For an even more extreme example, consider Andy Warhol's *Empire* (1964), a continuous eight-hour shot of the Empire State Building. (Time compression might have benefited *that* movie!)

To the extent that they combine to form a rich audio environment, sound effects can also help provide continuity, convincing the audience that a series of shots taken at different places at different times are happening before their eyes in one place, over successive moments, all occurring in the same audio space.

It's a truism that movie music should be felt and not heard. Like most truisms, it isn't quite true. Yet, unless you're producing a music video, the song isn't the main attraction. Remember, the function of music is to amplify and reinforce. Therefore, it must not overpower the thing it aims to support. An obvious example would be a love theme that's played too loudly, drowning out the dialogue that lets the audience know what the lovers are planning.

But, like a reliable supporting actor, sometimes music is called to center stage. Think, for example, how much less thrilling the soaring aerial shots in *Out of Africa* (1985) would be without John Barry's grand, swelling music score.

> Some other composers who wrote highly memorable music themes for blockbuster pictures include Vangelis for *Chariots of Fire* (1981), John Williams for *Star Wars* (1977), Maurice Jarre for *Lawrence of Arabia* (1962), and Max Steiner for *Gone with the Wind* (1939).

Concentric Regions of Effects

The most common flaw of the low-budget movie that aspires to commercial success is its failure to create an audio environment that is rich enough to meet audience expectations of realism.

When planning effects tracks that will achieve this level of realism, think of the requirements as a set of concentric circles (see Figure 5.1). At the core are the absolute essentials—sounds that match actions the audience sees on the screen. An example would be the clink of a teacup hitting the saucer after the actor has taken a sip. You must find a way to provide these sounds. The next ring corresponds to sounds that occur just off-screen—sounds that the audience would naturally expect to hear as a result of on-screen action. For example, when an actor storms out of the frame to leave the room, they will expect to hear the door slam behind her.

The sounds in the first two rings often have narrative purposes. The slamming door resolves the question of whether or not the actor is truly gone or waiting at the door for a reply. Unlike the first two rings, the third ring is truly atmospheric. It represents the wider world of sound, which may not have much at all to do with the action in the scene. Sounds in this imaginary world include city traffic, animal noises on a farm, or children at play.

Creating a Hollywood-style soundtrack is complex. And in the best of circumstances, it's one of the longest and most involved parts of the postproduction process.

But that process will take even longer if you don't start with clean production sound.

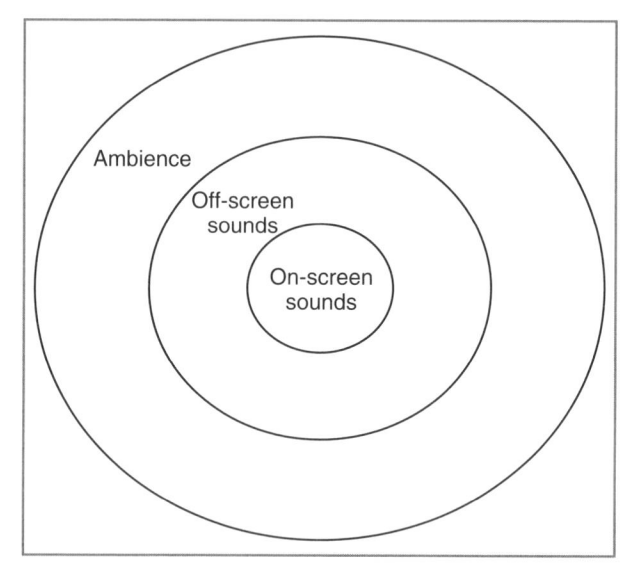

Figure 5.1
The sound designer must create a world of effects that includes sounds made by on-screen actions, sounds occurring just off-screen that relate to on-screen actions, and atmospheric effects occurring in the outside world. Another term for the outer ring is *ambience*.

Getting Good Production Sound

In a high-budget motion picture, the sound designer might not ever go near the set. But on low-budget DV productions, the sound designer, sound recordist, and sound editor might all be the same person.

Whether or not you're personally responsible for sound on the set, you can't get very far in audio postproduction unless you know the technical details of capturing good production sound:

- Matching microphones to the location
- Rigging different types of mics
- Using dual-system sound
- Eliminating unwanted production noise
- Avoiding ADR

Matching Microphones to the Setup

A sound technician must be able to select the type of mic that fits each setup. The goal is to capture the right audio perspective, or apparent distance between the actor who is speaking and the mic.

Besides the type of mic, a factor that affects audio perspective is the placement of the mic. Sound technicians refer to the distance between the actors and the mic as *air*.

In most cases, the audio perspective should match the visual perspective, or the viewers' apparent distance from the actors (focal length of the shot). That is, in a long shot, the audience will expect a lot of air, and in a closeup, much less. When a mic is very close to an actor, perhaps worn on her body or carried in her hand as a singer or interviewer might, the subject is said to be *close mic'd*.

For example, in a telephoto closeup the camera is actually quite a distance from the actors. But because the apparent distance from the viewer is close, the shot calls for a more intimate audio perspective.

> Frances Ford Coppolla's *The Conversation* (1974) has some scenes with unconventional audio perspective. In one scene, investigator Harry Caul observes lovers Mark and Ann from a hotel window as they stroll beneath him in San Francisco's Union Square. The audience watches the two in an extreme long shot, which corresponds to Caul's vantage point, but the soundtrack's audio perspective is very close and intimate—because Caul is listening to their conversation through a parabolic microphone that can pick up faint sounds from hundreds of feet away.

In general, the more air, the more ambient noise will be picked up from the environment. This can happen to a greater or lesser degree, depending on the type of mic and its pickup pattern (see Figure 5.2). A mic's pickup pattern is like the range and the field of view of an optical lens. The imaginary center of the pattern is the mic's axis, which is comparable to the camera angle. The hypercardioid, or shotgun, mic is the telephoto lens of audio gear. It can focus on relatively distant subjects and can reject surrounding, or off-axis, noise. A cardioid mic, typically called a *shortie*, is relatively omnidirectional, or accepts sound coming from all directions except directly in back of it. A lavaliere mic, (also called a *lav,* a *lapel mic,* or a *pin mic*) tends to be omnidirectional, but it doesn't matter because it's designed to be worn close mic'd on the subject—typically just a few inches from the mouth. A lav won't pick up much ambient noise because, at close range, the noise will be much fainter than the relatively high volume of the dialogue. (In technical terms, the signal-to-noise [S/N] ratio will be high.)

Rigging and Using a Boom Mic

The Hollywood-style filmmaker's staple audio pickup device is the boom mic. It's a shotgun mounted on a telescoping aluminum rod, or boom pole. The pole should be adjustable, about 8–12 feet long. (For an example of a shotgun mic, refer back to Figure 3.8.) A professional boom pole suspends the mic in a mesh of rubber bands called a *shock mount.* It serves as a shock absorber, damping vibrations and allowing the pole to be maneuvered without picking up the sounds of handling.

Whether used indoors or out, a shotgun is so sensitive that it's best to always use a windscreen, a foam-rubber sheath, to muffle extraneous sounds. A more durable windscreen that uses a system of baffles in a lightweight enclosure for the mic is called a *blimp* (see Figure 5.3).

Figure 5.2
The pickup pattern of a microphone is the surrounding space within which it will capture the best-quality sound. Within that area, the signal will be loudest and clearest, with the greatest fidelity and the widest frequency response (extending to the highs and lows of the human hearing range). In matching the mic to the job, the sound engineer must not only choose the pickup pattern that suits the situation but also know how to aim the mic for best results.

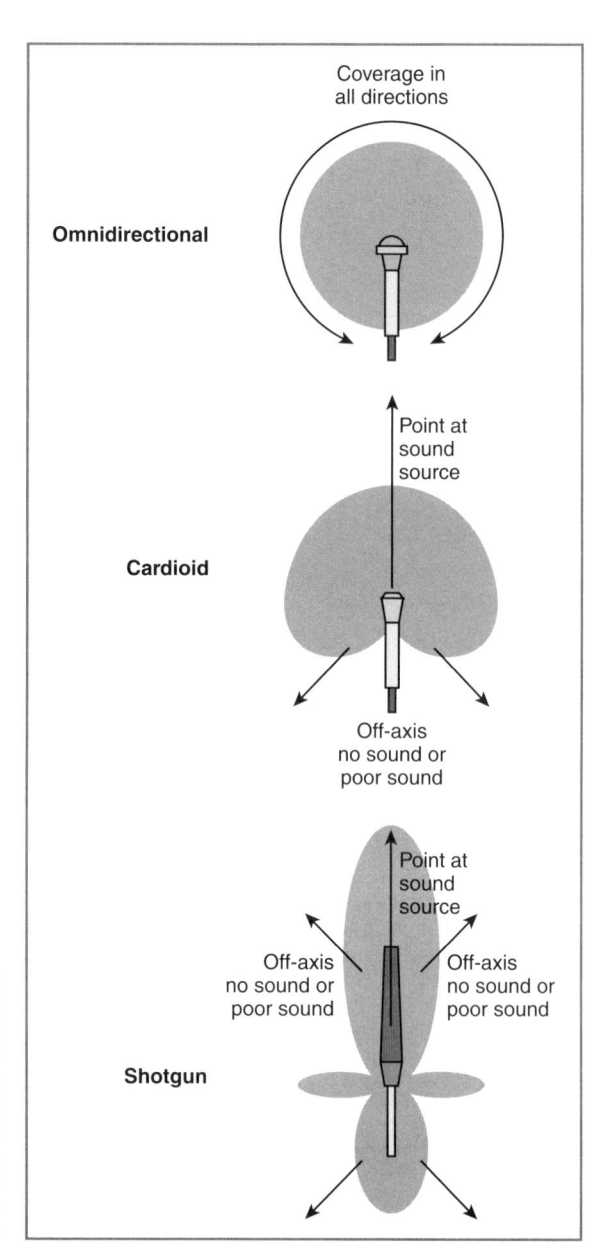

Figure 5.3
A blimp is a durable type of windscreen designed to enclose a shotgun mic with baffles that shield it from extraneous noise.

DV AUDIO MODES

There are no inherent audio problems that come with a choice either to shoot or to finish in 24p. If you select 24p mode in the camcorder, the audio synchronization for that frame rate is set automatically. If you convert from 60i to 24p in postproduction, the conversion process also maintains synchronization. However, a technical factor you should be aware of both when shooting and when editing is the digital audio bit rate. The DV recording standard permits four different audio recording modes, each at a different bit rate:

- AES/EBU standard, highest-quality stereo: two 16-bit channels at 48kHz
- CD quality, medium-quality stereo: two 16-bit channels at 44.1kHz
- Stereo, lower quality: two 16-bit channels at 32kHz
- Four-channel, lowest quality: four 12-bit channels at 32kHz

When you're on the set, you want to record at 48kHz, the highest quality stereo (typically used, as we'll describe, to record two copies of a monophonic track). In postproduction, when you import music and sound effects, these may come from CD sources, which will be at 44.1kHz. Most professional-level video and audio editing software will permit you to intermix sources recorded at different frequencies, automatically converting to 48kHz tracks. However, some don't. For example, versions of Final Cut Pro prior to 3.0 required you to go through a conversion step first to match frequencies of clips before you could insert them into edited tracks.

During a take, the boom operator holds the mic on its pole above the actors. The operator stands just outside the frame and must be ever watchful that the mic doesn't dip into the shot (a very common error, even on professional shoots).

Boom operation takes skill that comes with practice, so even though it's tempting to give this tedious job to rookie production assistants, you need an experienced hand. The boom operator should be familiar with the script and should continually adjust the boom to keep the mic aimed at whichever actor is speaking.

The recommended stance for the boom operator is to hold the pole over his head with hands spread about three feet apart (refer back to Figure 3.8). The operator's arms will grow tired eventually, regardless of the stance, but this one is easier to maintain for long periods of time.

> A careful boom operator should remove rings and jewelry from her hands and wrists. These might clatter against the pole during handling, making sounds that will be picked up by the mic.

During a take, the boom mic should be pointed downward at the speaking actor, on at an angle with respect to the pole. The correct place to aim the mic is at the center of the actor's chest. This is actually the place where the lower, richer tones of human speech reverberate. The higher frequencies emanate from the lips and nose, but these are easier to pick up off-axis than the lower frequencies emanating from the chest.

Aimed properly, the boom mic will record full, rich-toned dialogue with a minimum of ambient noise and just the right audio perspective for medium and close shots. In fact, a good mic is so sensitive and directional that you can use it in a location near a busy street, and the traffic noise will be so low in volume in relation to the voice that it might not be noticeable on the recorded track.

Beware, though, that a shotgun mic will pick up any sound occurring along its axis. So if you point a shotgun level with the horizon toward an actor (as is done when news videographers mount shotguns on their camcorders), the mic will pick up not only the actor in the distance but also all the sounds in the deep background behind her.

Professional mics, including the shotgun models, use three-wire XLR connectors (see Figure 5.4). All professional camcorders accept this type of audio plug. The third conductor in three-wire audio cabling carries a copy of the audio signal that is out of phase with the primary one. The effect is to cancel electrical interference that might get picked up along the length of the cable.

Figure 5.4
A professional XLR audio connector has three conductors: a twisted pair of wires surrounded by a braided-wire sheath. The second wire in the pair carries a copy of the audio signal. In technical terms, the secondary audio signal is out of phase with the primary. XLR audio equipment combines the two signals, which has the effect of canceling noise picked up over long cable runs. This is an old analog technology that's still in widespread use.

Most consumer and some prosumer camcorders have jacks for consumer audio gear. They accept either mini plugs (see Figure 5.5) or RCA plugs (see Figure 5.6). Headphones and some audio gear, such as electronic musical instruments, may use another type of plug, the ¼ inch audio connector (as shown in Figure 5.7).

Figure 5.5
Termination in a ⅛ in mini plug is a sure sign that a piece of audio gear, such as a mic, is a consumer-level unit that typically operates at −10dB. The audio input jacks of most consumer and many prosumer camcorders accept this type of plug.

Figure 5.6
An RCA plug is an older style of audio connector typically found on video and audio inputs and outputs on some camcorders, monitors, and VCRs.

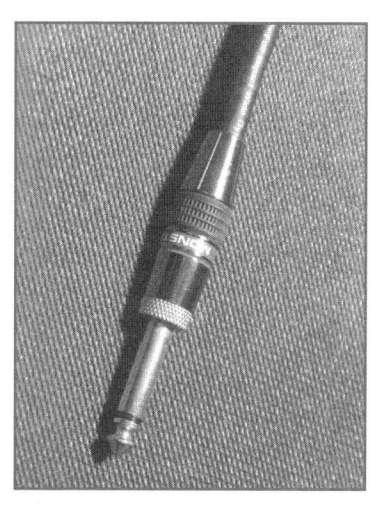

Figure 5.7
Not typically used on mics, the ¼ inch audio plug is commonly used with headphones and electronic musical instruments, such as guitars.

Besides the fact that pro-style plugs don't physically fit into consumer and prosumer cameras, you'll encounter another problem if you try to do this—the operating voltages, or line levels, will be different. In technical terms, professional gear operates at +4dB (decibels), consumer gear at −10dB. The solution is to use an audio adapter box, or line pad (see Figures 5.8 and 5.9), which accepts XLR inputs and provides output to a mini plug and also has a knob for reducing the audio voltage or line level.

> Doing the reverse—attempting to plug a consumer mic into a pro camcorder—will also be problematic. Even with an adapter plug, the difference in line levels will require you to boost the audio gain control on the camcorder +14dB. Turning up the volume this much will also boost the noise level considerably. And since consumer gear has a lower S/N ratio than pro gear to begin with, the result might be unacceptably noisy.

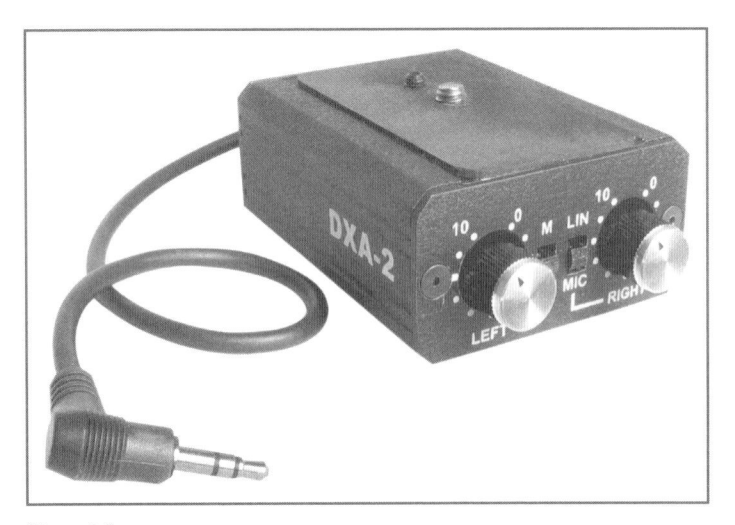

Figure 5.8
To use a pro mic with consumer-level audio inputs, the BeachTek DXA-2 XLR mic adapter screws onto the tripod mount at the bottom of a consumer or prosumer camcorder and plugs into its mini mic input jack. (Photo courtesy BeachTek)

Figure 5.9
The Studio 1 XLR-BP 3 Pro adapts as many as three XLR inputs, such as pro-style mics, to a mini camcorder input. Also serving as a mixer, it's worn on the camera or boom operator's belt. (Photo courtesy Studio 1)

Another way to adapt mic inputs, as well as to control their levels, is to pass them through a mixer (refer back to Figure 3.9). The primary function of a mixer is to blend the inputs from multiple mics.

Many types of professional mics require external voltage, called *phantom power*. Mic mixers typically have an output for phantom power (+1.5VDC), which is carried in the XLR cable. Or some boom poles have small battery compartments built in. Remember that, without phantom power, you will get little or no signal from a pro mic. So another mark of an experienced sound tech is to carry plenty of spare mic batteries.

> Coil the audio cable once or twice before fixing it to a boom pole with gaffer's tape. The purpose is to provide enough play in the cable so it won't become disconnected if someone tugs or trips over it. This prudent practice, useful for many types of rigging on the set, is called *strain relief*.

Another very useful feature of audio mixers designed for movie crews is a called a *talkback circuit*. It permits connection of several pairs of headsets, which may be worn by the boom operator, sound mixer, sound recordist, and the director. By listening to the take through headphones, a boom operator or one of the other sound technicians can warn the director of noise during a take, such as the sound of a passing truck or a crewmember's cough.

> Even if she hears a noise, the boom operator shouldn't interrupt a take. There may be plenty of good reasons to keep rolling. A silent hand signal to the director is all that's needed. (The director might want to keep rolling because much of the take might still be usable, or she doesn't want to interrupt the actors when they're in the moment. You never know what you'll end up using in the edit, but the hand signal will tell the second assistant camera to mark the log so that the editor knows to look for the noise. For more information on keeping camera and sound logs, see "Using Dual-System Sound" in this chapter.)

Rigging and Using a Shortie

Although never a good replacement for a boom mic, an omnidirectional cardioid shortie mic (see Figure 5.10) has three typical uses in Hollywood-style moviemaking:

As a handheld mic for singers and interviewers. In these situations, the mic will usually appear in the shot. Interviewers must train themselves to move the mic back and forth between themselves and their subjects, pointing directly at whoever is talking. In a heated conversation, this can seem like a lot of needless wagging of the mic, but it's just as important for getting clean dialogue as it is in good boom mic operation.

As a secondary atmospheric mic. An artful touch that adds a bit of complexity to the audio setup is to mount a shortie on a stand somewhere off-screen or to suspend it on a cable just above the set. Provided that the environment isn't full of extraneous sounds, the omnidirectional mic can capture the presence, or room tone, of the set. For example, its track will include not only the actors' voices (with a lot of air) but also the distinctive echo of a hallway. Certainly, it's possible to add these effects in postproduction, but a secondary mic can be particularly useful if you record its output on a separate track so that the sound

Figure 5.10
A handheld cardioid dynamic mic, called a shortie, is the right choice for singers and on-camera interviewers who work close mic'd with a mic that appears in the shot. The hollowed foam-rubber ball near it is a windscreen.

editor can mix it in at a low level with the production dialogue. It's also a standard technique when the situation calls for the actors to wear lavs. The second track with the room tone will help the editor balance the too-close perspective of the lavs.

As a plant mic. A plant mic is any mic that's hidden near the actors in a fixed position on a set—originating from the practice of literally hiding a mic in the centerpiece of a dining table. If indeed the scene is an intimate conversation in a restaurant, if the actors don't move around, and if there isn't much ambient noise, a plant mic can be a reasonable alternative to either using a boom or rigging the actors with individual lavs.

Rigging and Using Lavs

Pinning or clipping a lav (see Figure 5.11) to an actor creates the closest perspective of all—truly up-close and personal. Possible uses of lavs are

- **Interviews.** Pin a lav to the subject in one-on-one, on-camera interviews, especially if the subject will be moving around or if you don't want the mic (or the interviewer) visible in the shot.
- **Action scenes.** Put lavs on each actor who must deliver lines during an action sequence, such as a chase, where it would be difficult if not impossible to follow them with a boom. For safety, to avoid tripping over cables, these setups usually require wireless equipment.

A primary rule is to place the lav no more than 10 inches away from the speaker's mouth. Ideally, the mic should be concealed in the actor's clothing or even in his hair. However, the face of the mic should just peek out of its hiding place so it's in the clear and won't be muffled by fabric or hair. Tiny, flesh-toned lavs are available in a variety of shades for just this purpose.

Lav mics have thin cords that attach to thicker ones attached to an XLR jack. As with the boom mic's cable, a lav mic's cable should be coiled for strain relief and attached with gaffer's tape out of sight. The usual locations are on the back of a belt or in back of the leg with the connector taped to the calf or the thigh. The connector must be within reach of the actor so he can disconnect the mic by himself if necessary. (However, this should be done under supervision of a sound tech to make sure the audio setup isn't disturbed in the process.)

> No matter what type of mic is in use on the set, the director should call for quiet at the end of each setup and record a full minute of room tone. The sound editor will use the silence (which isn't silent at all and actually has unique qualities in each location) to fill in pauses in the edited dialogue and to otherwise cover audio edits.

Figure 5.11
This lav is actually rather large compared with some of the tinier versions, which can be scarcely bigger than a match head and flesh colored so as to be worn near the actor's hairline. Lavs usually require phantom power, which can be provided either by a watch-style battery in a compartment on the cord or through the XLR cable.

> Because attaching things to an actor's body can be a sensitive procedure, a lav mic is best affixed in the privacy of a dressing area and not on the set.

If you use more than one lav, putting a mixer in the setup is mandatory. But if you use more than two or three, all the cabling can become cumbersome. In these situations, you'll need wireless gear, but the setups can be quite complex.

Like shotguns, lavs require phantom power, usually supplied by a watch battery in a compartment in-line with the cord between the mic and the XLR connector.

> Have fresh spares for all types of batteries used on the set. Also keep a pocket battery tester handy so you can tell for sure whether a problem you're having is due to a dead battery or to something more troublesome, such as a cable with a hidden break, electrical or radio interference, or a blown AC power circuit.

Rigging and Using Wireless Mics

Wireless mics, typically lavs, may be necessary in complicated action scenes such as chases, fights, and dance numbers when the dialogue won't be as convincing if dubbed later. (Singing is almost always dubbed, unless the purpose of the video is to capture a live performance.) Normally, wireless setups are to be avoided because they're expensive, requiring a lot of gear, and they're much more complicated to operate. Furthermore, even though wireless can free the actors, in many ways it restricts the audio setup and can make the sound crew less mobile.

The basic wireless unit consists of a mic and portable transmitter, both worn on the actor's body, and a remote receiver connected to the input side of an audio mixer (see Figure 5.12). There's a separate receiver for each actor and transmitter, and each transmitter-receiver is on a different radio frequency (RF).

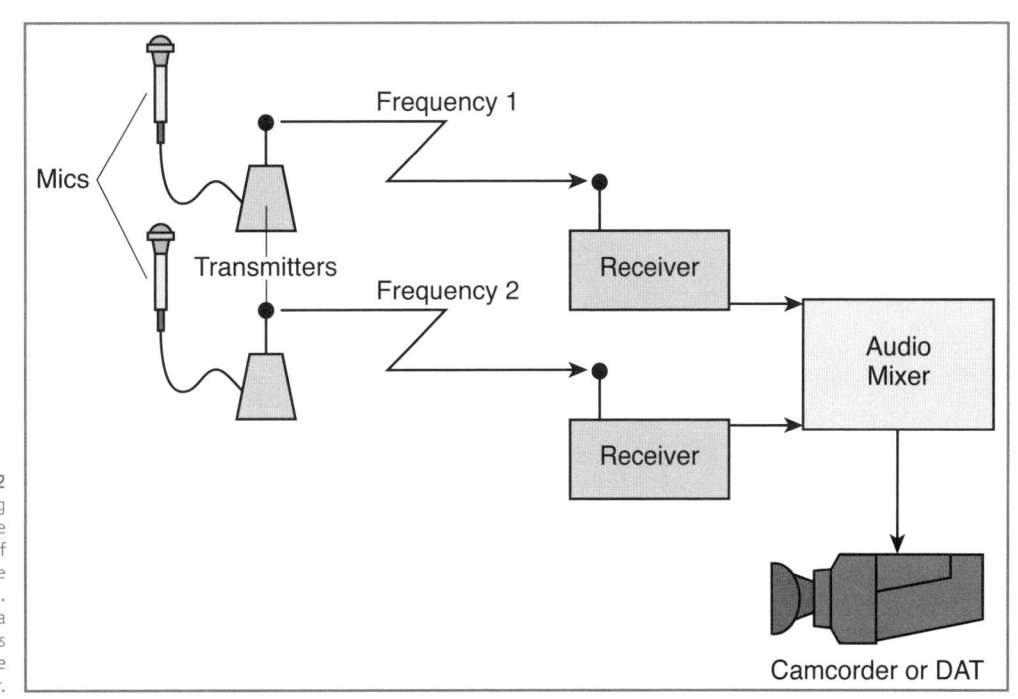

Figure 5.12
This diagram shows a wireless rig for equipping each actor on the set with a lav. You might use this setup for a crowd scene that has a lot of speaking parts. Each lav requires a wearable transmitter and a receiver at the base station. Each receiver, in turn, is plugged into a multichannel mixer, which combines the inputs into one or more mono channels for the camcorder and DAT recorder.

> **WIRELESS MICS AND MULTICHANNEL RECORDING**
>
> In the music industry, multichannel digital recording is commonplace these days, both in the recording studio and on location. Assigning each voice and instrument to its own channel and recording track gives the sound engineer a lot of flexibility when monitoring the levels of each channel and doing the mix in the studio. Prior to mixing, individual tracks can be looped (repeated to build repetitive sequences or rhythms), overdubbed (as when a singer accompanies herself, also called *double-tracking*), or simply replaced with a rerecorded or synthetic track—all without requiring any changes to the other tracks.
>
> Working this way on a movie set would require multichannel mixers and recorders. However, the common practice in movie production today remains to capture a clean monophonic dialogue track on the set and only then venture into multichannel in the postproduction studio. That's because, in a movie, most of the music and effects are created long after dialogue recording is done.
>
> However, technology is changing. The music industry had adopted digital work methods long before they were the norm in film and video, and in many ways music location recording is much more sophisticated. Multichannel recording on the movie sets could become much more prevalent, especially if the scene calls for several actors to wear wireless mics.
>
> (Because wireless rigs are used infrequently in movie setups, it's usually more economical to rent them than to buy them.)

Using Dual-System Sound

All digital camcorders can record stereo sound on tracks adjacent to and in sync with the video. Recording dialogue on the set in-camera will often give acceptable results, provided that you use good-quality mics and operate them properly.

In analog audio recording, it's permissible for the audio level to occasionally peak above 0dB. But in the digital realm, any signal above 0dB will be unacceptably distorted. Setting audio recording levels so they anticipate the loudest moments in a scene is therefore an important part of any sound check.

So, quality aside, recording audio in-camera has another serious drawback. During a take, you can't have the sound recordist and the camera operator competing for the controls. If you record in-camera, you have to pick an audio setting and stick with it throughout the take, and if any adjusting is to be done, it must take place at the mixer. That's all the more reason to use a mixer, but the situation is still less than ideal.

> The camcorder's automatic audio gain control (AGC) is another one of those "handy" intelligent circuits that more often than not makes bad choices. Its purpose is to compensate for high and low volume levels, boosting the gain when things go quiet and turning it down to avoid distortion when an actor shouts. But as with all auto controls, it usually can't react fast enough. The result is a problem sound engineers call *pumping*, as the gain wavers up and down, now straining to amplify the air conditioning, then clipping the actor's proud declamations. If you turn AGC off, you risk audio distortion if the sound levels go unpredictably high during a take. Even if you don't use dual-system sound, a good solution is to hedge your bets by splitting the mixer input (using a Y cable), recording the L (left stereo) channel at 0dB (normal) and the R (right) at –20dB. If levels peak above 0dB on the L channel during a take, the sound editor will have the option of using the R track instead (and possibly turning up its volume).

A much better solution, somewhat more expensive but far more reliable, is dual-system sound (refer back to Figure 3.10). In this scheme, mixer stereo outputs are routed to two recorders, one in the camcorder and the other an external digital audiotape (DAT) machine. In this setup, a sound recordist typically monitors both the mixer and the external recorder. The camcorder track is a backup, possibly recorded at a lower level than 0dB to protect against unanticipated peaking. (Remember, don't be concerned with capturing true stereo on the set. That's an effect to be created in post.)

The traditional approach in motion pictures is to shoot separate sound using an external audio recorder. Until recently, the workhorse recorders were Nagra reel-to-reel analog machines, now largely supplanted by DAT units. (However, Nagras are still used in extreme weather conditions.) In film editing, syncing picture and sound can be a major chore, a process facilitated by the second assistant's camera and sound log (see Figure 5.13). If you shoot dual-system HD or DV, the syncing process is quite easy (we'll describe how shortly), but it will go faster if you have an accurate log from the shoot that includes starting and editing timecodes for both video and audio.

> A particularly useful feature of high-end camcorders, audio recorders, and electronic slates is jam sync, an interconnection that synchronizes the timecodes on all recorders.

Eliminating Unwanted Production Noise

Consider that a real challenge for the sound crew on the set is to eliminate or avoid capturing *any* sound but dialogue, if at all possible. Ideally, everything the audience hears except human speech will be created in postproduction.

This is a major departure from run-and-gun video and from indie guerilla filmmaking. Creating synthetic audio environments is a Hollywood-style approach that complements 24p imagery, but it greatly increases the work and care involved in sound recording and finishing.

5. Thinking Like a Sound Designer

Date:		Oct. 9, 20XX	Title:	Neo's Ring		
Work Day:		Saturday	Director:	Pete Shaner		
			A.D.:	Caleb Cindano		

Cam Roll	Snd Roll	Set	Scene	Take No.	Start	Finish	Description
01	01	N.W. Anderson Bldg.	13	1	01000000	01000213	NG
				2	01000216	01000301	OK
				3	01000306	01000518	Noise?
				4	01000520	01000735	OK
01	01	Long Stairway	15	1	01000749	01001702	OK
				2	01001710	01002820	NG
				3	01002859	01003934	OK
				4	01004001	01005314	NG

Wild Tracks		Remarks
Birds	01005316	
Fountain	01005421	13-1 Traci off mic
		13-3 Car alarm
		15-2 Focus
		15-4 Bus rumble

Script Supervisor

Figure 5.13
Customarily kept by the second assistant camera operator, the camera and sound log records the start and end points of takes as camcorder timecodes. It's delivered to the editor along with the camcorder and DAT cassettes (still called *reels,* as in film) as a guide for finding and selecting takes.

This rule of minimizing noise on the set applies to sounds in all regions of the effects-world diagram. Even sounds that result from on-screen actions are to be avoided. For example, when the actor sets her cup on the saucer, the prop department should have it lined with a damp napkin—expressly to avoid the clink. When actors walk on hard flooring in a scene and their feet are not in the shot, the usual practice is to have them remove their shoes to avoid recording their footsteps. And when an actor reads a newspaper, the prop department will be careful to spray it with water until it's damp—to avoid capturing the annoying rustle of the paper.

Again, to runners-and-gunners, this can be a difficult mindset to acquire, but it will pay dividends in postproduction, as veteran movie sound engineers well know.

Avoiding ADR

If you don't succeed in capturing clean dialogue on the set, you may have to resort to postproduction dubbing, or automated dialogue replacement (ADR). In this rather tedious process, actors on a specially equipped sound stage lip-sync the lines as they watch the scene played back on a projection screen. There's nothing particularly automated about it. ADR requires lots of skill and patience, and even when done right, it's not always fully convincing. Usually, something doesn't quite match—audio levels, tone of voice, lip movements, or room tone.

The best fix for ADR is to avoid doing it entirely. And that simply means employing good audio practices on the set. However, you might not suspect that the usual reason to incur the time and expense of ADR isn't because there's distortion in the tracks. The most common problem is that dialogue is inaudible. And that can be because the boom operator didn't keep the mic aimed properly during the take.

> Of course, there are other good reasons to do ADR, including voiceover narration and off-screen dialogue, or dubbing to replace strong language or foreign-language tracks. It's sometimes also necessary to correct an actor's line reading or even to insert new material to clarify a plot point or make up for a shot that was missed or botched during shooting.

The Audio Postproduction Process

In professional feature production, the functions of picture editor and sound editor are separate. On some low-budget movies, an editor takes care of the visual continuity, the cleaning of dialogue tracks, and the building of music and effects layers.

Planning Layered Soundtracks

On the set, there's good reason to mix production sound. As the sidebar "Wireless Mics and Multichannel Recording," explains earlier in this chapter, the sound crew on the set typically captures nothing more complex than stereo dialogue tracks. And the stereo doesn't usually correspond to physical Left and Right channels. More often, one or more mics on the set are mixed to form a mono channel; then this channel is split between the stereo inputs of the camcorder or DAT. As many pro sound techs do, we advise setting these two tracks at different levels of audio gain: 0dB for the primary track and –20dB for a backup track, which the sound editor will use only if she encounters a distorted clip in the primary track.

But by the time you're in postproduction, all concerns about mixing should be put on hold—usually until after the picture edit is locked (declared final). During editing, your goal should be to reserve a separate audio track, if possible, for each musical instrument or orchestra section and for each discrete sound effect. Ideally, put the violins on one track, the crickets on another, and the summer breeze on yet another.

The objective is control. Separating audio tracks provides greater control.

So it should come as no surprise that an early task for the editor is to separate and clean the dialogue tracks. This step might seem nonsensical, in view of the crew's effort to mix the on-set mics in the first place. Certainly, if multichannel dialogue tracks ever become common practice, this aspect of the editor's workflow will change.

AUDIO EDITING TOOLS

Any prosumer-level, nonlinear editing (NLE) application—such as Final Cut Pro, Avid Xpress DV, or Sony Vegas—will have capabilities for multitrack audio editing. However, professional sound editors prefer more extensive tools of the type designed specifically for sound studios. This category of software is called the *digital audio workstation* (DAW), and the one most widely used in the movie industry is DigiDesign ProTools. (Avid is DigiDesign's parent company.) Although you can operate a DAW with just a computer keyboard and a mouse, ProTools also markets a line of control surfaces (see Figure 5.14). An audio control surface looks like a traditional analog audio mixing board, but in fact it's just a way of controlling the computer menu functions that's more comfortable for veteran sound editors.

Other DAWs include Apple Logic, Sony Sound Forge, MOTU Digital Performer, and Adobe Audition.

Figure 5.14
A ProTools control surface simulates the touch and feel of a traditional studio sound board, although it's equally possible to use a computer mouse rather than this array of sliders and knobs to adjust settings in the software.

Cleaning and Separating Dialogue Tracks

If the production dialogue is clean, clear, and understandable, this step won't be necessary. It's essentially a way to repair dialogue tracks that are marginally acceptable because of noise or low audio levels. In the digital realm, there's really no repair for the other prevalent problem—distortion. In a perfect world, any distorted track should be replaced, not repaired.

The editor's repair trickery begins with separating each actor's speech into a separate audio track. It's known as *checkerboarding,* and that's how the separated clips look on the timeline of the editing application (see Figure 5.15). (For a review of editing basics, including the use of timelines in nonlinear editing applications, see "An Oerview of NLE" in Chapter 7.)

Creating the dialogue checkerboard is fairly easy:

1. For each character in a scene, make one copy of the scene's entire audio track.
2. Delete the audio clips containing the other characters' lines from each track so that you end up with one character on each track, with gaps for the deletions.
3. If there are pauses between the actors' speeches and your editing software operates in nondestructive mode, you can simply drag the endpoints of each audio clip outward along the timeline to add handles, or a little extra footage, on either end of the separated dialogue clips. Otherwise, you can add short clips of room-tone one at a time, pasting them into the timeline, before and after each speech, to create the handles.
4. Create an audio cross-dissolve in the handle area of each clip. This has the effect of smoothing out the transitions between clips, and it also hides noises, such as coughs, intake of breath, and throat-clearing, that can occur at the beginning or end of an actor's speech.

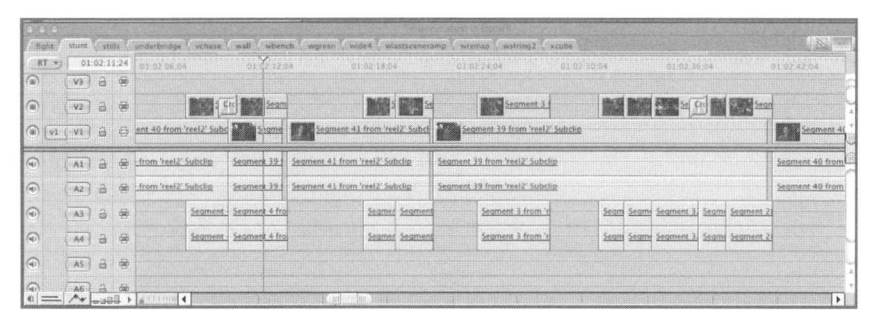

Figure 5.15
Separating actors' dialogue on different tracks creates a checkerboard pattern on the timeline. Once you've assigned each actor to a separate track, it's easier to do audio cross-fades to create smoother transitions and hide the noises, such as lip smacks, that can occur before or after an actor's line.

The basic goal of checkerboarding is to permit you to manipulate each character's audio as a separate track, just as you might work with different channels for each instrument and voice when recording a song in the studio. Checkerboarding has the added benefits of minimizing noise between speeches, as just described, as well as making it easier to replace bad audio clips with other clips of the same dialogue, either from another take or from ADR.

> A really effective tool for removing background noise when cleaning dialogue tracks is Bias SoundSoap Pro, a plug-in that works with many editing applications, such as Final Cut Pro. It utilizes a straightforward two-step procedure: 1) let it sample the room-tone clip that contains the unwanted noise (which it does with its Learn Noise function); then 2) have it digitally subtract any of this noise from any selected portion of an audio track. This procedure can remove traffic noise, wind, and even the whirr of the camcorder picked up by its built-in mic.

Covering Audio Mistakes

After all this effort of separating and cleaning dialogue, there may still be some undesirable noises on the track. Here's what you can do:

Delete any noises that occur in the clear. If a noise, such as a car horn, occurs in a scene but not under an actor's speech, simply delete it. In place of the deletion, the room tone will go dead. To fix this, add another track with an overlapping segment of room tone directly beneath the deleted segment. If the presence doesn't match the original track exactly, put fade transitions at either end of the room-tone clip.

Stack audio tracks to increase volume without distortion. If the level of a clip of production dialogue is too low, making the actor's line inaudible, you might not be able to increase audio gain enough without causing distortion. To remedy this, make a copy of the low-level audio clip, insert it in a new track on the timeline directly below the first, and sync them up. The effect of stacking the tracks this way will be to increase the apparent volume of the actor's line without adding distortion.

Cheat to hide unwanted effects you can't remove. If a noise, such as a ringing cell phone, occurs in the midst of an actor's speech and there's no removing it, keep it in. Introduce several other copies of the effect throughout the scene, including several before the troublesome noise occurs. This conditions the audience to the sound as part of the scene's audio environment, and by the time the offending instance is heard, they'll have learned to ignore it.

Recording ADR

If you feel you must dub actors' voices after the fact, the editor needs to prepare the following:

1. Make video dubs of all scenes that need dialogue replacement. You will need the video track and all production audio tracks for the scenes that need new dialogue. It's absolutely essential to include the production dialogue, which will serve as a guide track both for ADR actors and for the editor when attempting to sync the rerecorded tracks to the video.

2. Create an additional audio track, called a *streamer track*, that precedes each take with a cueing tone to warn the ADR performer when to start speaking. (The standard tone is called a *two-pop* and occurs two seconds before the cue.) Some editors prefer to use a sequence of eight beeps before the start of each take—three beeps, one second apart, a pause, then another three, then two. The start of picture and its accompanying sound cue go where the final beat would occur. It's really very easy for performers to get the knack of responding to this pattern of beats.
3. If the ADR involves music, the editor must also prepare a click track, which contains the musical beat.

The actual rerecording takes place in a specially equipped studio (sometimes called an *interlock stage*, a holdover from the days when projected film had to be synchronized with a separate sprocketed soundtrack). An ADR studio can be as small as a closet or as large as a modest-sized sound stage. The closet can work well as a voiceover booth for a lone narrator, but remember, it will have almost no room tone at all. A stage can accommodate more players and may have a presence of its own (which might or might not match that of the production set).

Another term for the ADR session is *looping*. The performer studies the scene as it plays back on a screen in the studio, while listening through headphones to the original production sound. The sound recordist then replays the take, and the performer listens for the cue and then repeats the (possibly corrected) line.

After the ADR session is done, the editor must cut the rerecorded clips into the show. As we've explained, it'll be easier to do the replacements if you've already checkerboarded the actors' speeches. During this process, the main challenge is to synchronize the new soundtrack with the lip movements on the video track. The usual way of doing this is to use the production track as a guide and adjust the new clip back and forth slightly in the timeline until the peaks of the waveforms line up vertically (see Figure 5.16). When you play back both audio tracks, if you hear an echo, they aren't in sync. When they are, mute the production track, turning down its audio gain to zero. (There's no reason to delete it. It might come in handy, you never know.)

> Here's another reason to record lots of room tone on the set. The editor will have to mix it with the ADR track so that the rerecorded dialogue will sound as though it were recorded on the same set as the production takes.

> Use the same make and model mic for ADR that you used on the set. You'll get a better match.

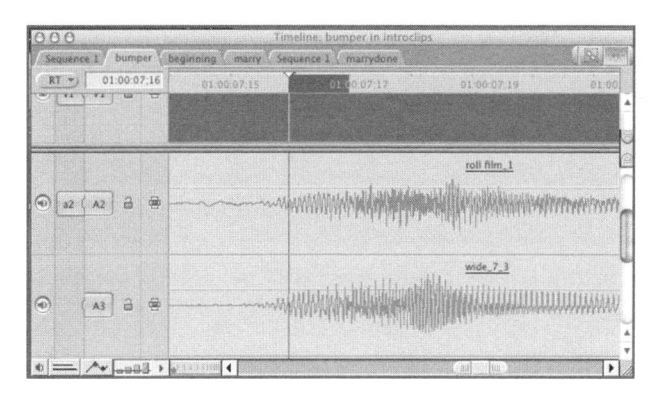

Figure 5.16
Audio tracks appear in the editing timeline as waveforms. You'll know that two identical or similar takes are in sync when the peaks of their waveforms line up vertically. (To use as a guide, the black bar displayed to the right of the playhead is exactly one video frame wide.)

A useful tool for aligning ADR tracks quickly and easily is Synchro Arts VocALign Project (see Figure 5.17 and www.synchroarts.co.uk), another plug-in. It forces the waveforms of two audio tracks into vertical alignment, and it can even lengthen or shorten the waveforms slightly to make a better fit. It even works when synchronizing a singing voice to a rhythm track or a foreign-language track to production dialogue (provided that the phrases have the same number of syllables).

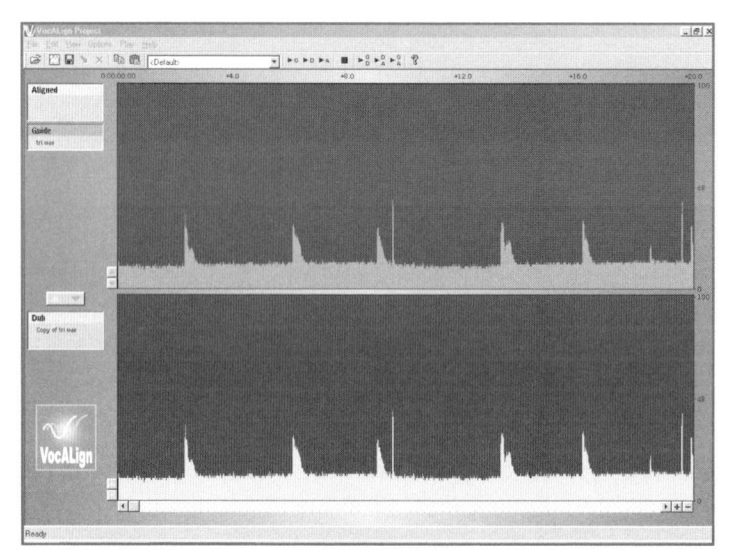

Figure 5.17
Synchro Arts VocALign Project is a software tool that can compress or expand the waveform of a dub track to match the timing of the waveform of a guide track. For example, the syllables of a dubbed voice can be made to align with lip movements in the video. This can work even if the guide track and the dub track are in different languages, provided that the dialogue in each contains the same number of syllables.

Creating a Spotting Table

When the dialogue is clean, by whatever means, and the editor is reasonably satisfied with his selection of takes and their pacing, it's time to begin adding music and effects.

As a technical tool in preparation for what can be a lengthy phase of postproduction, the sound editor creates a spotting table (see Figure 5.18). The table is simply a list of music cues (start of each new music clip) and individual sound effects, indexed by camcorder timecode. Most of the effects will be background effects or noises that, taken together, form the audio environment of each scene. The spotting table is nothing more than the editor's wish list for all the audio elements that haven't yet been added to the soundtrack. It will help the producer budget for sound editing time and music license fees. And if there's a composer and arranger, the spotting table is the editor's purchase order for music that has yet to be created.

> The term *walla* sounds like what the audience hears instead of actual background conversation in a restaurant or crowd scene. Some inexperienced directors actually tell actors to say, "Walla walla walla walla," but it's better practice (and more interesting for the actors) to actually improvise their own conversations, in character. That way, if the editor brings up background sound levels, the audience won't hear gibberish.

```
Production:   "Empire of the Zorg"                                         Director:       P. Shaner
Date:         1/02/XX                                                      Sound Designer: G. Jones
Scene:        Bar Fight                          Scene In:    01:05:06:21  Scene Out:      01:06:34:02
 Dialogue      In/Out       Music       In/Out       Source   SFX         In/Out       Source    Ambience    In/Out       Source
                                        01:05:06:21                                                          01:05:06:21
                            Honky tonk  01:05:38:11  Score
                                                              Breaking    01:05:38:11             Walla      01:05:38:11   Library
                                                              bottle      01:05:39:02  Foley
"Hey, you"    01:05:39:12
```

Figure 5.18
A spotting table is the sound designer's list of all music and sound effects cues in a show, indexed by timecode location. It will serve as a guide for the composer, as well as for sound editors who must research, create, and build the effects. In practice, the spotting table usually becomes two lists, one for music and one for effects. (*Walla* is the sound engineer's term for crowd murmur.)

Especially if the movie will be scored with original music, the sound editor typically prepares a scratch track, which inserts commercial or other prerecorded and readily available music clips as placeholders for the original music to come. The scratch track constitutes an agreement among director, producer, and sound designer about the "flavor" of the music to be delivered. It also makes test screenings seem more polished, which helps everyone better judge the movie's pacing. And it gives the composer an idea of what everyone else expects.

> Composers can be understandably leery of the expectations created by a scratch track. Consider how difficult a challenge it would be to surpass a famous piece of music or a popular song. Motion picture lore has it that Richard Strauss's *Also sprach Zarathustra*, the trademark theme of *2001: A Space Odyssey* (1968), was in the scratch track early on. Director Stanley Kubrick eventually decided there was no substitute.

Where to Get Music

An original music score, arranged for and performed by a studio orchestra, is a truly lavish production expense. Audiences expect it in a $100 million blockbuster, but most modestly budgeted project will have to find a more cost-effective solution.

Some of your options for building music tracks are the following:

Use prerecorded music selections from a music library. Sources include DeWolfe (www.dewolfemusic.com) or Opus 1 (www.opus1musiclibrary.com). You can pay either a per-drop license fee (for each music cue) or a flat fee to purchase unlimited rights to selections from a particular disc (or for a given production). Library music can sound bland, trite, or undesirably familiar. It can also be difficult to match the durations of clips to your scenes, especially in such a way that the pacing seems right and that music selections seem to flow together.

Hire performers to rerecord sheet-music selections. Licensing so-called rerecording rights to existing music will be both less expensive and less complicated legally than trying to clear the rights to a commercial recording. Using a commercial recording requires you to obtain rights (or clear) the composer's rights to the composition, the performers' rights to the performance, and whatever rights both of them conveyed to the music distributor that apply to your usage.

Hire a singer-songwriter. Some of these artists can improvise so well that they lay down a music track in a series of ADR sessions, watching the video and providing accompaniment.

Use music composition software. This is an increasingly attractive option, even for productions that might otherwise be able to afford original scoring. We've included a demo version of SmartSound SonicFire Pro software on the DVD, and we used it to build the music track of all our original shorts on the disc.

LICENSING COMMERCIAL MUSIC

Commercial music can be the most expensive option, even more expensive than commissioning a composer or songwriter to create something original for your show. The reason is that so much financial investment has gone into the promotion of a hit song, and once it becomes popular, it's priced according to its commercial value. Categories of rights that may apply to a single piece of commercial music are composition, arrangement, performance, and synchronization (using music in a soundtrack). Get help from the two main licensing organizations: Broadcast Music, Inc. (BMI) and the American Society of Composers, Authors and Publishers (ASCAP). You can search titles on their Web sites www.bmi.com and www.ascap.com and gather information about rights for selections by songwriters they represent. These Web sites also provide search services if you don't know the title of a desired cut or if you're not sure what you want. If you have a theme or genre, the search service can even provide a list of songs that you may not have heard of. You might also try asking for some of the lesser known works in hopes of finding something you like that won't command high fees.

Music Editing Tips

The finer points of music editing would take a book all by itself, but here are a few tips for incorporating music into your production.

Wait until the picture editing is done. Composers who write for the movies usually don't begin their work until the editor has done a fine cut of the picture, perhaps not even until after the picture is locked. At that point, the running times of scenes are fixed, and music can be fitted to them with frame-accurate exactness.

Cut to the beat. Refer to the audio waveform display in the editing timeline. Peaks will generally correspond to music beats. Listen carefully through headphones as you sync the music to the video, and cut on the downbeat (first and strongest beat in each musical measure). When you're cutting rapidly, as in a chase scene or fight, pick music with a strong beat and always cut on the downbeats unless you deliberately want to disorient the audience.

Backtime for precise cueing. When you are inserting a library clip and want its crescendo or climax to coincide with a video event, align those two elements first, the audio beneath the video, on the timeline. When you're composing original music or if you're building music with an application like SonicFire Pro, you can fit the duration of the music clip exactly to the scene, as well as time the climax to match the corresponding visual event. But if you're using library music (or any prerecorded clip), you don't have this kind of flexibility. In such cases, sound editors use a procedure called *backtiming*. That is, they align the music crescendo and the visual action first on the timeline. Then they work backward along the timeline, fading down the level of the music to zero at the beginning of the scene and raising it to an audible level just before the climax. A related technique called *sneaking in the cue* involves raising the audio level of the music selection very gradually from the opening of the scene.

How to Get Sound Effects

There are commercial libraries of prerecorded sound effects. Like music, effects are subject to copyright, and you must pay a license fee for their use. You can find ready-made sound effects at www.soundhunter.com. At this site, some of the selections are royalty free (but refer to the site for terms of use).

However, veteran sound designers delight in creating their own effects. They're aided in this effort by the basic fact of human nature that the ear is easily fooled. What's more, moviegoers are conditioned by experience to expect certain sounds that are not necessarily realistic. For example, in real life, walking through wet grass makes hardly any sound at all. But in the movies, the expected effect is produced by sound technicians called *Foley walkers* shuffling around in a bin of old magnetic tape. Similarly, the actual sound of an actor pulling on a jacket might not be discernible at all. But in postproduction, Foley artists will create the sound of rubbing fabric to enhance the perceived realism of the action.

> The bin (a small stage) where Foley walkers work is located in a type of ADR studio and is called a *Foley pit*, named for legendary Hollywood sound editor Jack Donovan Foley. Other materials that might be strewn in the Foley pit are gravel and corn flakes. Besides footsteps, Foley artists create sounds of all kinds, including turning doorknobs, door slams, and, you guessed it, the clinking of teacups.

No doubt in their everyday lives, sound designers are often listening for new ways to delight the ear. A manufactured sound effect is rarely done by simply pointing a mic at the real thing. (But if you do this on the set, it's called recording *wild* sound.) For example, crumpling cellophane can make a convincing rendition of a crackling fire, rapping a water glass with a spoon sounds like a melodic bell, shaking a box of cereal sounds like a battalion on the march, and an electric hair dryer can sound like a jet turbine.

> It can be a fascinating challenge to create sounds forfanciful things that don't exist in life. To create the laser blasts in the original *Star Wars* movie, sound designer Ben Burtt rapped a taut guy wire with a mallet.

The Mix-Down Process

When DME editing is all done, the mix-down process does what the term implies: A sound editor selectively blends the multiple layers of the rich soundtrack to create the specific, limited number of tracks required by the release format. The number of tracks and what they must contain will vary by distribution medium. For example, a common requirement for broadcast television is four tracks, which corresponds to two sets of stereo Left and Right channels. Dialogue goes on tracks 1 and 2 (stereo L and R), and music and effects are mixed to form tracks 3 and 4 (also stereo L and R). Playback or duplicating equipment mixes the tracks further, routing tracks 1 and 3 to the left speaker, tracks 2 and 4 to the right.

This arrangement is called *split tracks* because dialogue is kept separate from music and effects. The main reason for the split is to make it easier to replace the dialogue track with a foreign language or other alternate version, leaving the mix of music and effects unchanged.

Increasingly, commercial movie theater projection systems require Surround Sound, a multi-channel audio format developed and licensed by Dolby Digital. A common surround format is designated 5.1 (see Figure 5.19). It requires five separate full-range channels—Left, Center, Right, Left Surround, and Right Surround.

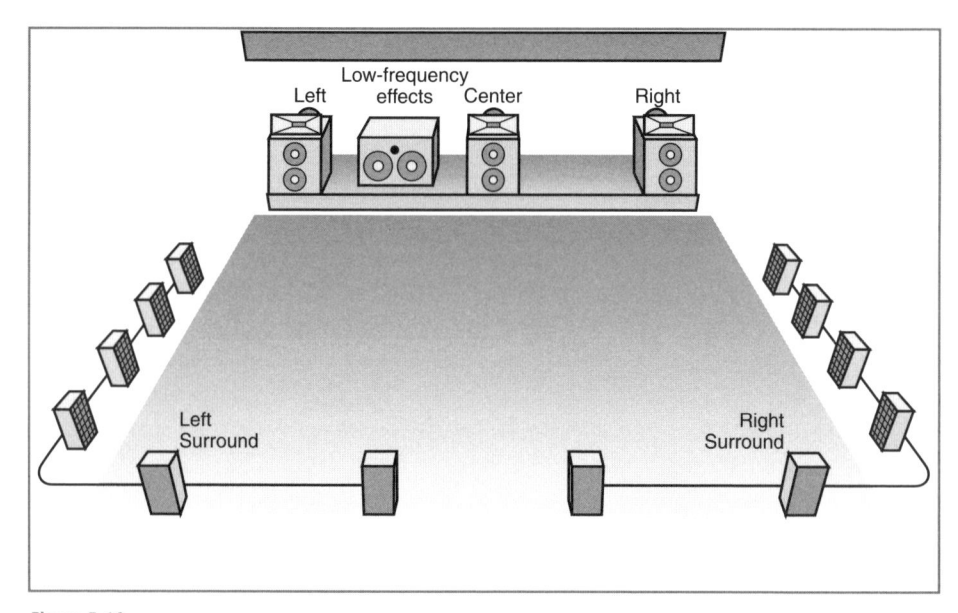

Figure 5.19
The Surround Sound 5.1 scheme requires blending of tracks and mix-down to five full-range channels and one LFE (subwoofer, or vibration effects) channel.

A sixth channel (the .1 in the label) is a narrow-bandwidth low-frequency effects (LFE) channel. It carries effects in the ultra-bass range that the audience can feel but not hear, such as the reverberation of an explosion or the shuddering of an earthquake temblor. (The speaker that produces this effect is called a *subwoofer*.)

As a sound editor, you must decide which voices, instruments, and effects go on which channel and at what audio levels. Recall that we said stereo effect isn't captured on the set, and neither are any of the surround effects. It's all a synthetic experience created in postproduction. Assigning tracks is straightforward. Consider the example of just two tracks, stereo Left and Right:

- Effects that have maximum separation occur only in one speaker or the other. So they are routed to the appropriate channel.
- Effects that should be perceived somewhere physically between the speakers are assigned to both Left and Right tracks, with the audio level higher in the speaker closest to the perceived location.

To achieve an artful mix, there are really just two basic rules:

1. Do the mix as you play back the tracks on speakers that are about the same size and position as the speakers in a typical playback situation. You must simulate what the audience will actually experience. For example, the final mix-down for a major motion picture is usually done in a movie theater that is equipped with an average-quality surround system. It's a common mistake to make judgments by relying on high-quality, studio-monitor speakers, when such an ideal listening situation might never occur in the real world. And, although an increasing number of home television sets have high-fidelity sound systems, remember that the sets in the vast majority of homes have tiny, 3-inch speakers that will do a very poor job of reproducing the bass frequencies. Low-budget filmmakers often have the opposite problem—they rely on their tiny computer speakers when doing a sound mix. Because of the poor frequency response of those speakers, the result is usually a music and effects track that is much too loud in relation to the dialogue. So, testing the playback on a real-world speaker system of adequate fidelity is absolutely essential to doing a reliable mix.

2. No matter what the release format, never mix dialogue with music and effects. Also, preserve your original multitrack audio. You might need it later if you need to make changes.

Wizards of Audio Know This

It's the sound designer's job to create realism where none exists. Of all the illusions a filmmaker must create, the soundtrack is the most synthetic and the most contrived.

In the reality of movie production, the actors may be performing on a studio backlot near a busy freeway. But for the screen story to work, the audience must believe they're on a nineteenth century battlefield, dodging a hail of shot and shell. Or the actors may be saying their lines on a studio sound stage where the only other noise is the key grip clearing his throat. But to watch this scene and be transported to a land of make-believe, the audience must sense they're in the hall of a mountain king, where underground rivers run and unseen creatures scurry about in the darkness.

> Examples of phony sound effects that have become Hollywood clichés are the sounds of punches and body blows in stunt fights. The sound of the bone-crunching payoff punch in many movie fights is nothing more violent than the breaking of a stalk of celery or the tearing of a head of crisp lettuce. In fact, the sound of a fist actually hitting someone's chin is a much less sensational thud. (We don't know this from firsthand experience, of course.)

chapter 6
Thinking Like a Director

Hey, anyone can direct a movie, right? Just follow these simple instructions, as voiced by captains of cinema over the years:

- Start out as a camera operator (George Stevens).
- Casting is 90 percent of the job (Sidney Pollack and many others).
- Know where to put the camera (Steven Spielberg).
- Photograph the actor's eyes (John Ford).
- A film should have a beginning, a middle, and an end, but not necessarily in that order (Jean-Luc Godard).
- Fire somebody on the first day of shooting, just so everyone knows you mean business (Mel Brooks).
- Always have a reason for every decision you make (Pete Shaner).
- Make all your mistakes in a loud, clear voice (Gerald Jones).

On any movie set, the director is the person who makes the decisions. Crew, actors, and production staff all look to the director for the last word on any detail, creative or logistic. Do you like her hair? Is this lighting effect what you're after? What about his performance on the last take? Is this fabric okay? Do you want to try to get in one more setup before the sun goes down?

The director isn't necessarily a hands-on expert in any of these areas, but ultimately he is expected to have an opinion, the deciding one. If you're responsible for making the ultimate creative decisions on your digital video production, whether you're working by yourself news-style or film-style with a cast and crew of thousands, you should know how professional directors think.

And if you're anyone else on the cast or crew, it's a wise career move to learn how a director thinks, if not actually read her mind.

Of course, there's no single word of advice, or even a book full of them, that will make a great director. But personal views of famous directors aside, those who've been schooled in the studio system would all agree that Hollywood-style filmmaking is a careful, meticulous process.

That hasn't always been true in the culture of run-and-gun videographers. And it's not necessarily the way digital filmmaking is going.

With the encouragement of producers and distributors, fledgling directors are rushing to shoot and edit their movies more cheaply and more quickly and quicker on digital video. That's fine as far as the democratization of the medium is concerned, but along the way it may be tempting to ignore some of the hard-won wisdom of the old studio work methods.

If you want to direct a movie that distributors and audiences perceive as polished and commercial, you should know how workmanlike pros have evolved their craft over the years. That's not to say you must imitate them or adopt their aesthetics as your own. But they usually had good reasons for the choices they made, and so should you.

This chapter surveys production from the director's point of view, emphasizing the traditional Hollywood approach, occasionally highlighting how going digital might or might not change the way you make your movie.

THE DIRECTOR'S STAFF

On a fully crewed movie shoot, the director has several highly experienced assistants, each with a unique set of skills and responsibilities:

First Assistant Director (AD) is the director's primary assistant and supervises operations on the set. She has control over the shooting schedule and is accountable for keeping to it. At any point, if the crew isn't shooting, the AD is expected to know exactly what it's waiting for and how long it will take.

Second AD assists the First AD and is usually responsible for some kind of record keeping and for getting cast members to and from the set on time.

Unit Production Manager (UPM) reports to a line producer and oversees the budget, hires crew, and approves payments. If the shoot has a second unit (for shooting establishing shots, inserts, and so on), it will have its own UPM.

Location Manager scouts and contracts for locations, as well as supervising set construction on site. It's his job to make sure that the crew leaves the location in as good or better condition than they found it.

Production Assistants (PAs) are administrative aides and all-around helpers, jokingly called *go-fers* because they are at the beck and call of the director and her staff.

On some projects a producer or line producer might assume the functions of UPM or location manager instead.

Selecting Material

If you're setting out to make a low-budget, digital-video movie, chances are you want to tell your own story. The director's vision, after all, shapes the whole creative process and is often the motivation for starting the project in the first place.

> With some justification, screenwriters complain that directors in the studio system get too much credit for being the auteurs, or authors, of the movies. But in the early twentieth century, directors were highly paid clock-punchers assigned to projects by the front office. A handful—including Alfred Hitchcock, John Ford, and Howard Hawks—had such individual styles and content that they stood out from the studio employees.
>
> The concept of the director as the author of the film is a European idea that eventually caught on in the popular mind, ultimately raising the status of directors in the industry.
>
> One director who flaunted his style was Frank Capra (*It Happened One Night, It's a Wonderful Life*), who encouraged the notion that his movies had "the Capra touch." Apparently, his longtime writing collaborator Robert Riskin got so disgusted hearing this that he stormed into Capra's office, dropped a stack of blank paper on the desk, and exclaimed, "There! Put the Capra touch on that!"

If, instead, you're directing on assignment, a producer probably handed you a script and asked what you could do with it. The producer's second question, if not the first, would be whether you think you can bring it in for a specific amount of money (some shockingly low figure, we'll bet).

But whether you're deciding which of your own stories to tell or which offer to accept, here's some practical advice on low-budget commercial realities:

- Fewer locations, fewer characters
- Less talk, more action

Fewer Locations, Fewer Actors

To make your project more feasible financially, there are ways to reduce the budget without skimping at all on the quality of your imagery.

To make the production budget go as far as possible, keep the number of locations down. This will almost certainly require some rewriting of the script. For instance, if you're planning an ultra-low budget production, try setting most of the action in the same house. This way, if you shoot mostly interiors in smaller rooms, you can use smaller lighting kits and fewer setups. And you won't lose time transporting the entire cast and crew and all your gear from one location to another.

24P: Make Your Digital Movies Look Like Hollywood

> We did the Aqua Tan commercial shoot (see clips on the DVD) in a rented mansion on the beach in Santa Monica. Its owner maintains it as a location for movies and commercials. It has so many rooms, all with different themes in décor, that scenes shot in them can look like different locations. To these options, add the backyard with its veranda (where several of our scenes took place), a swimming pool, the beach, and the Pacific Ocean. And, the impressive spiral staircase in the main lobby served as a kind of grand entrance and fashion runway. This type of location is perfect for minimizing transportation and setup delays so you can work on a compressed schedule without sacrificing safety or quality.

Using a small cast and conserving on the number of speaking parts will also simplify production and reduce expenses. This is another good reason to rewrite the script. Besides economizing on payroll, having fewer actors will put less of a burden on transportation, makeup and wardrobe, and catering.

However, there's another good reason to reduce cast size that's unrelated to saving money. Consolidating character roles in the script can make your story more compelling. While it's rare for screenwriters to make the mistake of having too many heroes, challenging the leading character with too many opponents is a common script flaw. As a rule, the more singular and powerful the opponent, the more exalted the hero.

So, consolidating several villains into a single opposing character at the writing stage can both heighten the drama and save you production money.

Less Talk, More Action

The old saying that talk is cheap applies to movie production. Once you've paid to transport cast and crew to the location and rigged the set, letting the camcorder roll as the actors expound is about as inexpensive as anything you can do. It's also potentially the most boring for the audience.

There's another old maxim: Show, don't tell. And that's still good advice for filmmakers.

So why, if talky scenes are cheap to shoot, do we suggest cutting back on the dialogue?

We're also on the subject of making your project more feasible, and it's a matter of what will sell. Movie distributors tend to think of "talking head" movies as not being suitable for the wide screen. That's partly because of a long tradition of television drama that favors tight closeups of actors' dialogue. (Pick any soap opera as a good example.) In fact, a common put-down of screenplays among studio executives is the comment, "It's small screen," meaning it's too talky, a story for television.

But even more important for the low-budget filmmaker is the harsh reality that dialogue-heavy movies don't travel well. For international audiences, talky stories, whether comedy or drama, aren't as popular as more action-oriented fare. Cultural differences can prevent an audience from identifying with—or even understanding—translated dialogue or subtitles.

But everyone understands a good fight or a thrilling chase.

> The international market represents perhaps the best way for an indie filmmaker to recoup production expenses, especially if domestic theatrical release is limited or if box office revenues are marginal or disappointing. However, international distributors have a quirky way of screening potential new products. At the annual American Film Market (AFM) in Santa Monica, buyers go from room to room to sample video versions of new movies. More often than not, they ask to see the movie in fast-forward, with the audio turned down. Apparently, they reason that if they can understand the plot, so will their audiences, no matter how bad the translation.

Yes, everyone understands a love story, too. But here's the key to deciding when dialogue can carry a story. The audience might not remember or even pay attention to spoken words, but strong, underlying emotions will always be unmistakable. If dialogue carries emotion, it works. If instead it tells a complicated story about something that's happening off-screen, it's a snore.

> Some of the most commercially successful movies fuse exciting action with heightened emotion. For example, one of the most popular actors of all time in international markets is not Sir Laurence Olivier or Marcello Mastroiani, but action hero Charles Bronson. The classic formula of his blockbuster movies, such as *Death Wish* (1974) and *The Evil That Men Do* (1984), was revenge against vicious, irrational cruelty. At the opening of these screen sagas, someone dear to him would be brutally murdered by bad guys. The rest of the movie was his fierce quest for the culprits and delivery of his own brand of street justice. You can say what you wish about the morality of this type of story, but audiences in countries all over the world consistently voted for these gritty movies with their ticket money.

Production Planning and Scheduling

In the early stages of preproduction, the director may work with the writer to suggest ways of consolidating the locations and character roles in the script. At this point, the script starts its evolution from writer's draft to shooting script. The early writer's drafts, which concentrate on refining story and character, have unnumbered scenes and don't specify shots. This format is called a *master scene script*.

As preproduction planning continues, sequential scene numbers are added to the script and perhaps also notation of essential shots at crucial story points, such as establishing shots and emotional close-ups, as well as cutaways and inserts that show reactions or props needed for important plot clues. (It's still not a shot-by-shot description—that comes later.)

When the shooting script begins to emerge with numbered scenes, an experienced production manager (PM) does a script breakdown (see Figure 6.1). Using one breakdown sheet for each scene, the PM lists its required elements: location, set, characters, props, special effects, and so on.

Based on the breakdown sheets, the scheduling process is essentially a matter of shuffling and sorting scenes, grouping them so that needed resources (a leading actor, a fog machine, a trained animal) can be used as much as possible on continuous shooting days.

While the proposed schedule will be worked out between the PM and the line producer, the director needs to understand the process because she will ultimately have to approve it—and live by it—as the detailed plan that will control what happens on each day of the shoot.

The basic principle of movie scheduling is to sort and re-sort the elements of the breakdown, arranging the more expensive elements on successive days as much as possible. For example, scenes are first rearranged and grouped by location (such as a house), which is usually the most constraining factor, then by sets (such as rooms) within that location.

Script Breakdown Sheet

Date: 08/01/XX

Production Company: Idle Dreams Productions
Production Title: "For a Few Dollars Less"
Breakdown Page No.: 4
Scene No.: 2
Scene Name: Bettina's Confession - Kitchen
Int/Ext.: INT
Day or Night: DAY
Page Count: 2

Cast:
Bettina
Bob

Stunts:
None

Extras/Atmosphere:
None

Special Effects:
None

Extras/Silent Bits:
Cable Guy

Vehicles/Animals:
Dog "Wilmer" walks through

Wardrobe:
Cable co. uniform
Bettina tennis togs

Props:
Tools (Cable guy)
Kitchen stove (practical)
Toaster (practical)

Sound Effects/Music:
Record wild clatter, pots and pans

Special Equipment:
None

Makeup/Hair:
Nothing special

Production Notes:
Does Bettina need a tennis racquet?

Figure 6.1
For each scene in the shooting script, a breakdown sheet lists the required elements on shoot day, including cast members, stunts, extras, live special effects, vehicles, animals, wardrobe, props, live sound effects, special equipment, makeup and hair, and any production notes to be discussed with the director.

Each attempt at sorting the scenes goes to the next finer degree of detail. Here are the PM's scheduling priorities, in descending order of importance:

1. Location
2. Different sets within each location
3. Exteriors before interiors (saving interior shooting as a contingency for rainy days)
4. Days before nights (you'll all lose less sleep this way)
5. Principal actors scheduled on successive days
6. Continuous scheduling of special equipment, vehicles, animals, stunts, and effects

A MAJOR SCHEDULING CONSTRAINT: ACTORS' AVAILABILITY

Besides location, perhaps the biggest constraint on your schedule will be the actors' availability, which is subject to union (SAG or AFTRA) rules and industry practice. (Scheduling conflicts for stars can also be a huge headache.) Your options for booking and scheduling actors include:

- **Run of show.** Actors will be available and on call for the duration of the shooting schedule; used mainly for principal roles.
- **Weekly.** Producer can drop actors from the payroll and pick them up later if the unpaid interval is at least 10 days; not used much on low-budget shooting because schedules aren't long enough to apply this rule.
- **Day player.** Actors are scheduled for specific days and paid a per-diem fee.
- **Children.** Labor regulations vary, but many states limit the number of hours children can work on the set. To comply with these laws, you may need to hire academic tutors and social workers, as well. (The studio's solution? Hire identical twins and schedule them at different times.)

If you're working with nonprofessional actors and not paying them, these complexities might not be necessary. However, with union approval, it can be possible to use professional actors under deferred pay contracts. If you do this, remember that the amounts you pay eventually must be calculated based on union rates and working rules, so the UPM must keep accurate daily payroll records, even though there might be no cash outlay for salaries during the shoot. For more information on employing union actors for experimental and low-budget productions, see www.sag.org.

As a general rule, you'll want to shoot all the scenes at a given location on successive days. But scheduling would be fairly simple if location and transportation were the only factors to consider. You can probably assume your principal actors will be scheduled nearly every day of the shoot. However, because of union rules and pay scales, it can be cost effective to hire supporting players by the week. (See the sidebar, "A Major Scheduling Constraint: Actors' Availability," on the previous page) In view of this, it might be a better plan to sort all scenes involving these weekly players into the first week, even if it means extra location moves, and then drop them from the payroll and return to the first location to get scenes involving only the principals in the second week.

As we've said, DV productions are often fast and light on their feet due to smaller crews and lighter equipment. Staying at one location, you can possibly shoot as many as eight script pages per day. Another way to think of it is that, working at the same location, you can usually shoot two or three master scenes in a day, each with several setups.

When you factor in other requirements, such as hiring special-effects crews and expensive equipment for particular scenes, the scheduling process can grow quite complex. That's where scheduling software such as Entertainment Partners Movie Magic Scheduling comes in (see www.entertainmentpartners.com). It lets you try different what-if scenarios to see where you can save time, money, or both.

> As you plan your shooting, remember that each time you move the camera to a new position, it can take anywhere from 15 to 45 minutes to relight.

> Planning to shoot at night? Due to lighting technicalities, as well as the comfort of cast and crew, it can be more practical to shoot day-for-night. Still, the only way to capture an authentic after-dark look is to shoot after dark. If you do insist on shooting at night, remember this: If you schedule 12 hours of nighttime shooting, be prepared to get only as much footage as a nine-hour daytime shoot. For some reason, crews work slower at night, even when they're well rested.

Planning Your Shots

At the most practical level, the director's main task is to deliver coverage, or all the shots the editor needs to assemble the screen story. Ideally, adequate coverage should also include several choices for each edit.

The time-honored film-style Hollywood approach to getting coverage is the master-scene shot plan. If you use this approach, the shooting script doesn't necessarily need to be broken down into specific shots because the master-scene approach will cover all the basic possibilities.

Despite what we've said about emphasizing action in your shooting, the master-scene approach evolved for shooting dialogue between two actors. However, the practice of retaking the same event from multiple viewpoints can be applied to almost any situation.

For each scene, the director and the DP must choose camera positions, angles, and lenses to capture the following shots, usually in this order:

Master scene. In a dialogue scene, it's typically a medium shot (MS) of two actors, framing them from about the knees up, also called a *two-shot*. The master scene captures the entire scene from beginning to end without interruption. Traditionalist directors will get the whole scene in the can, whether or not they plan to use all of it in the edit. That's because the master scene is the editor's all-purpose alternative for any other take that's unusable.

Closeups (CUs) of first actor. The setup for the first actor's CU comes in closer and reframes his head and shoulders. Relighting from the MS will usually be necessary to get the key light just right on his face. Another term for an actor's closeup is the *single*, or a *clean single*. A variation that includes some of the other actor's body in the frame is called a *dirty single*, which has become a standard style of shooting. The purpose of a dirty single is to show the other actor's body language, such as nodding of the head or gestures, as he reacts to the first actor's speech.

It's the mark of a rookie director to shoot only the actor's speaking parts in his closeups. It's equally important to capture the emotions that play on her face as she reacts to what the other actor says. In fact, the editor may want to cut away from the speaker as soon as possible so that her lines play under her partner's reaction shots.

Extreme closeups (ECUs) of first actor. These shots may frame the actor's head or might come in so close as to frame only the eyes. ECUs can be incredibly powerful, but they should be used sparingly for emotional climaxes. So, unlike CUs, for which you should cover all the actors' lines as well as their reactions, you need only shoot the ECUs you intend to use in the edit.

> To save time or to get around talent scheduling problems, you might be tempted to shoot a clean single without the other actor being present. But that will leave the on-camera actor delivering lines to a stand-in or to empty space, neither of which is likely to evoke an interesting performance. Even PAs can be poor stand-ins because they won't necessarily give the actor any emotion to react to. Certainly, a skilled actor can imagine what's not there, but why make the job more difficult?

> A famous variation of the CU is the Warner's closeup, which frames the actor's face from chin to top of forehead. Named for the studio that wanted a way to showcase the glamour of its actors, its purpose was to fill as much of the frame as possible so as to make the star seem larger than life.

Closeups and extreme closeups of second actor. These shots are called *reverse angles* with respect to the shots on the first actor. They will require setting up from the opposite camera angle and relighting to get the key and fill on the second actor's face just right. When setting up for the second actor's takes, a careful director will not cross the stage line (see "Stage Line," later in this chapter). For intercutting of closeups to work in the edit, camera angles should correspond to the actors' relative heights and eyelines. For example, if the first actor is taller, the camera should be looking up at her, as the second actor does, and the reverse angle should look down on the second actor. Generally, if the first actor's CUs are dirty singles, the shots on the second actor should also show just as much of the other actor's body. Most people have an intuitive sense of what's right for matching singles just from years of watching movies that have been meticulously shot and edited according to master-scene technique.

After masters and closeups, the remaining shots before moving on will be the following:

- Inserts (ECUs of hands, objects, and gestures, as well as shots of important actions, such as hiding a clue in a drawer)
- Establishing shots (such as an extreme long shot, or ELS, of the building or location)
- Wild sound effects (actual sounds that occur in the location environment or as a result of actors' actions, such as the slamming of a car door)
- Room tone (as a last take before you move on, call for quiet on the set and record for about a minute)

WHO SAYS DON'T PUSH IT?

In the best of circumstances, you'll move the setup still closer and vary the camera angle to move from CU to ECU and then relight. However, if you're on a budget or in a hurry to catch the fading daylight, a shortcut is simply to stick with the CU setup and use the telephoto zoom to reframe for the ECU. Called *pushing in*, it's a common practice in television, but some film-style purists regard it as a mark of carelessness. When you figure that pushing in could save you the 30 minutes or so it would take to change the setup and relight, it can be a useful work method for DV crews that are trying to shoot as many pages as possible in a day. Since pushing in is a quick and easy move, it also doesn't tire the actors by requiring them to wait around for the new setup, and it can even help you keep the dramatic momentum going in a scene. (It's also possible to go from MS to CU by pushing in, but you might not save as much time because it's so important to relight for the CU.)

The Elements of Shot Design

All the creative and technical decisions that go into shot design comprise a director's style, and there are almost as many styles as there are directors. Although these styles vary considerably, there are just 10 options in shot design, which you can use in any combination:

Framing, or the size of the subject, has three basic variants: closeup, medium shot, and long shot. The uses of each are part of the master-scene scheme.

Lens selection, or focal length, also has three: wide, normal, and telephoto. In general, telephoto shots flatter the face, and wide angles tend to distort facial features, swelling brows, nose, and lips and exaggerating expressions (which can be useful for shooting comedy, but not much else).

> Decisions about focal length can also affect depth of field. Wide lenses have great depth of field; telephoto, or long lenses have shallow depth of field that permits selective focus.

Camera angle has three options: low (below the subject), neutral (level with the subject), and high (above the subject). Low angles tend to exalt, or lend power to, the subject, and high angles diminish the subject.

So, that's nine variations so far, in the categories of framing, lens selection, and camera angle. The tenth factor is:

Camera movement can be used in combination with any of the other factors. Moving the camera during the shot is a hallmark of the studio movie style. Audiences have come to expect it, even though, like a good musical score, most of the time its effect should be subliminal. It can add fluidity to actions on the screen, enhance continuity between shots, and reinforce rising or sinking emotions by soaring or diving. Its many variations include: panning and tilting (see Figure 6.2), zooming (Figure 6.3), dollying (Figure 6.4), trucking (Figure 6.5), and craning (Figure 6.6).

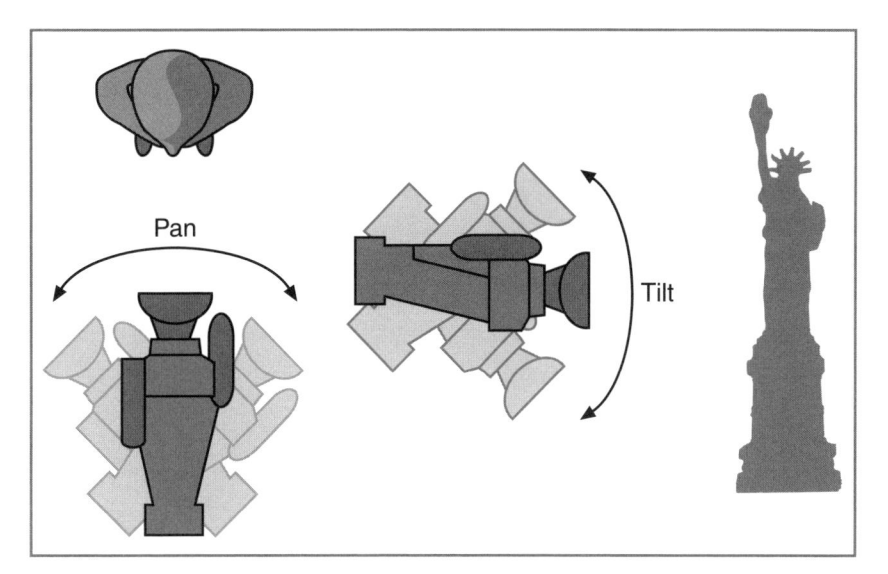

Figure 6.2
With reference to a camera mounted on a tripod or other stationary mount with a moveable head, panning moves side to side within the same horizontal plane, and tilting moves up and down within the same vertical plane.

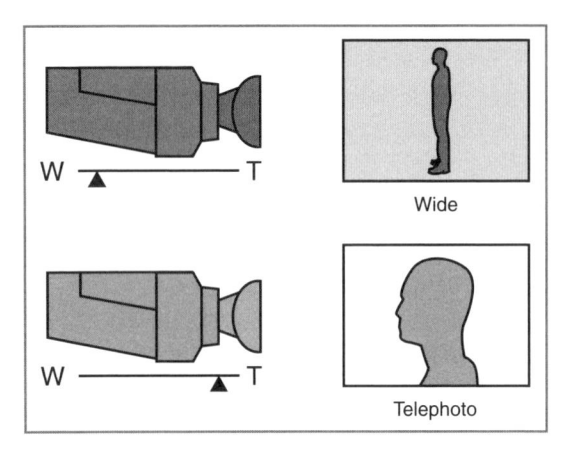

24P: Make Your Digital Movies Look Like Hollywood

Figure 6.3
Zooming is accomplished with a lens having continuously variable focal length, from wide (W) to telephoto (T).

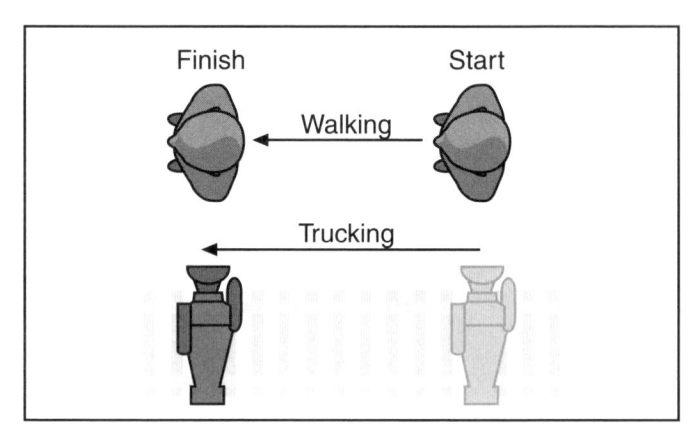

Figure 6.5
Similar to dollying on tracks, trucking keeps pace alongside a moving subject.

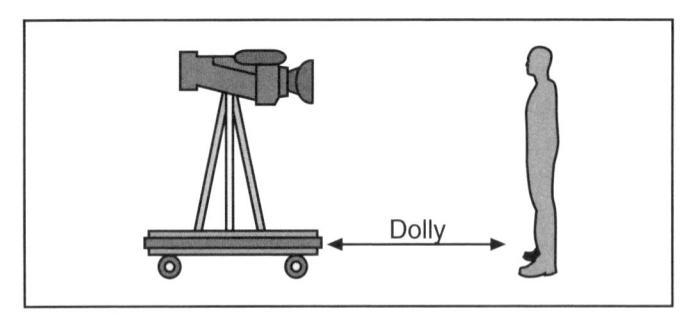

Figure 6.4
Traditionally done with a rolling camera mount on tracks, dollying moves toward or away from the subject.

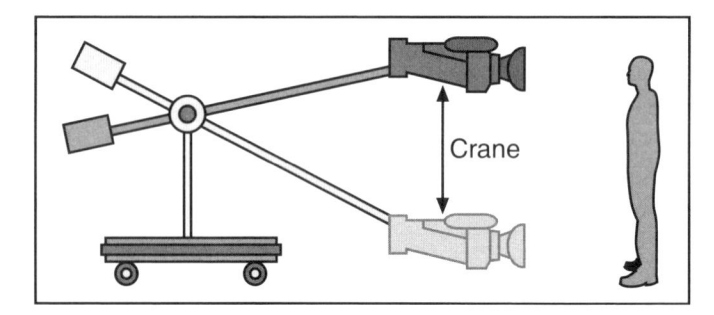

Figure 6.6
Craning raises or lowers the camera by a lever action. (A short crane mounted on the back of a dolly is called a *boom arm*.)

6. Thinking Like a Director

110

SHOT DESIGN TERMINOLOGY

Here are some fine points of shot design, along with terms to describe them.

Establishing shot. Remember that this term describes a storytelling function rather than the design of the shot. Although commonly an ELS of a location, it could just as easily be the ECU of keys in a jailer's hands that establishes the following scene in a lockup.

Over the shoulder (OTS). This shot centers one actor in the frame as viewed approximately, but perhaps not literally, over the other's shoulder. In a traditional approach, it's a type of dirty single, a CU of the speaker's upper torso that includes the side of the listener's head. The reverse angle on an OTS shot should complement and seem opposite to the height and eyeline of the first.

Perhaps the most commonly used over-the-shoulder shot is the movie fistfight. The camera is placed over the shoulder of the opponent while the facing attacker swings his fist as if hitting the opponent's jaw. The opponent snaps his head backward as if hit and the sound of a punch is added in post. This stunt was invented not by a director but a great stuntperson, Yakima Canutt, John Wayne's stand-in.

Insert. The insert is a shot that's briefly intercut with a longer scene to show an object or some other meaningful detail. Traditionally, it's a CU or ECU. An example would be a CU of a newspaper headline inserted into a dialogue scene in which two characters are discussing the news. Tight inserts don't show surroundings of a particular location or set. Savvy production managers take advantage of this and often schedule all inserts at the end of a production or at some other convenient time, usually done by a separate, less senior crew, called the *second unit*. Studios sometimes shoot all their inserts on separate, smaller sound stages called *insert stages*.

Cutaway. A cutaway is any shot that takes the audience out of a scene, usually to add information. For example, we see a man hurry off-screen and then cut away to his wife in another location glancing anxiously at her watch. Or during a shot of two characters walking on the beach, you might cut away to a shot of a seagull floating over the waves. Although using a cutaway is ultimately an editing decision, you won't have the clips to work with if you don't plan the shots in advance. Stock footage or clips from a film or video archive can be an economical source of cutaways, particularly if the duration of the shot is so short the audience won't have a chance to study it for details that might not match.

Point of view (POV). A POV shot shows the audience what one character sees and helps them identify with him. In most other types of shots, the actors must stay focused on each other, not on the camera. But in the POV and its matching reverse, each actor must look straight at the lens. One use of the POV is the horror-movie stereotype that shows the concealed monster's view of the unwitting victim. (At screenings, cinema buffs have been known to yell, "Watch out! There's a camera operator in the bushes!")

Blocking the Action

A term inherited from live theater, *blocking* describes the actors' movements on the set. Your ideas about blocking a scene will have a big impact on camera placement and other decisions you make as you plan the shooting.

First of all, you want to limit the actors' movements so they won't stray beyond the boundaries of the set or move into areas that would be out of focus or poorly lit. Secondly, blocking is a storytelling tool. Effective blocking is every bit as important, sometimes more so, than dialogue in conveying information and emotion to the audience. For example, it's not necessary for an actor to deliver a verbal refusal if she just makes a furious exit. That way of telling the story is not only more interesting and compelling than dialogue, but it can also improve pacing, forcing you to advance the story quickly by cutting to the next scene.

Blocking should be repeatable from one take to another, or your shots might not match when the editor cuts them together. Also, if there's too much variation in blocking from one take to the next, you might not know whether you've captured the scene the way it was written or the way you intended to visualize it. And, if you permit spontaneous variations in actors' blocking on the set, you must be prepared to spend more time in the edit finding ways to match the assembled takes.

How Much Structure?

The task of blocking your scenes raises a question that will affect all other aspects of shot design: How much do you need to structure the shoot in advance? Put another way, how much improvisation will you tolerate on the set?

> A strong preference for either structured or improvisational shooting has a major influence on a director's overall style. Directors who favor structure plan each shot carefully in advance and in detail. Then, on the set, they stick closely to their plan. Famous examples include Alfred Hitchcock and Steven Spielberg. Improvisational directors permit experimentation on the set, including alternate line readings by actors and impromptu blocking. Directors who are noted for their improvisational styles include Robert Altman and Francis Ford Coppola.

Filmmakers who improvise a lot often criticize directors who favor a structured approach for a lack of spontaneity due to blocking that's worked out in advance. Improvisational directors trust their actors to sense where their bodies want to go in the heat of the moment. The resulting action may well be more realistic, more inventive, and more interesting to watch than the writer's or director's preconceived ideas about how the action should play.

But waiting until you get on the set to work out the blocking is risky. Some directors get away with it, but it's challenging to set camera and lights if you don't know exactly where the actors are going to be.

A good compromise is to allow plenty of time for rehearsals. Hold preproduction sessions to read through the scene with actors. Let them play it out, and watch how they naturally want to move. Then, after rehearsal, but well before shoot day, you can design your shots and draw up your shot plan with its blocking informed by the rehearsal process.

Graphic Tools for Visualizing the Story

Tools for working out the story on paper in preproduction include the storyboard (see Figure 6.7) and the shot plan drawing (Figure 6.8). The more structured your directorial approach, the more you'll want to rely on such drawings at the preproduction stage.

Storyboard

A good storyboard bears a strong resemblance to a comic strip. It shows the sequence of shots as thumbnail sketches, usually with dialogue written beneath. A storyboard artist must work closely with the director as they interpret the script visually and must have a firm grasp of the principles of cinema shot design.

A storyboard is much like the film buyers' fast-forward look at a movie. It tells you whether the story makes sense without dialogue, gives a sense of flow and pacing, and highlights any breaks in the continuity.

Figure 6.7
The storyboard helps the creative team think through the visual logic of the story, and it can help them reach agreement about the preproduction planning that will follow. (Illustration courtesy of Chris Pechin, www.famousframes.com.)

When a storyboard emerges from the script, collaboration among the creative team can begin in earnest. The art director, set designer, and production manager can begin to get an idea of how the look of locations and sets can support the story, and the DP can begin to discuss the mood of the scenes with the director and see how scenes flow from one to the next, affecting how the audience should perceive the time of day in each shot.

Shot Plan Drawing

All the elements of shot design culminate in the shot plan drawing, a diagram of your camera setups, blocking of actors, and shots for a scene.

Although both tools help the director work toward specifying shots, the storyboard and the shot plan have different purposes. The storyboard helps the creative team see how the story will play on the screen. In a bird's-eye view, the shot plan shows how the action will play on the set and how the actors will use the playing area. A good shot plan follows through on the visual ideas in the script and storyboard. It anchors your shot designs within the real constraints of a particular set.

Because it details each setup and shot, the shot plan also helps you make sure you'll get all the coverage you need. When you're working film-style, you'll be shooting out of sequence. In the frenzy of production, it's all too easy to lose track.

Deriving the Shot List

Following from the shot plan, a shot list itemizes the shots you intend to get, in the order you intend to get them. If you're working from a storyboard and didn't do a shot plan to accompany it, you'll have to give some thought to the order of setups and shooting.

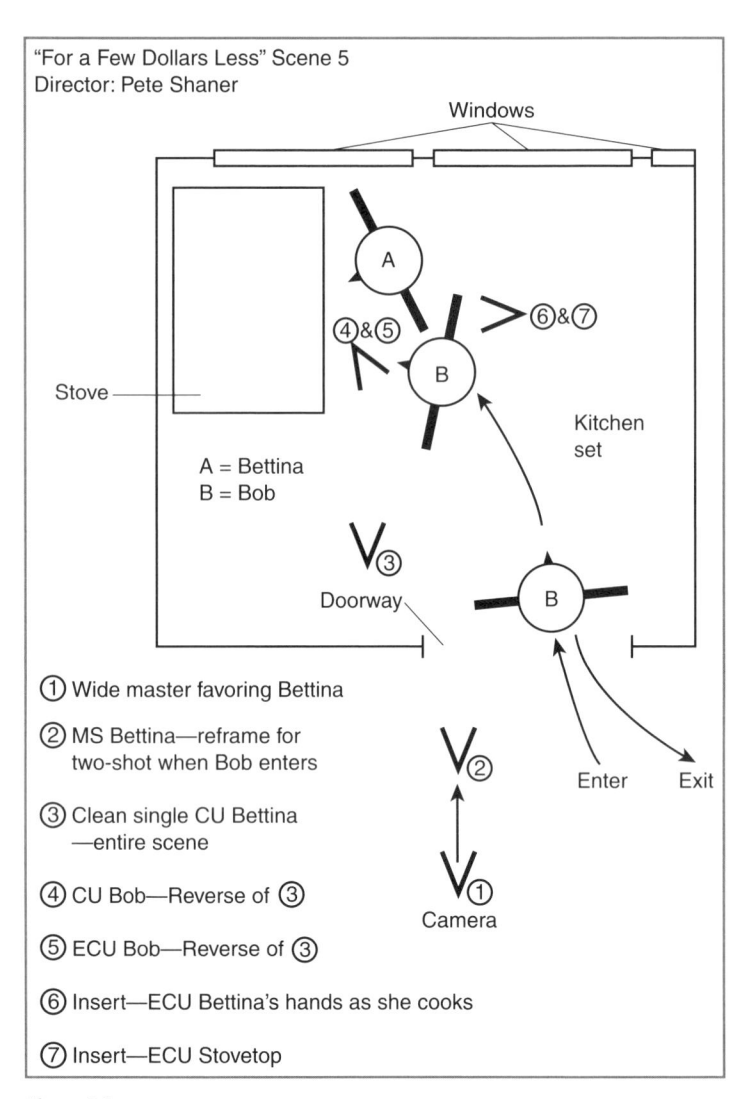

"For a Few Dollars Less" Scene 5
Director: Pete Shaner

A = Bettina
B = Bob

① Wide master favoring Bettina

② MS Bettina—reframe for two-shot when Bob enters

③ Clean single CU Bettina —entire scene

④ CU Bob—Reverse of ③

⑤ ECU Bob—Reverse of ③

⑥ Insert—ECU Bettina's hands as she cooks

⑦ Insert—ECU Stovetop

Figure 6.8
The shot plan is an overhead view of the set, showing one or more camera setups and the specific shots for each. Unlike the storyboard, the shot plan is tailored to the practical realities of a real location. The plan shows how the visualization conceived in the storyboard will be captured as a series of takes on the set. Notice also that the order of shots in the plan is grounded in classic master-scene technique.

To derive the shot list from the shot plan, start by listing the shots in story sequence, then sort them by master shot, and finally by increasing degrees of closeup. (Notice that the order exactly follows master-scene shooting technique.) For example, the shot list for a two-character dialogue scene would look like this:

1. Master two-shot: Bob and Bettina in the Living Room
2. All Bob's CUs
3. All Bob's ECUs
4. All Bettina's CUs
5. All Bettina's ECUs
6. All inserts
7. Next master shot: Bob and Bettina in the Kitchen

> The classic approach to shooting in master-scene technique is to start with the widest shot and move ever tighter. The entire set is lit correctly for your first shots. As you move in closer, you need fewer lights, with fewer adjustments. This approach minimizes relighting and saves time. However, there will be occasions when you should do the opposite. Particularly when working with inexperienced actors, children, or animals, the subject's repetitions in close might not match the master-scene takes. Even an experienced actor might give all her tears in the early takes and have none left for the extreme closeup. In such cases, if you need that special quality in the tight shot, shoot all the closeups of that subject first.

As preproduction planning continues, you'll probably re-sort the list several times, grouping shots by location, interior or exterior, day or night, scene, setup, and shooting day. Again, it's wise to shoot exteriors before interiors, regardless of their sequence in the story. That way, if it rains, and you can't shoot the exteriors, you'll still have shots you can get indoors.

The director can then use the shot plan and shot list as a basis for discussions with the DP and crew about the details of camera setups and lighting.

Preserving Continuity

Continuity is a visual sense of how shots flow logically when they're assembled. An assembled sequence should give a unified, convincing impression of uninterrupted time, space, and action. For example, showing an actor's hair parted on the left in one scene and parted on the right in another would be a break in continuity. If she wears a purple dress in one shot and yellow pants in the next shot (of the same scene), that's another break. Ultimately, continuity is an editing issue, but you can't get it right unless you plan your shots with the concept in mind.

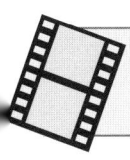

> As with other aesthetic aspects of shot design, directors can disagree on the importance of maintaining continuity. To paraphrase director Oliver Stone (who used stronger language), "Continuity is for people with no guts."

On a fully crewed movie set, the script supervisor watches each take, makes notes on problematic details (such as mismatched clothing), and advises the director of possible breaks in continuity. If your production can't afford a full-time script supervisor, continuity should be the concern of the director or camera operator.

But the time to begin thinking about continuity is at the very earliest stages of visualizing the script. There are three key principles of continuity to keep in mind when designing your shots:

- Stage line
- Screen direction
- Time dependencies

Stage Line

The stage line is an imaginary line drawn between two actors on the set (see Figure 6.9). To assure visual continuity, all your camera setups in a scene must be on the same side of the line, or axis. If you fail to follow this rule (also known as the *180 degree rule*), characters will swap sides on the screen during a scene, which can be disorienting to the audience. If you stay on the same side of the stage line, Bob will always be on the left side of the screen and Bettina will always be on the right, no matter how you frame them. This can be difficult to visualize if you're new to the concept, but it's easy to spot the error on the screen.

Figuring out the stage-line rule can become complex if the scene includes three or more actors. In this situation, there are effectively multiple stage lines, one between each pair of actors. One simplified approach is to find a central element, such as a table, and shoot the scene from just two setups, one on either side of the table, respecting a single stage line drawn through the table's center (see Figure 6.10).

But there aren't any hard and fast rules for handling the stage line in multiple-character scenes. Your best guideline is your own intuitive sense of continuity, gained from watching movies all your life. Here's our best advice, which is more of a guideline than a strict rule: *Actors should always appear to be looking toward the person they're talking to,* even if that person isn't in the frame. If the listener is off-screen, decide where he is in relation to the speaker and maintain that imaginary stage line. If the actor's eye contact doesn't seem logical, find an alternate setup. This is where a detailed storyboard helps, especially as you discuss the problem with the actors and the DP.

Some filmmakers deliberately experiment with crossing the stage line, but be prepared for a challenge in the editing room if you decide to try it.

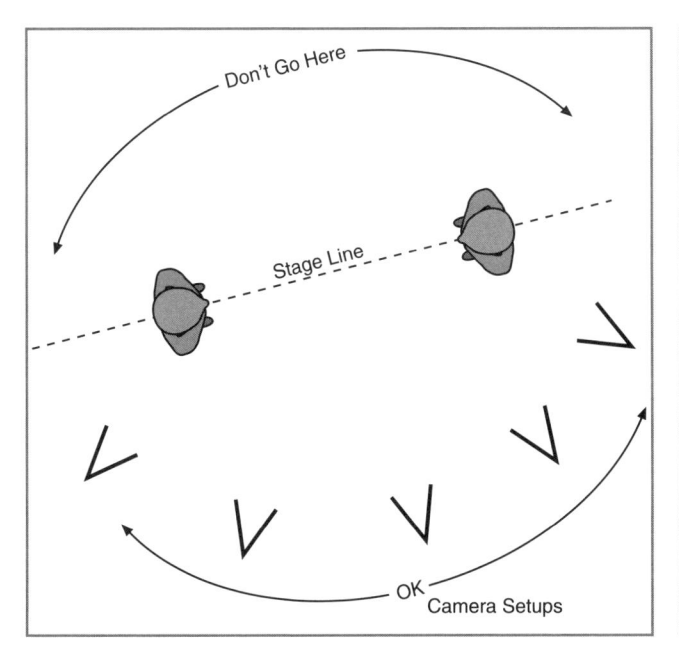

Figure 6.9
The rule of not crossing the stage line with the camera when shooting a scene also applies during editing. Selecting takes from either side of the line will cause actors to jump inexplicably from one side of the screen to the other.

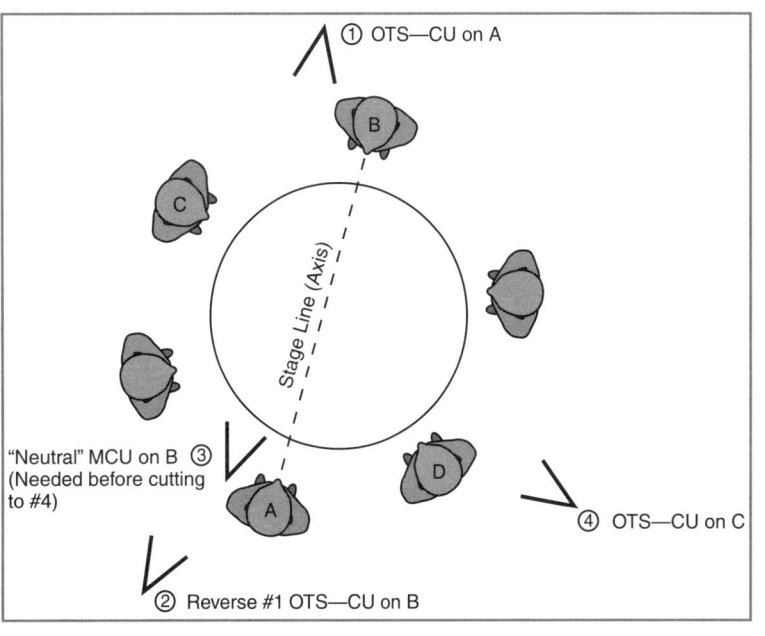

Figure 6.10
The family at the dinner table or the locker-room poker game is a difficult scene to shoot because there are potentially as many stage lines as there are pairs of actors. A practical approach is to draw a line down the middle of the table and insert a neutral angle (looking at the head of the table, for example) before you cross it. In any shot, actors should always appear to be looking toward the person they are talking to.

Screen Direction

The path of a subject through the two-dimensional space of the movie frame is its screen direction. Stated as a basic rule, respecting continuity of screen direction requires maintaining a consistent point of view and frame of reference for the audience. For example, if a character is walking from left to right in the first shot of a sequence, and you cut away for the second shot, when you return to the character in shot three, he should still be walking left to right, not right to left.

As another example, think of an actor walking down the sidewalk (see Figure 6.11). Her goal is the front door of an apartment building, but that door isn't shown in the first shot. In the first shot, we see her walking from right to left. In the next shot, we see her friend waiting anxiously for her at the building entrance. To preserve continuity of screen direction, the friend must be looking to screen right expecting her approach. For best effect, the building entrance should be on the *left* side of the frame, to establish it as the ultimate goal of the walker. Compose the shot so that most of the air, or empty space, in the frame is in front of the expectant friend. The audience will get the idea that the walker will enter the frame there.

If you want to show the actor approaching the building entrance in a series of shots, you must always show her moving from right to left. The only way to change screen direction without confusing the audience is to interpose a neutral shot, showing the actor coming right at the camera or moving directly away from it. Then you can show her walking from left to right in the next shot. However, if you now cut back to the friend waiting at the entrance, he must be looking to screen left.

Some aspects of screen direction are rooted more in moviemaking convention than in reality. For example, if you're cutting back and forth between two sides of a telephone conversation, it will look more natural if one character holds the phone to her left ear and the other to his right.

As with other principles of continuity, some filmmakers deliberately violate screen direction. But we don't advise confusing your audience this way.

Time Dependencies

A time dependency is created when an effect viewed in one scene is caused by an action in an earlier scene. An example is a burning cigarette. If the actor's cigarette is burned down to the butt in the first shot, it will be a break in continuity to see him holding a freshly lit one in the next, unless you insert a shot of him lighting up again.

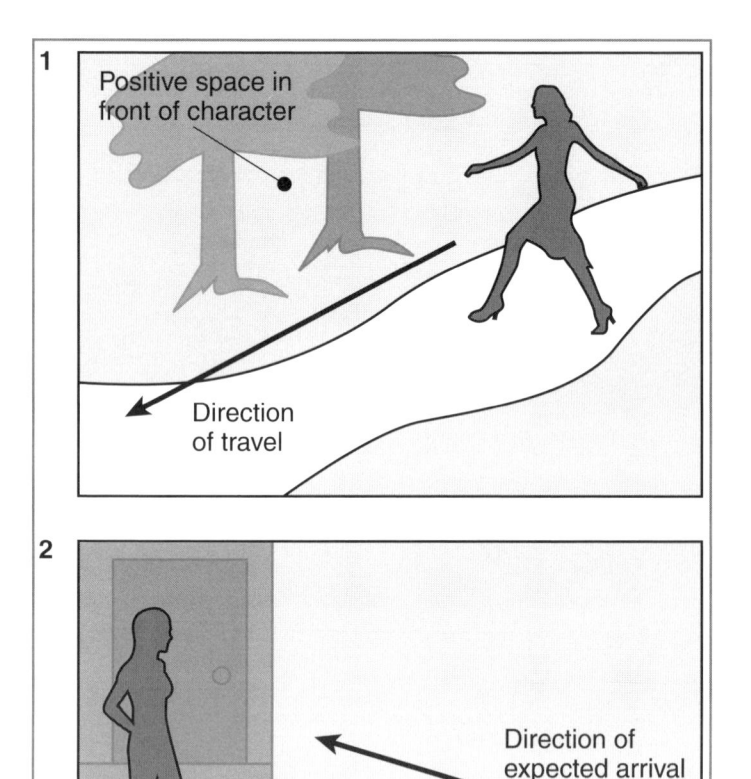

Figure 6.11
To preserve continuity of screen direction, shots of the woman hurrying home and her expectant friend must match the expectations of the audience.

There are two basic ways to deal with this problem: one time-consuming, one not. A production assistant can start several cigarettes burning at various times, and then hand one of appropriate length to the actor just before a take. Or, unless the cigarette is essential to your story, a much easier fix is to simply eliminate the time-dependent element from the scene.

What's Your Shooting Ratio?

A director's shooting ratio is the number of takes she shoots divided by the number of shots that end up in the movie. It's a measure of both her work efficiency and her creative style. Directors who structure their shooting tend to have lower shooting ratios, around 4:1. Improvisational directors, who permit more experimentation and therefore "waste" some footage, might shoot 8:1 or even higher.

In preproduction, shooting ratio is a matter of philosophy that will affect scheduling and budgeting. After shooting has wrapped, it's a measure of what actually happened.

The more structured your shot planning and shooting style, the better you'll be able to stick to a schedule and a budget. You'll know what shots you need to get, and you can stop shooting when you get them. A downside is that, from a creative viewpoint, your scenes can lack spontaneity. And if happy accidents occur on the set, as they often do, you might not be open to taking advantage of them if you insist on your preconceived ideas.

At its worst, a structural production style may lead to cutting in-camera, meaning that you shortcut the master-scene process. You stop at one good take of the shots you know you'll need, or you shoot only what you expect to see on the screen. In theory, the editing will be a matter of simple assembly.

As a rule, cutting in-camera is bad practice. You won't have any options in the editing room, and the actors will only get one chance to do it right. And, if you find that you need a workaround for a shooting mistake, you just won't have any other usable takes.

Improvisational directors have the opposite problem: When do you stop? Can you tell how much coverage is enough?

Here's a cautionary word: Digital video production encourages experimentation, improvisation, and higher shooting ratios. Removed of the burden of worrying about the expense of film raw stock and processing, the video director can let the camcorder roll and do take after take. That flexibility can be a good thing, as long as you stay on schedule.

But if you want to be able to shoot eight pages per day instead of three or four, you can't afford to overshoot. So, from the standpoint of delivering a picture in a limited amount of time and on a limited budget, a structured shooting approach—the way things have traditionally been done on the studio lot—can give you enough discipline and predictability so you don't blow your budget.

There's another consequence of improvisational production: Editing will take much longer. There will simply be too many takes to choose from. You don't want a reputation for being a dump-truck director, who overshoots like mad, then dumps a ton of footage on the hapless editor, who will struggle long hours to make some sense of it all.

Improvisation, Casting, and Rehearsal

It might seem odd that going digital would affect how you work with actors, but it does. We've already pointed out that shooting tape encourages improvisational styles and experimentation on the set. And, unlike film, there really isn't any direct cost to shooting a few more takes if the director or actors want to try an alternate approach to the material.

In fact, it's perfectly reasonable never to call "cut" as you roll through one take after another for a given setup. This will take some discipline, since the cast and crew will want to relax between takes. They can and should, but if you intend to keep rolling, you should inform the actors that they are, in effect, always on camera. Some actors choose to stay in character anyway, and a continuously rolling camera is one more reason to live the part. So, warn them you'll keep the camera rolling, but occasionally stop recording and let everyone take a break (which may simply be when you move to the next setup).

> Here's another reason to keep the camera rolling between takes: An actor's impromptu actions, such as handling wardrobe or props, can play as meaningful reactions. For example, pulling on a coat or setting down a coffee cup might not carry any particular emotional weight on the set. But edited into a sequence, the action might play as disgust, decisiveness, or indifference. The lesson? Every bit of tape you shoot is potential material for the editor. (But to be fair, let the actors know the camcorder is rolling.)

Furthermore, improvisational styles are becoming more commonplace, both in the movies and on television. The acting is more naturalistic, more offhanded, less formal. In the old days, actors developed deliberate techniques for giving the "illusion of the first time," delivering lines as though they just thought of them. But when they're improvising, many readings *do* occur in front of the camera for the first time. Directors may want to tolerate or even encourage realistic alternate line readings and blocking, especially if the underlying emotion comes through.

> Naturalistic acting is most associated with television because of a reliance on tight closeups, where the slightest expression registers. At the opposite extreme is live theater, where actors might have to shout just to be heard in the back of the hall. However, subtle, expressive acting is older than the talkies. In 1926, director Clarence Brown claimed that when he first worked with Greta Garbo in the silent picture *Flesh and the Devil*, he would direct her to express emotions and feelings in a certain way. But from his vantage point behind the camera, he thought Garbo's famous face remained stoic and unchanging. Yet when he screened the same scenes later and her face filled the frame, he was astonished to see every expression he'd asked for.

This all impacts your casting choices, rehearsal methods, and style of working with actors on the set. Above all, you want actors who don't get locked into performances or line readings, and you want them to both act and react. In particular, you want the camera to capture their facial expressions and body language as they watch and listen to their partners in a scene.

And since digital productions are often low budget, you may be working with actors who have little or no professional training. On the one hand, their freshness and naturalism might be innate, but on the other, they might not do *anything* the same way twice, including your careful blocking to keep them framed correctly in the shot. A common problem with inexperienced actors is a reluctance or inability to react at all on camera. Perhaps assuming that acting is all about speaking, they tend to deliver a line and then go stony-faced, awaiting the next cue.

So, to find the right actors in the first place, consider conducting your casting sessions this way:

- Pick a scene that involves both acting and reacting, speaking and listening.
- Videotape auditions and study reactions.
- Have the actor read with another actor, someone who can give them emotion to react to as well as simply cue their lines.
- Ask for at least three readings: 1) with no coaching (to see what their instincts are), 2) with some direction (to see how the performance changes), and 3) giving an opposite direction (different objective or attitude). An actor whose readings and reactions are much the same all three times is either locked into a preconceived idea about the part or simply doesn't respond to direction.

Carry this mindset into the rehearsal process. Remember that the goal should be for the innovative performances and the inspired moments to happen for the first time when the camera is rolling. Therefore, meet with actors in advance of shooting. You probably can't be on the set, but at least simulate its size and furnishings as closely as possible. Discuss the actors' parts with them and answer their questions, and let them try on wardrobe, handle props, and block the scene within the playing area.

> Experienced actors often ask, understandably, "What's my motivation?"—to which the legendary Alfred Hitchcock reportedly replied, "Your salary."

What you shouldn't do is over-rehearse. Or let the actors lock onto their characterizations.

Even experienced actors may be uneasy reporting to the set without feeling that they've "nailed" their portrayals. Reassure them that you want them to make discoveries—in *front* of the camera.

Transportation, Setup, and Logistics

As you move out of preproduction and actually get ready to shoot, remember that, as the ultimate decision-maker, the director is also primarily responsible for the safety of cast and crew. Yes, a digital production that uses few if any movie lights can take advantage of simplified logistics and can move fairly quickly from setup and from one location to the next. But hurrying invites accidents. Setting up requires rigging lights and sound, set dressing, cast preparations, color balancing, and sound checks. You should budget time for gaffers to take safety precautions, such as sandbagging stands and taping electrical lines to the floor.

When moving locations, it can take just as long to strike a set as it did to set it up in the first place. It's not just a matter of ripping everything down; you have a responsibility to return the facility to its original condition. Allow sufficient time for cables to be coiled and tied, gear to be lashed down in trucks, props and wardrobe to be gathered up, inventory to be taken, and for cast and crew to get from here to there without tripping over any of it.

> Here's one way to be in a big hurry without incurring risk. If you've got the crewmembers, vehicles, and equipment to spare, you can pick up speed by dispatching a separate crew to the new location to start setting up while you're wrapping the shoot at the current location.

Also, in thinking about your shooting schedule, remember that moving to another location usually requires starting there the next day. Transporting, unloading, and setting up at a new location can easily take several hours. Don't skimp on that time. If hurrying doesn't cause an accident, it's just as likely that the crew will forget a valuable piece of rental gear or a crucial prop will go missing.

Controlling the Set

All your preproduction planning is done, the show is cast, the crew and the equipment are booked, the location is prepped, and a call sheet (see Figure 6.12) has been issued for day one.

Hollywood-style moviemaking has a highly formal procedure for controlling the set. With an army of people to manage, lots of expensive and cumbersome gear, and a tight schedule to keep, this procedure helps the shooting day go as smoothly as possible. It promotes efficiency, thoroughness, and safety.

It also lets everyone know who is in charge at all times.

Even if you're working on a smaller-scale production with less formal procedures, you should know how the drill goes on a studio lot.

As preparation begins for a new scene (which may or may not be on a new set), the director claims the set, announcing he's taking over from the first AD and the setup crew. He sends the technicians on a break so he can discuss the scene with the actors and give them his full attention. Stand-ins observe.

The actors run through the scene for him once or twice. Although the principals have probably rehearsed it previously, this may be the first time they've been on the set with the full cast. It may also be the first time supporting players have even met the principals. The actors have the opportunity to ask questions and work out kinks in the scene. The director may ask for walk-throughs, in which actors literally walk through their blocking, saying their lines but not really performing, concentrating on use of props, business with wardrobe, and changes to blocking.

At this point, the director recalls the department heads for a rehearsal for the keys. Keys, in this context, means key personnel. Each of them will be looking for small details in the action they might have missed and late changes as a result of reblocking. At the same time, the first AD, who is always thinking ahead, is estimating how long it will actually take to shoot the scene and how he can prepare for the next setup. Also during this time, the director, the DP, and the first AD make a final decision on the sequence of shots (making sure, for example, to first get all the shots involving a particular day player or special effect).

Figure 6.12
The call sheet is intended to answer most questions from anyone in the cast or crew about what will be expected of them the next day. It gives a general on-set reporting time for the crew and the expected time for the camera to roll on the first setup, as well as specific call times for individual cast members who require extra time for makeup and wardrobe. Prepared by the first AD, the call sheet is issued just prior to the wrap of the previous day's shoot so it can be distributed to everyone. The other elements in the sheet coincide with those in the script breakdown.

Call Sheet

Production:	For a Few Dollars Less	Shooting Day:	MONDAY
Producer/PM:	Gerald Jones	Date:	8/1/XX
Director:	Pete Shaner	Crew Call:	7:00 AM
AD:	Caleb Cindano	Shooting Call:	7:30 AM

SET	SCENES	PAGES	CAST NOS.	LOCATION
Kitchen	2	2	1,2,3	Cindano House
Living Room	1	4	1,2	
Exterior	Establish			

NO.	CAST MEMBER	PART OF	MAKE-UP	SET CALL	REMARKS
1	Cindi Melman	Bettina	7:00	7:30	Tennis togs
2	Roger Chan	Bob	7:00	7:30	Pajamas / bathrobe

ATMOSPHERE / EXTRAS	PROPS	SPECIAL INSTRUCTIONS
Cable Guy	Tools	Cable co. uniform
Wilmer the Dog		With animal wrangler

OTHER CALL TIMES:			VEHICLES & OTHER:
Director	6:30	Camera	
First A.D.	6:30	Sound	
Second A.D.		Grips	
PA		Electric	
Craft Services	10:00	Art Dept.	
Script Super		Make-up	
DP	6:30	Wardrobe	

NOTES AND CHANGES:
Lunch 12:30PM 1:30PM - Walkaway to local restaurants

This rehearsal having concluded and any issues resolved, the second AD takes the actors to makeup and wardrobe. The director turns the set over to the first AD and leaves to do administrative tasks and individual conferences. Stand-ins walk through the scene as the DP tells the grips how to set the lights. Meanwhile, the first assistant camera (AC) moves in to spike (mark) actor's positions.

The first AD calls the actors back, and the director reclaims the set. In a final tech rehearsal, the DP makes sure the lights are set properly, the AC checks her focus marks, the property master makes sure props are in place and actors are handling them correctly, and the other creative and tech heads make sure everything is ready.

Having completed these steps and satisfied that everything is ready, the director or first AD calls, "Places!" Then the director calls "Roll camera!" After the sound recordist announces "Speed," the director calls "Action!"

At the conclusion of a take, even well after the last line has been delivered, the action continues. The actors remain in character, and no one on the crew makes a sound—until the director decides at last to call "Cut!" Delaying the call provides some extra footage for the editor's convenience, as well as giving an opportunity to catch actors' improvised reactions on tape. Some of the most interesting movie moments can occur just when you're otherwise tempted to turn the camcorder off.

Slating and Timecode

As the director calls "Action," the second AD is standing in front of the camera lens holding a slate, or clapper board (see Figure 6.13). The slate has handwritten notations of the scene number and take number. The beginning timecode is also indicated, either by handwriting or by a digital readout from the electronic slate's internal clock. If you're shooting dual-system sound, the sound of the clapper creates a peak on the sound track by which the editor can synchronize the video track with the audio track.

A careful director will slate every take. If you fail to slate a shot at the beginning, show the slate at the end of the take, but hold it upside down. This is

> On a traditional set, calling "Speed" occurred after a slight delay during which the camera and analog tape recorder reached full speed. In practice, with camcorders and DAT players, the units are at speed scarcely before the operator's finger lifts off the Record button. However, the practice of calling Speed persists, partly because it acknowledges that the equipment is actually recording, and partly because that's the way it's always been done.

Figure 6.13
A "smart slate" features a mechanical clapper and a digital readout of the timecode. The LED is controlled by an internal electronic clock. This model also connects the clock to an output jack that provides jam sync signals to synchronize camcorders and DAT recorders that support this feature. (Photo courtesy Denecke, Inc.)

Color Plate 1: This shot has two areas of blown-out whites, which are totally overexposed, containing pure white pixels (100IRE). The intense light at the top of the frame is an example of a highlight you might want to permit for aesthetic reasons. But you can't get away with the overexposed shirt on the right. Any way you look at it, that's a mistake. And you can't fix it by adjusting levels in postproduction because there's no pixel information to recover from that area. Solutions on the set include increasing the fill light on the other subjects (and reducing the exposure) or asking the wardrobe department to find the actor a colored shirt. And to make sure that the only overexposed highlights are the ones you intend, turn the camera's zebra function on, if it has that feature. Zebra bars will appear in the viewfinder on overexposed areas and will disappear when you reduce the exposure to the correct level.

Color Plate 2: Here's what can happen when you follow our advice about setting camcorder white balance manually before each setup—but you forget to do it. Judging from the overall blue color cast in the first shot (a), the previous setup must have been indoors under tungsten lights, which are decidedly orange. Moving outside, the light on the scene is from the sun, which has daylight color balance, definitely blue. Resetting the white balance is simply a matter of pressing the White Balance button on the camcorder while shooting a white card that fills the frame. As shown in example (b), the result is to adjust the color response of the camcorder CCDs in relation to pure white. Unlike overexposure, this type of mistake when shooting is usually easy to fix in postproduction. In an application such as Apple Final Cut Pro or Adobe After Effects, the repair involves much the same procedure—adjusting the colors in the picture in relation to a pure-white area, such as a shirt collar, a highlight, or even the actor's teeth.

Color Plate 3: When shooting video, there's enough soft daylight coming into this room from the frosted windows so that you can avoid using any movie lights at all. From this camera angle, shooting actors on the couch, use a bounce board at the position indicated by the orange line to reflect light back toward their faces and fill shadows. If you take this approach, remember that the lighting levels in the room will change throughout the day as the sun moves across the sky. If instead you decide to use movie lights in this situation, you will have the problem of mixed lighting, combining the blue cast of daylight with the characteristic orange cast of the tungsten movie lights. To correct the color, apply sheets of color temperature orange (CTO) gel to the window panes to change the temperature of the incoming light to more nearly match that of the movie lights.

Color Plate 4: You might be able to shoot film in this spot (a), but not video. Between the highlights of the bright sun and the shadows in the shade of the tree, the required exposure latitude is greater than the five f-stop range we recommend. Moving into the shade (b) both softens the light, which can be very flattering to your subjects' faces and brings the overall contrast range within acceptable limits for video.

Color Plate 5: When you shoot exteriors in full sunlight, you have to make your own shade to soften the light and reduce contrast in the image. To shoot this scene in a convertible for the Libby Lavella music video, we rigged a large silk in back of the car (a). The cloth acts like a sail in the slightest wind. To prevent it from tipping over, we not only weighted the C-stands down with several sand bags, but we also secured the frame with ropes. The camera angle from the front of the car (b) used bounced light as the key on Libby's face.

Color Plate 6: Here's our rig for shooting the chroma-key shots in *Neo's Ring*, when Traci is magically transported to exotic locales. The actor stands under the horizontal panel of stretched silk, which provides soft daylight as the key on her face. A portable green screen is rigged on sandbagged stands in the background. The camera setup will be where the technician is standing on the left. When shooting the screen, you have to be careful to light it evenly, avoiding any shadows, or the compositing in post will be much more difficult.

Color Plate 7: In *Neo's Ring,* Traci is composited using the green-screen technique with some vacation footage Pete shot in the Yucatan. She exits this scene by ducking behind a wall, an illusion created in postproduction. For a description of how this was achieved.

Color Plate 8: Setting the shutter speed slower than the frame rate is the secret to creating the characteristic motion blur of "bullet time," as demonstrated in this fight scene from *Neo's Ring*, making it appear as though the agent has supernatural powers as he jumps through space to circle around behind Josh. In general, you'll get the cleanest results when you edit at the same frame rate you shot. That is, if you shoot 24p, you should also edit at 24p to prevent the effect called *tearing*. However, this scene was shot at 60i using a Canon XL1 camcorder, edited in Final Cut Pro at 60i, then converted to 24p as a final step in post using Red Giant Magic Bullet, and it plays smoothly.

called *tail slating*. Reasons to deliberately skip the front slate and show it at the tail might include wanting to start the camcorder quickly to capture an actor's sudden burst of emotion or shooting an ECU so tightly that the slate won't fit in the framing.

Each time you start a new DV cassette, set the timecode, which follows the format HH:MM:SS:FF (hour, minute, second, frame). On many prosumer and most professional camcorders, you can set the first two digits of the timecode manually. Although the default timecode begins with "00," experienced camera operators learn to set the hour digits to "01" on the first tape they use, "02" on the second tape, and so on, incrementing the hour code for reach additional tape. That way, each shot on each tape (reel) has a distinct timecode, and no two frames in the clips will have the same timecode.

A traditional method for keeping track of takes, held over from film production, is the camera and sound log (refer back to Figure 5.3). On a film shoot, the purpose of the log is to make it easy for the editor to match up a film clip with its corresponding audio track on a separate roll of magnetic tape. But if you're recording audio in the digital camcorder (single-system sound), a camera log isn't necessary, at least not for that purpose, because the audio track is already in sync with the picture on the tape. However, your editor will want to know which scenes are on which reel, so it's a good idea to keep a log of starting and ending timecode indexes for each take, even if it's just annotations in a script. (Follow the numbering scheme just described.)

If you're shooting dual-system sound, your editor will need the camera log so he can match up DV cassettes with corresponding DATs.

On the set, the second AC is responsible for keeping the camera log, recording information reported by the camera operator, and labeling tapes. If you don't have a second assistant on your crew, give this job to whoever slates the takes.

> If you don't use a slate and you're shooting single-system, the camera operator can wave his fingers in front of the lens before each take. Editors can spot this easily when shuttling through the takes in fast forward or rewind. If you're shooting dual-system, he can clap his hands in front of the lens to create the sync mark on the audio track.

Getting Elements for Digital Effects

If you want to do any digital compositing in postproduction, you'll have to do some careful planning so that you capture the elements you'll need. For example, you'll have to plan carefully for digital mattes, the equivalent of film double exposures.

In conventional photography, a matte is a device placed over the camera lens to mask a portion of the scene from being exposed. The purpose is usually to permit a double exposure, adding another image later in the masked area. In both analog and digital video, matte shots are achieved instead by a compositing process called *keying*. In postproduction, the editor can select a specific color in the scene for which a second scene will be substituted. If the color is pure black or pure white, the process is called *luminance keying*. If the color is green or blue, the process is called *chroma keying*. Luminance keying can work fine for titles, but if you're shooting a moving subject, keying on white or black will be difficult because changing highlights and reflections can be mistakenly interpreted as part of the matte.

The process of keying a moving subject is called a *traveling matte*, or *travel matte*, and the most reliable way to create it is with a chroma key color of green or blue. In theory, keying can be done with any color, but the reason to use green or blue is because they don't normally show up in your subject's skin tones. The most common type of traveling matte shot is to use the chroma key color as the background. When you composite the shot in post, your subject can appear to be transported to another place, such as a remote location or a fantasy set.

Getting the lighting just right is the biggest challenge when shooting the background key on the set. The main problem is keeping the chroma key color from showing up where you don't want it, especially on the subject. If this happens, the second scene will "bleed through" the first when composited. A particularly troublesome spot is the outline of the object, where its edges border on the background and pick up its reflection. (For more information on keying in postproduction, see Chapter 8.)

It's the DP's job to get it right, but a good director should know what's required:

Choose your key color, selecting either green or blue, depending on the color least likely to appear in the rest of the shot.

Dress the set with the key color. Use special chroma key–colored fabric or paint. One handy accessory is a small chroma key screen that folds to a compact size (see Figure 6.14 and Color Plate 7).

Figure 6.14
A portable green (or blue) screen is just the right size to serve as a chroma key background for a medium closeup. We used this rig to shoot Traci's magical travel scenes in *Neo's Ring*. Traci's closeups on the set were combined in post with vacation travel footage of a Hawaiian beach and the Mayan ruins of Yucatan Mexico.

Avoid sharp edges where the background meets the ground or floor, if it will appear in the frame. In the studio, walls used for mattes have a cove base, or curved bottom, to soften the corner. Allowing a sheet of heavy chroma key paper to curve gradually near the floor will achieve the same thing.

Light the chroma key background evenly, avoiding highlights and shadows that might not be included in the matte.

Set the chroma key background at an angle with respect to the lights and the camera lens, and check the viewfinder or monitor to make sure you're not getting any reflections from it.

Use backlights or rim lights to emphasize the subject's edges and separate it from the background. Some cinematographers recommend using a gel of the opposite color from the chroma key on these highlights. That is, if the chroma key is blue, use a straw (pale yellow) gel: if green, minus-green (magenta).

Don't use soft focus or autofocus on your subject and check manual focus carefully. Crisp edges are essential to achieve a clean composite in post.

Don't use costumes in the key color or makeup or props with that color, or anything on the set with shiny parts that could reflect it.

Don't stand the subject too close to the background, where it might pick up reflections from the key color.

Particularly if you plan extensive keying, shoot some tests during preproduction and take them through the compositing process. Watch for the problems we've mentioned. If you're not sure whether an object might contain or reflect the key color, include it in your testing. As with most production technicalities, there are ways to fix some of these mistakes in post, but it will be less bothersome and usually less expensive to simply prevent them by taking care on the set.

It's All the Director's Fault

In theory, the director deserves the title of auteur because nothing should appear on the screen unless she decides to put it there. Of course, in a world that can throw you both happy accidents and production snafus, the wise director knows that luck also figures in.

So it follows that, as a director, you should not only have a reason for everything you do, but you should also be perfectly willing to take credit for whatever happens, intentional or not. "Did you like that?" said with a knowing wink should be the director's response to any and all criticism.

After all, who else knows you didn't plan it that way?

> In *The Manchurian Candidate* (the original version, 1962), audiences noticed that one of Frank Sinatra's monologues was out of focus. Director John Frankenheimer claimed it was the best of all the takes they did that day and said he'd decided to keep it.
>
> However, he also admitted, years after the fact, that another of his famous shots was unintentional. For this shot in *The Train* (1964), the audience POV is at ground level between the rails. A train comes straight toward us and then derails with engine and cars hurtling off-screen, ending with the amazing image of a giant freight-car wheel spinning a few feet from the camera. Asked how he had staged the shot so expertly, Frankenheimer confessed that the wreck was real, and the crew had forgotten they'd left one of the 12 simultaneously running cameras on the tracks. The footage he used was recovered from the debris.

chapter 7
Thinking Like a Veteran Editor

Above and beyond all other talents, an editor is a storyteller. Oft-repeated wisdom in Hollywood says that a movie is written three times: first when the writer creates the pages, then as the director coaches the actors and creates the imagery, and finally by the editor, who must build a coherent story from disconnected parts.

But it isn't only a creative job. Much of the work is about as meticulous as repairing a cuckoo clock. In the realm of digital video, the editor must be one of the most well-versed technical experts on the postproduction team. That's especially true when the goal is to edit in 24p and to seek a polished commercial look. And if the effort must also culminate in film transfer, the editor must thoroughly understand not only the wizardry of computer video and television engineering, but also the arcane arts of the film laboratory, with its precisely tailored film stocks and carefully controlled chemical brews.

> Traditionally, movie editors didn't have to know much about what happened in the lab. It was their job to cut, to be the storyteller who could keep track of a bewildering collection of celluloid scraps. It's only with the advent of the independent film genre and low-cost NLE software that editors have had to become tech wizzes. Some veteran studio picture editors are still in the dark about digital video.

We don't expect everyone who aspires to make a movie to be a hands-on editor, any more than we'd expect a director to be a master cinematographer. In fact, particularly for directors, it can be a wise move to leave the editing to someone else, even if you think you're perfectly capable of doing it yourself. Consider the truism about a movie being written three times. When you've wrapped the shooting, you'll have been in the forest so long you'll have your favorite trees. Another pair of eyes, with new perspective, can give you some objectivity about what and how to cut.

We suspect that you're no stranger to computer-based nonlinear editing (NLE) systems. Even die-hard shooters of film have been converting their footage and editing on DV for many years. Of course, there are some techno-averse filmmakers who would as soon supervise the edit as watch the making of sausage. If that's you, you won't be able to hide your eyes if you want to be successful shooting or finishing in 24p. Besides some of the material in this book on cinematography, this chapter is about as technical as we get.

But we'll try to keep it clear and understandable. We won't attempt to teach you how to edit, but we'll give you a good overview of the NLE process, just in case you've been living in a cave.

And then we'll roll up our sleeves and get into the details of media conversion and lots of other wizard's tricks for getting down to the fine cut of a video movie that looks like film.

An Overview of NLE

There is a variety of high-powered desktop NLE software packages on the market, including Adobe Premiere Pro, Apple Final Cut Pro, Avid Xpress, Pinnacle Liquid Edition, Sony Vegas, Ulead Media Studio, and quite a few more.

There is very little difference in the way different NLE desktop systems work, and no difference at all in the quality of the DV files they create. DV is DV. In fact, speaking only of technical quality, an entry-level application such as Apple iMovie or Pinnacle Studio produces movie files in which the imagery and sound are every bit as good as you'd get with any other NLE. As with other software applications, differences among the products come down to how sophisticated you can get in customizing and fine-tuning the results.

Of course, when you're aiming at delivering a product that could turn heads in Hollywood, you'll want all the sophistication you can get.

However, that doesn't mean the software has to be difficult to learn or to use. No matter which NLE you choose, your workflow will be much the same, and the essential steps aren't complicated.

We'll use Final Cut Pro (FCP) for our examples. The application has four basic windows, or workspaces (see Figure 7.1):

- Browser
- Viewer
- Timeline
- Canvas

24P: Make Your Digital Movies Look Like Hollywood

Figure 7.1
Here's how the Final Cut Pro workspace can look on a single monitor. However, many editors prefer to spread it out over two screens. This can be done on a Mac that has two video outputs and monitors. The Apple OS X operating system will treat the two displays as one large workspace. (Windows also has this capability.) The left screen might show the browser and bins; the right screen might have the viewer and canvas windows side by side with the timeline below.

The browser shows and manipulates folders and media files on the computer's hard drive. Initially, the browser is empty. When you open an existing project or load clips for a new one, the browser will show a list of the clips. You can create a text description for each clip you upload. The browser is very similar to a computer disk directory, and you can create and use folders not only for storing your clips but also for organizing them in groups. These folders are called *bins*, analogous to the film editor's term *trim bin*, which refers to a physical container that holds film clips.

The viewer gives you a preview of the clip you're currently working on and provides controls for adjusting its in and out points (called *trimming the clip*). The in point is the timecode location at which you want a clip to start, and the out point is the timecode at its end. Because the viewer has a separate set of playback controls, you can run a selected clip without affecting either the canvas or timeline.

The timeline is a graphic representation of the edited sequence starting from the left and flowing to the right. It shows the assembled sequence of clips in your movie as a set of parallel video and audio tracks. Clips inserted in the timeline appear as horizontal bars, the length of bars corresponding to the durations of the clips. The playhead is a special cursor that marks your current position on the timeline. Unless you set an explicit in point for a clip, inserting it into the timeline will occur at the current position of the playhead. (It's also called the *edit point*.)

The canvas provides a preview of edited clips in the timeline. The display shows the frame at the current playhead position in the timeline. Referring to this display, you can view your entire sequence as you build it, whereas the viewer shows you individual clips. If your computer supports output to a video monitor, it will usually display whatever is in the current window—the viewer or the canvas.

The editing process for achieving a first assembly proceeds as follows:

1. Capture clips from the camcorder cassette into the bin.
2. Trim a clip in the viewer.
3. Insert clips in the timeline.
4. Optionally, add transition effects between clips.
5. Play back the edited sequence in the canvas.

Editors' work styles differ, but here are some of the finer points of each step:

Capturing clips. You start by connecting your camcorder to the computer via its FireWire cable. There are three alternative ways of transferring the video clips from the DV cassette you shot into the computer: 1) You can mark in and out points as you capture each clip, one at a time; 2) You can transfer the entire cassette and let the program detect in and out points whenever you turn the camcorder on and off (called *automatic scene detection*); or 3) You can mark in and out points as you preview a long segment or the whole tape (called *logging clips*) and then capture them all in a single batch operation. You can save time in this batch operation by fast-forwarding between the in and out points as you mark them, then walk away and let the program capture all the clips as the camcorder plays unattended.

Trimming clips. If you marked in and out points during capture, it may be unnecessary to do this step before you insert the clip in the show sequence. You want to leave yourself some extra footage on either side of the clip to allow time for transition effects, such as dissolves, and for use as handles when you are polishing audio (see Chapter 5 for more information on the use of handles in audio edits). If you uploaded clips using automatic scene detection, you'll probably want to mark the in and out points more precisely. The viewer has a pair of buttons for marking in and out points (see Figure 7.2). Or, you can press the I (in) or O (out) keys as you watch the clip play in the viewer.

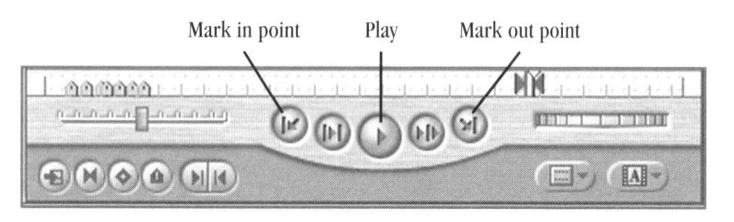

Figure 7.2
The viewer in Final Cut Pro has its own set of playback controls, which resemble those on a VCR or deck. As you play back, or scrub through, a clip, you can mark the in and out points by clicking the Mark In and Mark Out buttons or by pressing I and O on the keyboard.

As you begin a rough cut, don't trim clips too tightly. It's a common mistake among rookie editors to attempt to trim clips too tightly before they are assembled in show sequence. If the clip is trimmed too short, you can't start it any earlier or end it later or dissolve in or out without going back to recapture it from the original tape.

THE IMPORTANCE OF ORGANIZING YOUR CLIPS

The better you organize your clips in the browser window, the better and faster your editing will go. Filenames of clips should have descriptive labels, which you can type into the browser either before capturing or afterwards. (If you use automatic scene detection, the filenames will be Clip01, Clip02, etc. initially and you can change them later.) The more descriptively and precisely you label your clips, the easier it will be to find just the take you want. Also, make use of the OK/NG marker in the Log and Capture window to rate each clip; you can search on these tags later. Include anything that was distinctive about the take in your description. Select Log Clip to enter descriptions of the clip such as, "Best acting but noise in audio."

You can rearrange clip descriptions in the listing (by dragging clip names around in the display), create and name folders to hold similar clips, and even nest folders within folders.

We suggest setting up a folder scheme that corresponds to your shot plan. For example, each folder might be a different scene such as "Bettina's Kitchen." Within that folder you can create several subfolders to hold the shots from each setup, named for instance:

- Bettina-Bob two-shot master
- Bettina singles
- Bettina ECU
- Bob singles
- Bob ECU

This structure follows the logic of the script and the shot plan, and it helps you visualize the flow of the story line and the shots you'll need to build it. For example, in the organization just listed, if you don't have any OK clips in the "Bob singles" folder and you can't find any on your original tapes, you know you don't have any good reaction shots of Bob from this scene, and you'll have to find ways to fill in those gaps.

Inserting a clip in the timeline. When you've selected the take you want to use and trimmed it so the in and out points are about right, you can insert it in the timeline. You can achieve the insertion in several ways, and none is more correct than the others. It's just a matter of the editor's work style. You can drag a clip's filename from the bin and drop it at the desired location on the timeline. Or you can drag the image of the clip from the viewer and drop it on the timeline. Or you can drag from the viewer window and drop it onto the canvas window (see Figure 7.3). If you do this, you'll be presented with a menu of options for adding a transition effect. (All other methods of insertion create a straight cut between clips.) Remember that the canvas displays the frame at the current position of the playhead in the timeline. So, when you drop a clip onto the canvas, the insertion will be made at the timecode location indicated by the playhead.

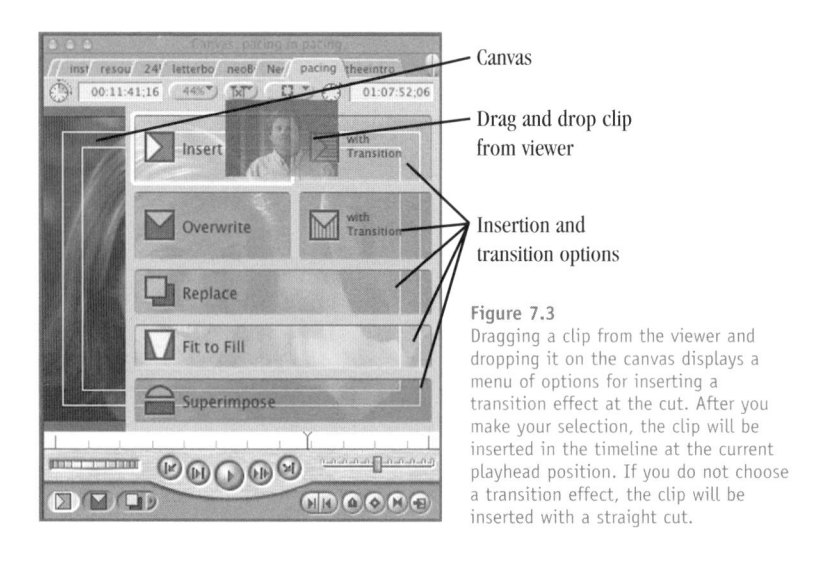

Figure 7.3
Dragging a clip from the viewer and dropping it on the canvas displays a menu of options for inserting a transition effect at the cut. After you make your selection, the clip will be inserted in the timeline at the current playhead position. If you do not choose a transition effect, the clip will be inserted with a straight cut.

> As you begin to do finer cuts, you'll be working mostly in the timeline. At this point, the advice about keeping your trims loose no longer applies. Ultimately, you want scenes to play the way you'd attend a Hollywood party: Arrive late and leave early. To hold the audience, cut into a scene already in progress and cut away the instant you've established the plot point or delivered new information. Get out before things get boring.

Adding a transition effect. If you didn't select a transition effect when you inserted a clip (by dropping on the canvas), you can add it later by clicking the cut in the timeline between the clips and making a selection from the Effects menu. There are lots of options for controlling the duration and behavior of a transition. However, to adhere to classic Hollywood-style storytelling, you should restrict transitions to cuts and dissolves. Even then, use dissolves sparingly to indicate the passage of time.

Film students have a saying, "If you can't solve it, dissolve it." Dissolving is often an easy way to fix a bad cut. The lesson here is not to resort to dissolves whenever you're stuck. Quite the opposite—too many dissolves in your show is a sign that your cuts lack continuity.

> In FCP, the most common type of dissolve is called a *cross-dissolve*. A transition that involves fading in and fading out is called a *dip-to-color dissolve* in which the color is black.

As you insert clips, the timeline shows the sequence of the scene you're building. (You can expand or compress the view of the timeline on the screen so that it represents the whole show or just a few shots or a few scenes.) Each parallel layer on the timeline is a separate track. At minimum, there will be one video track and two audio (stereo) tracks. When you shoot sync sound (as you always do in DV unless you're deliberately shooting MOS), the audio tracks drop into the timeline in perfect sync with the picture. You always have the option of unlocking the dialogue tracks and manipulating them separately, which you need to do when performing split edits, for example. As you add music and effects, the video tracks will have several audio tracks below them on the timeline. (For more information, see "Split Edits" later in this chapter and the advice on building soundtracks in Chapter 5.)

Playing back the edited sequence. The diligent editor will spend a lot of time replaying edited sequences to get the pacing just right. Rewinding, in the analog video sense, isn't necessary in NLE unless you want to see a clip played back in reverse. To play back a sequence of clips you've assembled in the timeline, move the edit point to the start (or press the Home key to go to the starting frame) and select the Play button in the canvas window. If you added any transitions or did any compositing that requires the program to generate new frames, you probably won't see them on playback (depending on the speed of your computer). The canvas will display the message "Unrendered" instead. This is done to avoid delays during routine playback when you're concerned primarily with pacing rather than quality of imagery.

Minus some specific menu commands and keyboard shortcuts, that's pretty much the entire process of assembling a sequence of takes to build your screen story for the first time. From here on out, editing is mostly about tweaking by ever-finer degrees of detail.

Technical Editing Issues in 24P

The frame rate and scanning mode you chose when shooting will affect how you edit. You will also make different technical choices in your edit, depending on whether you plan to distribute primarily on video or on film.

Other than choosing either 60i or 24p when you shoot, during production you don't need to be concerned about what's going on inside the camcorder. But when you edit, some technical issues of DV recording come into play. To make intelligent choices during the edit, you need to appreciate some of these finer distinctions:

- ◆ Timecode
- ◆ Pulldown
- ◆ Pulldown removal and deinterlacing
- ◆ Interlacing and tearing
- ◆ Rendering and prerendering

Timecode

The camcorder records an index that keeps track of each frame according to a time scale. The index is the timecode. Its format is HH:MM:SS:FF, for hour, minute, second, and frame. When you upload a clip into the NLE, the timecode goes along with it. Since it can be confusing to try to deal with duplicate timecodes, it's good practice on the set when you load a new cassette to manually set the HH index to the reel number (if your camcorder has this feature). All timecodes on the first reel (hour-long cassette) will therefore start with 01, the second reel with 02, and so on. If perchance you forget to reset the hour, the camcorder will default to 00, and unless you forget *twice,* you will never have any duplicate timecodes.

However, you can still experience errors in recorded timecodes, called *timecode breaks*. These breaks can occur when you:

- Rewind the tape to play back on the set and don't return to the starting position—or, worse, tape over a take. If this happens, the timecode sequence will continue to run properly, but the clips will appear to be out of order on the tape.
- Camcorder battery failure or power disconnection when it's on can also cause a timecode break.

> You'll also get timecode breaks if you set the camcorder to Time Of Day timecode. Most consumer cameras don't have this feature, but prosumer and professional cameras do. It's useful in certain situations, such as syncing two or more cameras so their timecodes run concurrently. Shooters of reality shows, live concerts, and events rely on this feature all the time. But you'll get a timecode break every time you stop and restart the camcorder.

Timecode settings within the NLE can be confusing, but they needn't be. In normal camcorder mode, DV recording is done in drop-frame (DF) 60i for standard NTSC video. Drop-frame is something of a misnomer because no frames are actually dropped. For reasons having to do with the advent of color television broadcasting, NTSC video runs at 29.97 frames per second, rather than exactly at 30. The 29.97 is called *drop-frame rate*, and it's a trick of timecode numbering. In every minute except the tenth minute, the recorder drops two frame numbers. By this scheme, drop-frame video is said to be *wall-clock synchronized*. That is, an hour of video footage, as measured by its timecode, will have an actual running time of one hour by the clock.

If your eventual output is video, whether via television broadcasting or electronic projection, you can stay in DF mode from shooting through editing and output, even if you shot in 24p. If, however, your goal is film out, you may want to use the camcorder option of shooting in nondrop-frame (NDF) rate so that film frame counts and running-time estimates will be accurate. Another reason to be concerned about DF versus NDF is when incorporating PAL footage, which is NDF. (As we emphasize in Chapter 9, if you're going for film out, be guided in the technical details of your shooting by the requirements of the film transfer house you've selected.)

We'll have more to say about format conversions shortly, after acquainting you with the related mysteries of pulldown schemes.

Pulldown

The term *pulldown* describes an old physical method of converting film to video, but the term is still in use to describe the electronic process that does much the same thing.

Back in the days of analog video, film laboratories that offered film-to-tape transfer services used a scheme of 3:2 pulldown to convert 24fps motion-picture film to 30fps video so that the movies could be broadcast on television (see Figure 7.4).

In 3:2 pulldown, the first frame of film is recorded on the first two fields of video, the next frame is recorded on the succeeding three fields of video, the next frame on two fields, the next on three, and alternating between two- and three-field captures for the length of the movie.

Now known as the *Standard Method* for 24p, 3:2 pulldown is used in camcorders to record video captured at 24fps as 60i DV recordings. If your goal is video output, you can edit the uploaded recordings in 60i just as you would any other video show. But if you're working toward film transfer, you'll want to actually cut at 24p, using the simplicity of matching edited frames to output one-for-one.

> Another reason to convert and edit in 24p is to achieve frame-accurate edits. Then, if you need 60i output, you must convert it back.

An option on some camcorders, such as the Panasonic AG-DVX100a, is called *24p Advanced Method (24pa)*, which performs pulldown inside the camcorder prior to recording by a scheme of 2:3:3:2 (see Figure 7.5). The only reason to shoot in 24pa mode is because you intend to edit in 24p.

The purpose of the advanced method is to permit more accurate recovery of true 24fps footage within the NLE. It was developed to support 24p camcorder shooting mode so as to provide a conversion method to 60i that did not involve interlacing of fields from different frames. When the 60i is converted back to 24p, entire frames are dropped. To use this feature, you need an NLE that supports 24p Advanced, such as Final Cut Pro or Sony Vegas.

> Pulldown used to refer to the physical pulling down of film sprockets in an optical gate. Nowadays, a digital intermediate is made of the film, and the pulldown process is performed on the computer-based imagery.

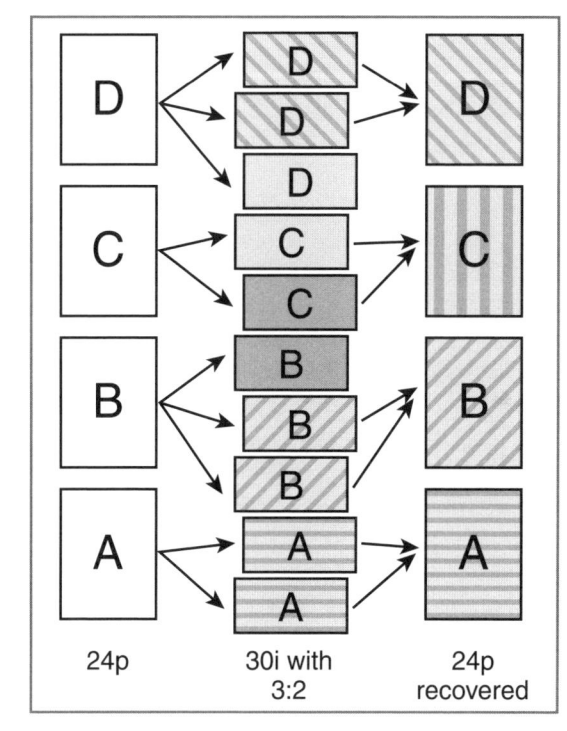

Figure 7.4
In the 3:2 pulldown scheme, also called the *24p Standard Method*, the first frame A of film (or progressive video frame) is copied to the first two fields of 60i video. The next frame B is copied to the succeeding three fields, and the copying continues, alternating between two- and three-field increments.

Pulldown Removal and Deinterlacing

Any NLE that supports DV can be used to edit footage shot at 24p and recorded at 60i. If video output is your primary goal, and you're willing to work around a few messy edits, that's really all you need to know.

Some NLEs, such as Final Cut Pro and Sony Vegas, give you the option of editing in 24p. Doing so will help you achieve frame-accurate 24fps editing, which has two main benefits:

- Editing in 24p avoids messy edits that can result from accidentally cutting on interpolated frames in 60i.
- It also provides one-for-one frame matching for film transfer, assuring not only that you're cutting the video the way it was shot, but also that the film-transfer house will be less likely to introduce artifacts by having to do any interpolation on your frames.

Pulldown removal discards the extra fields added by the 3:2 (or 2:3:3:2) process. However, converting 60i DV footage to 24p (or any progressive mode) can use a different type of transformation: Deinterlacing can combine two fields to generate each progressively scanned frame. Deinterlacing 60i can yield an approximation of 30p, but the result won't be the same as shooting 30p in-camera, and it certainly won't be equivalent to shooting in 24p. When you deinterlace 60i, fields are unlocked, every other field is discarded, and a process of field doubling is applied to fill in the missing scan lines. Field doubling won't restore full resolution (because all of the detail information isn't there), and motion won't always look right because some of the visual information is being discarded. For much the same reasons, it's not advisable to shoot in 30p and then try to convert to 24fps in post.

Interlacing and Tearing

Whether you shoot 24p or 60i, if you edit in 60i, you will occasionally have to deal with a messy edit. This occurs when you attempt to cut on a fast action that changes markedly from one field to the next, an effect called *temporal displacement*. For example, if you cut on an ECU of a hand reaching quickly for a knife, the result can be tearing. The hand was in one position in the first field and moved noticeably before the second field was captured. The combined frame shows two blurred instances of the hand that show up on playback as jitter.

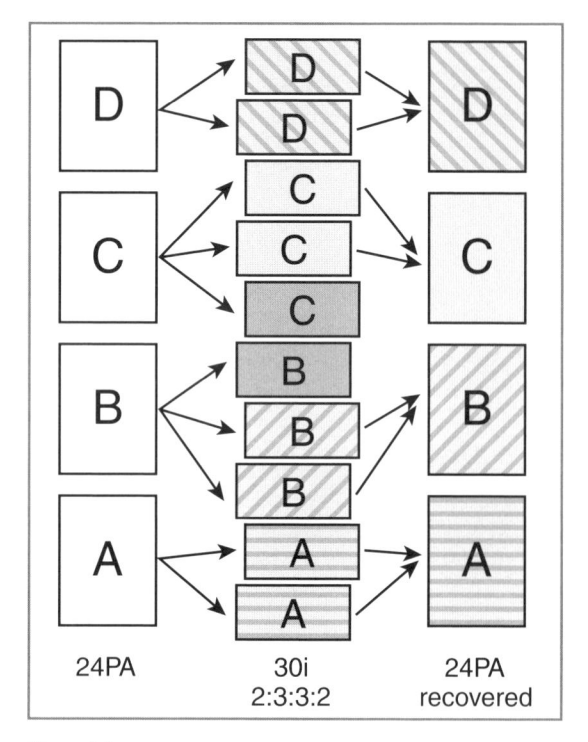

Figure 7.5
In the 2:3:3:2 pulldown scheme, also called the 24p Advanced Method, or 24pa, the first frame of film (or progressive video) is copied to two 60i video fields, the second frame to three fields, the third frame to three fields, and the fourth frame to two fields, then the pattern repeats. This conversion method can't be used to create final NTSC output, but it is useful for prerendering because it recovers 24p frames faster and more reliably than the Standard Method (3:2).

For footage shot in 24p, the process of pulldown removal can eliminate this problem. If you edit in 24p, you'll always be cutting on clean frames. Any artifacts you see will be the result of the way the camcorder captured the image (controllable by varying shutter speed), not because of pulldown or interlacing.

Rendering and Prerendering

Within NLE, prior to output (such as printing to tape), the rendering process generates frames that don't exist in the original footage. These include transition effects such as dissolves, as well as composites and titles.

Some canned effects provided with NLEs are prerendered. That is, if you don't customize them by varying their durations or other parameters, you'll see them on playback right away, without having to go through a rendering step. Prerendering can also be an intermediate step during the edit. You can choose to render an effect so you can judge it while playing it back. The more you prerender during editing, the less time the system will take to generate finished output.

If you edit in 24p and then choose to output NTSC video, rendering will have to restore 3:2 pulldown to create a valid DV file or recording. When you shoot 24p, you'll always have better results editing in 24p as well, even if you're outputting to video, provided you can spare the time it will take the computer to perform the extra rendering (which might be hours).

ACCELERATOR CARDS

Pulldown removal also requires rendering. However, when used in conjunction with Final Cut Pro, the Aurora Igniter card removes 3:2 pulldown fields in real time (and reinserts the 3:2 when you play back or output).

This product is just one example of an accelerator card, a computer hardware add-on that performs functions otherwise done in software. Hardware will always be faster than software, although it's usually much more expensive and can't be modified or updated as easily.

Various accelerator cards are available for Mac and PC systems. Some perform 3D graphics calculations, and others do rendering for NTSC output. The purpose of an accelerator card is to reduce or entirely eliminate rendering time so that the editor can see results right away, in real time during playback.

As you become more professional in your editing, you will probably want to upgrade your system with one or more accelerator cards. When a client or producer is looking over your shoulder, or when a deadline presses, you just won't be able to afford the rendering time.

If your NLE supports 24p Advanced, you can choose to prerender with 2:3:3:2 pulldown. Always prerender with this option if you will be doing further edits, and prerender the entire show with it prior to printing to tape. Even though printing to tape will use the 3:2 scheme, you'll get smoother motion and cleaner edits if you apply 2:3:3:2 first.

Another important advantage of 24p Advanced is that it requires less rendering time. In fact, with Final Cut Pro and a fast G4 or G5 Mac, pulldown removal or prerendering with pulldown can be done in real time.

> Cutting HD is beyond the scope of this book and certainly not in the category of low-budget production. HDV is an attractive alternative, and some of the prosumer NLEs will handle it, including Final Cut Pro HD and Sony Vegas. Most of what we say about editing 24p DV applies equally well to HDV, with the added caution that HDV is a highly compressed format (MPEG-2). You may experience more interpolation problems and tearing even in the best of circumstances because of missing video information in the recording.

Converting from 60I to 24P in Post

As we mentioned in Chapter 1, it is possible to shoot in plain-vanilla 60i and convert to 24p in postproduction. You might want to do this because:

- You didn't have access to a 24p camcorder when you were shooting.
- You want to incorporate 60i footage into a show you shot and edited in 24p.
- You want to preserve a 60i version of your show that doesn't have film look. (You might choose this option for documentary footage that will have a dual use, both as television news and as source material for a movie.)

A software application that converts 60i to 24p reliably is Red Giant Magic Bullet Suite. It's a plug-in for Adobe After Effects. Besides converting the frame rate and doing some nice interpolation on motion effects, Magic Bullet also lets you apply filters to create film-look effects such as grain, jitter, letterboxing, and color correction.

You can apply Magic Bullet Suite after your 60i edit is done. It does the conversion in a rendering process that, for a feature-length production, will probably take many hours, even days, depending on the processing power of your computer. If your distribution medium is video, you can output a DV file (.MOV extension). However, if your output is film, you can generate an After Effects project file (.AEP). The .AEP file won't be editable in your NLE, but it's somewhat higher in quality than DV because it uses the After Effects Animation codec, which creates an uncompressed image stream. (For more information, see Chapter 9.)

Other applications that apply various film look filters but do not convert frame rates are Magic Bullet Editors and DigiEffects CineLook. Magic Bullet Editors is a version of the product that plugs into various NLEs, including Adobe Premiere Pro, Apple Final Cut Pro, Sony Vegas, and Avid Xpress. This version of Magic Bullet contains the Look Suite, which lets you apply grain, aged film, letterboxing, and other effects. Since it's a plug-in, one of its advantages is being able to apply these effects within the NLE as part of your editing tasks.

> Among the NLEs, we believe Sony Vegas is the only one that will actually permit you to convert 60i to 24p without a plug-in. You could therefore do the conversion prior to editing and cut at 24fps. Combined with the Magic Bullet Editor plug-in, Vegas is a cost-effective alternative to purchasing Final Cut Pro, Magic Bullet Suite, and After Effects.

Using an Edit Decision List (EDL)

An edit decision list (EDL) is a holdover from the practice of using NLEs to cut film projects. You needn't be concerned with it when editing DV unless you want to incorporate film clips into your edit. (Creating an EDL may also be necessary if you need to move your project between platforms, such as from Final Cut Pro to Avid.)

The EDL is a text file exported from the NLE that specifies edits and transitions as events, indexed by timecode. The main purpose of an EDL originally was as a guide for film lab specialists called *negative cutters* who physically cut the camera negative to conform it to the edited electronic version of the show. (Increasingly, this job is done instead in the digital realm with a digital intermediate, and the negative is never cut physically.)

Cinema Tools in Final Cut Pro has its own EDL system, which handles all the EDL requirements, and the same with Avid Xpress. Broadware Slingshot Film Trakker is another software tool that will convert a 60i edit to a 24fps decision list.

Editing Hollywood-Style

Whew! Having delved into the minutiae of editing in 24p, let's leave the video engineers to talk amongst themselves and discuss creative flair in editing.

As we've said more than once, the challenge of achieving a polished Hollywood look isn't entirely—or even primarily—technical.

It's also about imaginative use of the medium.

As you think about the job of assembling your screen story, refining its logic, and heightening its emotion, here are some editors' tricks that make the Hollywood product stand apart:

- Split edits
- Jump cuts
- Speed ramping
- Match cuts

Split Edits

Increasing your use of split edits can add polish to your cutting, improve the flow of scenes, and even solve problems of coverage. For example, an actor may be talking to another actor off-screen. The dialogue comes from the off-screen actor while the audience views the silent reactions of the listening actor. If the audio cut precedes the video in the timeline, it's a J-cut. If the video precedes the audio, it's an L-cut. (You can remember this by the J or L shape created at the split on the timeline.)

Split edits are tedious when cutting film, but they are extremely easy to do in an NLE. You begin by making a simultaneous cut; then you select either the video or audio cut and drag it forward or backward along the timeline (see Figure 7.6).

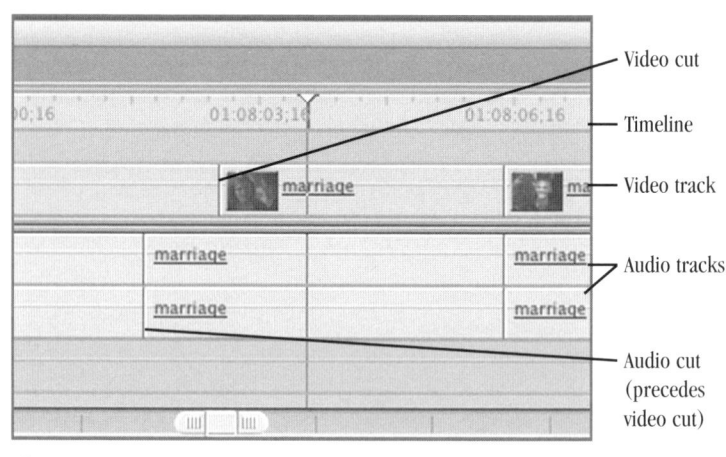

Figure 7.6
To perform a split edit in Final Cut Pro, unlock the video and audio clips and then drag the cut to the left or right along the timeline to change the in and out points.

> In *Out of Sight* (1998), director Steven Soderbergh used an audacious and clever series of split edits to show the developing romantic attraction between characters played by Jennifer Lopez and George Clooney. The two sit in a darkened, elegant club conversing, and steadily the dialogue slides out of sync and the sequence becomes enhanced with dissolves. A clearly focused scene progressively breaks up into a dreamy, stream-of-consciousness montage. Normal time breaks up and flows unusually, all because the visuals can go anywhere while the dialogue continues to play beneath them.

It's often more interesting to watch the person who is listening than the one who's talking. That's why capturing reactions on the set is so important. In fact, reaction shots are the key to an actor's performance, and listening well and reacting naturally are some of the most valuable skills a film actor can have.

A split edit can also hide an uneven or perhaps a bad performance by shifting attention away from the bad actor as much as possible. Conversely, you can enhance a good performance by repeatedly cutting back to the good actor's emotional reactions.

There are other dramatic uses for split edits:

- Segue into a scene by starting music or dialogue of the new scene as the old scene fades.
- Tighten up the tension and pick up the pace with fast cutting.
- Cover mistakes made in directing or cinematography by inserting mismatched or oblique shots that do not match the narrative, using split edits to keep the dialogue going.

> Sometimes, a stony reaction speaks volumes, but here's an incident in cinema history when perhaps it went too far. In *Spartacus* (1960), Peter Ustinov starred as Lentulus with Laurence Olivier as Crassus. Both were very restrained and cool actors, masters of the British stiff upper lip. In a later interview, Ustinov confessed that when he and Olivier discussed how they would play their parts, Ustinov said, "I've decided to do nothing." Olivier replied heatedly, "But you can't! *I'm* doing nothing! We can't *both* do nothing!" But that's what they did. Watch the movie to see how the editor cut the scene.

Jump Cuts

Film historians describe a major shift in cinema style that appeared with the French New Wave in the late 1950s and early 1960s. Jump cuts—abrupt transitions that defied conventional notions of continuity—were employed extensively by Jean Luc Godard in his cinema verité films to challenge the conventional aesthetics of film. A jump cut is a deliberate violation of continuity of time or space, or both. Often, it's an abrupt jump forward in time, which plays as though the transition occurs in real time. When first developed, the jump ran counter to traditional Hollywood and European classical cinema, which took pains to use seamless edits (so-called *invisible cuts*) that didn't make the audience feel disoriented or uncomfortable.

Since the New Wave, this kind of editing has become mainstream. Editors and directors routinely use jump cuts to shorten perceived time, abbreviating action sequences from a long single take to a series of short, fast cuts. Today, jump cuts are common in both action sequences and commercials. They can be used to add energy to scenes that need to be fired up or to advance the story quickly. Jump cuts can even be used throughout an entire film, provided that a lot of fast-paced shooting was done during production.

> Jump cutting and shock video are semantically different, although people occasionally confuse them. Shock video refers as much to content as to style. In the early 1960s, much shock material was sexual, typified by soft-core pornography made popular by Russ Meyer and other filmmakers. Shock video available today includes everything from hard-core pornography to actual scenes of murders in progress.

Speed Ramping

Speed ramping is another type of cutting that's very difficult to do in film but easy in digital video. Imagine a scene with the actor walking down a hall to a door. The whole scene might take some 10 or 15 seconds. With speed ramping, the actor walks for a second or two, then the editor accelerates the central part of the scene to get him to the door faster. Music videos use this process quite often. It's achieved in the edit by time bending, by which frames can be dropped and blended during acceleration. (For more information on time bending, see Chapter 8.)

Match Cutting

Match cutting can be a thematic technique, and you can't do it unless the director gives you the footage. However, you can keep an eye out for happy accidents you can use as you upload the takes. The principle of match cutting is simply to juxtapose shots in two different times and places so they appear to be joined across time and space. For example, you might cut on an actor leaving the door to his house and immediately entering the door to his office, with a continuity of action that makes the viewer think he's simply stepped into the next room. The audience might know full well that the office is across town, but the continuity of motion carries whatever momentum has been established in the first scene into the second.

> The esteemed movie editor Walter Murch holds that, as a rule, scenes should be joined so that the viewer's eye is going the same direction right before and right after the cut.

When Is the Final Cut Final?

Most editors never truly feel they are finished. At some point, a producer or a distributor or the need to meet a deadline takes the picture out of their hands. There's always something left to tweak, and since NLEs make the process both nondestructive and fluid, you can keep making changes until you keel over from lack of sleep.

But if you want a telltale sign, the edit is finished when the pacing seems right. Inevitably, the editor's rough cut will seem both slow and erratic. Besides the care that will be given to building sound effects and music, most of the editor's work in postproduction will be to cut scenes that don't advance the story, shorten scenes that overstay their welcome, and fine-tune in and out points to keep the action moving, sustain emotion, build suspense, and stimulate excitement.

By the time the pacing *does* seem right and the polish of music and effects are there (even if the music is a scratch track), the director and the editor will have completely lost their objectivity about the project. They've both been in the forest way too long.

Difficult as it might be at this point, you must screen the movie for people who have no stake in it. Relatives and friends don't count. They will love it, and for all the wrong reasons. Producers, clients, and investors can't judge; they just plain care too much.

Do what the major studios do. Round up a test audience, preferably composed of people who never heard of anyone on the production team.

If they laugh, if they cry, if they don't walk out—maybe, just maybe, you're ready for prime time.

WHAT IS CHARACTER?

As one of the movie's skilled storytellers, the editor must never forget the importance of character. Audiences respond to a star picture after picture because of some strongly attractive quality they see in the star's character. But in movies, as in life, a person's character is judged by what people see her do, not necessarily by what she says. Odd as it might seem, long, flowery speeches don't create character.

As a quick shorthand for building character in a movie, veteran screenwriters had a favorite ploy. This sure-fire technique should be obvious from the term "pet-the-dog scene."

Hollywood's reliance on character in screen stories helped build the star system. When Howard Hawks prepped *El Dorado* (1960), actor Robert Mitchum claimed that Hawks called one evening saying he'd always wanted to direct a film with both Mitchum and John Wayne. Mitchum replied, "Great! What's the story?" Hawks had no idea what the story would be. "Nobody cares about the story," he said. "It's the characters that matter."

The lesson for the editor? Cut dialogue when you can. Find actions that tell the story, even if the director didn't shoot it that way.

chapter 8
Thinking Like a Special Effects Wizard

The original *Star Wars*, produced on film and released in 1977, was a milestone event in the history of cinema. It resurrected the B-movie, science-fiction genre and pushed it into the category of top-line, mass-market blockbusters. Almost a decade before that, another sci-fi magnum opus, *2001: A Space Odyssey*, had played to a wide international audience, but its special effects were so incredibly time consuming and expensive to produce that the picture actually discouraged major studios from financing more of what the executives disparagingly called "space westerns." Before *Star Wars* set box-office records, the conventional wisdom in Hollywood was that sci-fi, like children's stories, appealed to a loyal but decidedly narrow market.

Star Wars set the pace for an onrush of sci-fi and fantasy movies aimed at the widest possible audience. And they all relied heavily on synthetic visual effects. Some of these effects used animated physical models, while others were digital creations that did not exist outside of a computer. They were intended not only to fool the eye and help the audience suspend disbelief, but also to simply dazzle the senses.

After *Star Wars*, special effects became center-stage entertainment.

Today, it's impossible to conceive of a blockbuster without its generous offering of "eye candy." And some degree of stunning visual wizardry is now expected in any big-budget movie, regardless of genre.

> Creating special effects requires a practiced visual sense and an understanding of the principles of design. Director Sam Peckinpah, later dubbed the "Master of Violence" for his gritty action-adventures, got his start in show business as a set dresser. He worked on the old Liberace TV program, where he swept floors and set the pianist's trademark candelabra on the piano.

The low-budget digital filmmaker who aspires to create special effects that will rival the Hollywood product would seem to have an impossible task. Even considering the power and economy of desktop CGI, how can you compete with a movie made on a $100 million budget?

If you have the time, skill, and inventiveness, you can.

> Think we're overstating the case? Check out two shorts produced by special-effects zealots with desktop tools and apparently a *lot* of time on their hands: *405: The Movie* (2000) by Bruce Branit and Jeremy Hunt (www.405themovie.com) and *Duality* (2001) by Mark Thomas and Dave Macomber (www.crewoftwo.com). As good as you guess these underground efforts might be—they're better!

But remember that special effects are all about trickery. An effect doesn't necessarily have to be expensive to deceive (and satisfy) the audience completely. For example, the first *Star Wars* wasn't produced on a shoestring budget, but many of its effects were both resourceful and cheap. When the camera pans quickly over a sea of heads in a crowd scene, even today's visually jaded audiences won't guess that the field is a table crammed with thousands of painted cotton swabs—a reliable cast of extras that stood faithfully for hours on end!

The mindset you need to think like a special effects wizard actually hasn't changed since the days of the earliest silent movies.

The purpose of a special effect is to make the audience see and believe something you can't shoot with a camera.

In this chapter, we'll survey some of the impressive digital tricks you can achieve with a moderately powerful but not particularly special PC. They range from image transformations you can apply with a click of the mouse to complex motion composites that are limited only by your patience and creativity.

Applying Film-Look Filters

Designed to work within an NLE application such as Final Cut Pro or a postproduction tool such as Adobe After Effects, a filter is a type of plug-in menu selection that applies a predefined set of creative options, such as colors, textures, and effects designed for artistic impressions or technical transformation. You'll get the idea from the names of just a few of these filters: watercolor, fogged glass, neon glow, lens flare, paint daubs, torn edges, smudging, stained glass—and there are hundreds more.

Film-look filters can be applied in postproduction to a selected clip or sequence literally at the click of the mouse button. In the most straightforward examples, the effect is applied to the entire frame and to every frame in the sequence. With only a bit more fuss, you can select an area, such as a bright sky or the shadow of a tree trunk, and apply the effect only to the selection. In theory, the application is sufficiently "smart" to detect the moving edges of the selected shape as it changes from frame to frame. However, in practice, the process can be more than a bit messy.

A major subset of these predefined, or canned, filters is film-look effects. They include grain, dust, scratches, stains, shutter blur, even hairs in the projection gate. As we discussed in Chapter 2, another artifact of film projection that audiences notice only when it's entirely missing in video is bob and weave, or jitter. Curiously, jitter, however slight, is another characteristic that audiences have come to associate with "quality," and many film-look filters now include the effect.

> The more erratic the motion in the clip, the less reliable this edge-detection function will be. At worst, if you want to be selective about the areas to which an effect will be applied, you'll have to repeat the selection and filter frame-by-frame. The more carefully you shoot with the requirements of digital mattes in mind, the less likely you'll have to doctor your frames one at a time.

> It's easy to make any video, even one shot, plain-vanilla 60i, look much like an old 16mm film print. Just apply a selection of film-look filters in a not-too-subtle way to simulate film grain, faded color, scratches, hair, and bob and weave.

DigiEffects CineLook is a set of plug-ins for After Effects. Among its film-look filters is a set called *StockMatch*, which transforms video colors to more nearly match those of specific film stocks, including Kodak Ektachrome and Fuji Fujichrome. Be aware, however, that this transformation is largely an aesthetic one. It's designed to make your video *look* as if it were shot on film. But it's not meant to actually prepare your footage for film transfer, and it won't assure that these film stocks will reproduce your video colors any more faithfully.

Manipulating Time and Space

In the special effects wizard's bag of tricks are many ways to alter normal perceptions of time and space. Of course, as we pointed out in Chapter 5, the flow of time in a movie is totally artificial. A typical feature film compresses the events of days or even years into about two hours of viewing time. This compression is achieved primarily through the basic process of cutting and assembling clips in the edit. However, special effects can further warp the perception of time within a clip and in ways the camera simply can't record. (For more information on altering the flow of time, see "Time Bending," later in this chapter.)

A factor in the viewers' perception of time is the expected speed at which people and objects move through space. We've already discussed how varying frame rate and shutter speed in the camera can affect the apparent speed—and enhance the excitement—of an action scene.

But the important distinction here is how people and objects move *through space*. Many special effects aim to manipulate space in ways that straightforward photography or videography cannot.

Special effects artists have three different ways of thinking about space. These are abstract notions of geometry on which all CGI is built:

- Two-dimensional (2D) images
- 2½ dimensions (2½D)
- Three-dimensional (3D) space

2D Images

The optical image that the camera records on the surface of its CCDs is two dimensional. Any depth the viewer perceives in the picture is an illusion. As we discussed in Chapter 4, the cinematographer has a few basic ways of manipulating 2D depth:

- Choice of camera lens: Wide lenses expand the field of view, opening up the shot, and telephoto lenses narrow the field of view and compress distances.
- Selective focus, achieved with long lenses and shallow depth of field.
- Back and rim lighting, which can make the subject appear to stand out from the background.

The only spatial transformation you can achieve in 2D space in postproduction is distortion. Using an application such as After Effects, you can compress the X and/or the Y dimension (see Figure 8.1), or you can distort it by using a filter that applies a shape, such as a spherical distortion (see Figure 8.2).

Figure 8.1
Compressing a 2D image along its X axis (horizontally, as shown on the right) causes the picture to appear vertically distorted (compare with the original image on the left). This isn't an effect you'd normally do, but it serves to illustrate how pixel data can be manipulated by changing its geometry.

Figure 8.2
Image manipulation can be performed on specific areas of an image rather than on the image as a whole. CGI software tracks the shape through successive frames, so you can avoid the tedium of applying the effect to individual frames. Applying spherical distortion to the area of the actor's face (original on the left, distortion on the right) causes an effect similar to shooting her with an extremely wide angle lens.

$2^{1}/_{2}D$ Imagery

After Effects, one of the most widely used special-effects software tools, and many other image-manipulation applications use the scheme of 2½D, which is based on a virtual stack of picture planes, or layers (see Figure 8.3). Each layer is a 2D image, composed of X×Y pixels. But in addition to its 2D properties, each layer has a Z-axis value, or priority. Since the end product will simply be a 2D image on the movie screen, the layers must be combined, or flattened. A layer's priority determines how it will be combined. For example, higher-priority layers obscure, or hide objects on, the layers beneath. As a further option, a layer can have the property of transparency, which can permit objects on lower-priority layers to show through. The degree of transparency, as well as its tint and other properties, can be adjusted so that the transparent layer can work much like a photographic transparency, a sheet of colored gel, or an optical filter.

Digital video compositing is the process of combining two or more 2D layers in a 2½D scheme to form a single, flattened 2D image. In an application such as After Effects, the computer literally adds RGB pixel values of one layer to another, to a greater or lesser degree, depending on the covering layer's percentage of transparency (0% is opaque, and 100% is clear).

For example, chroma key digital mattes are done exactly this way. If the key color is green, the RGB values of those pixels in the first layer are treated in the compositing as though they were zero. When the pixel values in the second image are added to the first (the matte containing the key color), those values simply replace the green. Also, any non-green pixels in the first image have higher priority than the corresponding pixels in the second image, so those pixels are unchanged in the final output. The net result is that imagery in the second layer completely replaces any green pixels in the first layer.

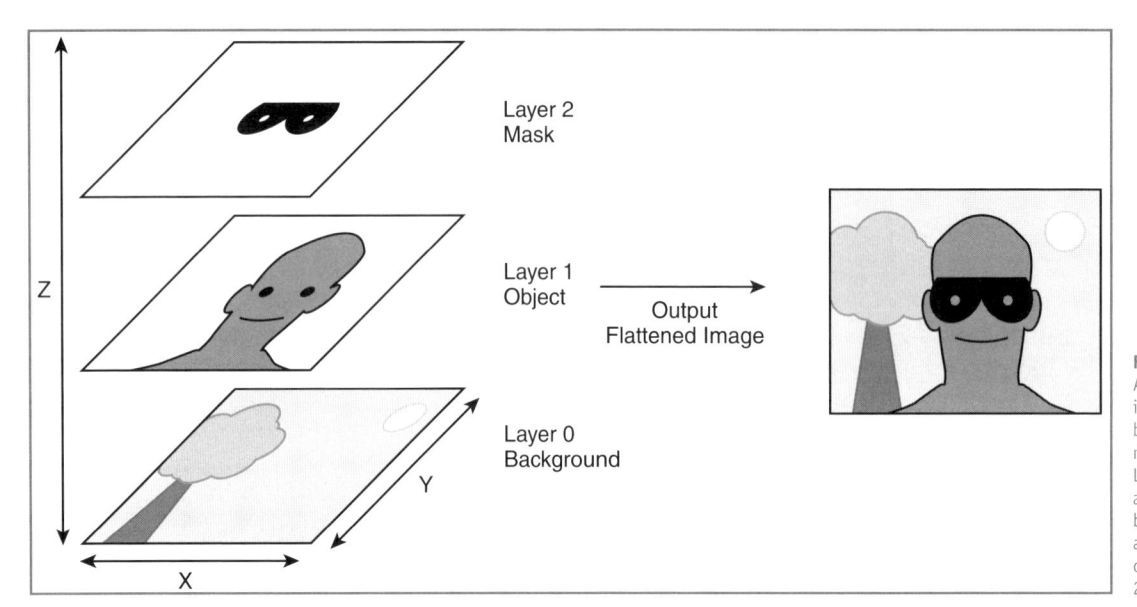

Figure 8.3
Adobe After Effects and other video image manipulation applications are based on a scheme of 2½D, in which multiple 2D images form layers. Layers on top can partially hide or affect the appearance of the layers beneath. The final output from the application is a movie clip containing a sequence of flattened 2D images.

CASE STUDY: TRACI'S DISAPPEARING ACT

In *Neo's Ring*, we composited Traci shot against a green screen with vacation footage of a Mayan ruin. When Traci first appears in the distant location, she's in the foreground, the carved walls of the ruin in the background. Notice, however, that when Traci exits the frame, she disappears *behind* one of the ancient walls (see Figure 8.4). This was done in After Effects by making a copy of the background layer, deleting all but the leftmost wall from the image, making the area of the deletion transparent, and then placing that layer on top. That put Traci on the middle layer, sandwiched between the portion of the wall in the foreground and the scene in the background. When she exits, she's obscured by the portion of the wall contained on the top layer.

Figure 8.4
In a digital matte scene in *Neo's Ring*, Traci appears to exit "behind" a wall in the ruin. This is achieved by copying the background layer that shows the ruin, cutting out a portion of wall, and making everything else on that layer transparent. When Traci stands at center screen, her image shows through the transparent area of the top layer. But the portion of wall on that top layer hides her body when she moves to the left edge of the frame (see Color Plate 7).

3D Space

Also called *three-space*, 3D CGI uses an entirely different virtual scheme for its geometry. Like 2½D representation, 3D specifies location in space according to X, Y, and Z axes. But as it is in physical measurements of the real world, the Z-axis is a full spatial dimension rather than a stack of layers. In three-space, a picture plane is simply any 2D slice, which can be made anywhere within the space, taken from any angle (see Figure 8.5).

Since the output of film and video cameras is limited to 2D images, the movie special effects designer doesn't have any 3D imagery of live scenes to work with. For this reason, much of the 3D special effects work you see in the movies is done in the field of animation, where images are totally synthetic. Computer applications for creating synthetic 3D imagery for digital video include Alias Maya, Corel Bryce 3D, and NewTek Lightwave 3D.

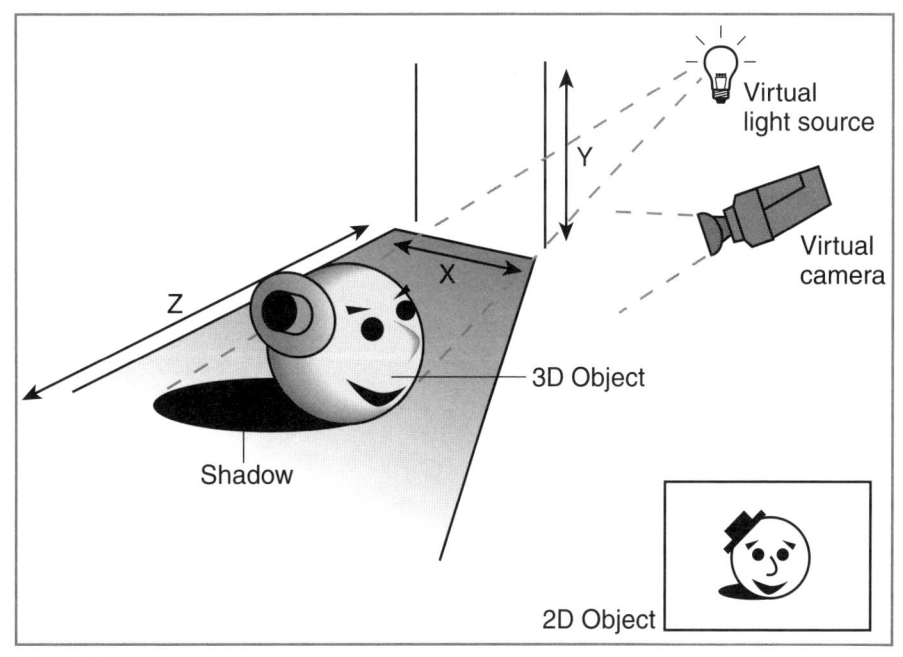

Figure 8.5
Virtual 3D animation applications such as Corel Bryce can create objects within a geometric space of X, Y, and Z dimensions. This scheme permits you to create solid objects. The object's shadow can be generated if you specify the type and direction of a virtual light source. The output video image is any 2D slice through that space, at any angle, taken from the vantage point of a virtual camera you move around the imaginary set.

There have been contrived (and expensive) efforts in filmmaking to capture full 3D live-motion footage. One technique involves surrounding a stunt location with tens of 35mm still cameras and then firing them all at the same moment to freeze an action in space. The still images are then animated and combined in post to create a pan around the frozen scene. So-called *bullet time*, a technique made famous in *The Matrix* (1999) and its sequels, used this scheme, but with a difference. The shutters of the cameras were fired in rapid succession, creating an ultra slo-mo sequence to which whizzing bullets frozen in space were added by compositing. The audience sees the actors step slowly through the shot as the bullets stay suspended around them.

Applying the Same Effect to a Sequence of Frames

Most of the tools and filters of 2½D image manipulation are contained in Adobe's workhorse still-photo editor Photoshop. After Effects presents you with many of the same tools and menu selections, but with the added capability of applying an effect to a sequence of frames in a video clip. This is possible because of two powerful capabilities of CGI software.

Edge detection. You can apply an effect to a selected area, or shape, within a frame. Your selection defines the boundaries, or edges, of the shape. The application can then track and identify the shape through successive frames and apply the effect to each, even though the shape is continually changing with the motion of the scene. The application does this by detecting abrupt shifts of brightness and color between adjacent pixels. These are the edges of the shape. However, the edge detection function is far from perfect. For example, if the shape you've selected is a piece of sky, the application probably won't be able to detect that an actor's upraised arm suddenly appearing in the shot has split the sky into two separate shapes. Or, if you select an actor's face for color correction, the software will totally lose track when the actor turns his back to the camera. For these reasons, the CGI artist sometimes must intervene within a series of frames to indicate to the computer where a drastically transformed shape is located and then reapply the effect and continue on to the frames in the rest of the clip. At worst, and this is rare but it happens, you will have to apply an effect one frame at a time.

Keyframing. A technique that has many different uses in both editing and special-effects creation is termed *keyframing*, also called *interpolation* or *tweening*. In the process of keyframing, you select the first frame of a sequence to which you want an effect applied, and then you select the last frame. The application applies the effect to all the frames in between, interpolating the positions or degree of change in each so that the overall transition is smooth. To add further sophistication, depending on the type of effect, you can usually vary the speed or even the acceleration at which the effect is applied. For example, keyframing can be used to animate an object's movement across the screen (see Figure 8.6). To add flair and realism, veteran animators add acceleration in the beginning of the move and then decelerate toward the end. These accelerations and decelerations are called *farings* in the animation business, a feature now built in to computer animation software. In After Effects, such accelerations and decelerations are called *easing in* and *easing out*.

> To be precise, keyframing is the identification of first and last frames, and tweening is the interpolation process of generating the transitional frames. However, many designers use the terms interchangeably.

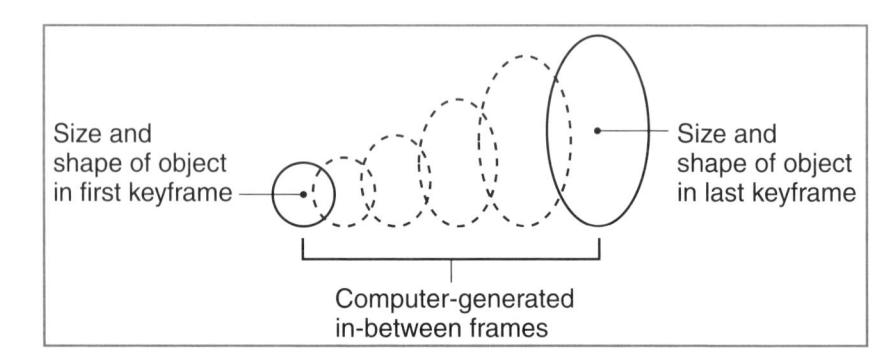

Figure 8.6
In the CGI process of keyframing, you select the first and last images in a transition or animated sequence. The computer then performs tweening, generating all the frames in between.

It's one of the much-touted features of Final Cut Pro that all of its transition effects, such as wipes and dissolves, can be customized by keyframing. That is, you can fine-tune the degree, speed, and acceleration of the effect.

Another very familiar—and quite stunning—keyframe effect is called *morphing*. You've undoubtedly seen it in horror movies where a character's face gradually transforms into the face of a werewolf or goes through some other type of extreme distortion. This is a straightforward effect you can easily achieve in After Effects. You provide the starting and the ending images, and specify the duration of the transformation, and the computer will generate all the in-between frames.

> All NLEs and special-effects applications include some canned effects. In general, the more sophisticated the application, the more ways it will provide for you to customize those effects. Entry-level software permits only limited modification of predefined effects.

The more complex the morphed objects are, the more an intermediate step is needed. The morphing will be more dramatic to the extent that you map, or specify point-to-point correspondences, between the two images. Using a mouse or a stylus, you select a point on the first image and then indicate where that point will end up at the end of the transformation. You repeat this process to map all the distinguishing features on the image. In effect, you're telling the computer where the eyes, ears, nose, and mouth are on both faces.

The Art and Craft of Combining Imagery

Most of your work in creating special effects for the movies will rely on compositing images in 2½D in an application such as After Effects. We've already covered most of the basics of one type of compositing, digital mattes, in our discussion of chroma keying in Chapter 6. There are many more tricks to this part of the trade.

PLANNING FOR COMPOSITES ON THE SET

It might seem elementary, but you can't achieve most special effects in postproduction if you don't plan for them during the shooting. In particular, to do mattes and other types of composites, you must storyboard them meticulously, discuss them in detail with your creative and technical teams, and make sure you get all the required elements in the can.

If you're doing chroma keying, some extra logistics will be involved in acquiring, setting up, and lighting a special green or blue backdrop (or using special chroma key paint on the set). As a rule, green works well for exteriors and blue for interiors. In either case, you must select wardrobe and set dressings carefully to make sure that the key color doesn't show up in unwanted places.

Improvising Effects with Luminance Keying

If you plan ahead carefully and shoot against a green or blue screen, chroma keying is the most reliable way to create digital mattes. But recall that there's a somewhat older technique called luminance keying that uses a white, black, or grayscale area as the key color. Originally developed for supering titles, luminance keying can be tricky because natural highlights or shadows on the subject are more difficult than color to control and can be mistakenly interpreted as part of the key. Luminance keying is particularly hard to do on moving actors on which the lighting is changing from moment to moment as they dance around in the light.

However, you still may be able to achieve some impressive effects by using luminance keying. In particular, it's the one keying method you may be able to try if you *didn't* plan ahead during the shoot. For example, consider a series of exterior shots in which the sky is overbright. It's straightforward in post to increase the video levels in the overexposed areas so that they blow out completely, becoming pure white. (In technical terms, that's a video level of 100IRE.) Using luminance keying, you can then use the level of 100IRE as the key color and matte in another shot of a gorgeous sky, such as a sunset, to serve as the background.

If you try this, be forewarned that other highlights in the shot can be included accidentally in the key. There are at least two possible solutions for this:

◆ In After Effects or another application that lets you apply effects to selected areas within the frame, adjust the levels of just the highlight areas to make them less than 100IRE, which will exclude them from the matte. Leaving 100IRE as your key color, recombine the imagery.

◆ Create a traveling matte by drawing a shape in After Effects that covers the troublesome area like an opaque patch. Then recombine the imagery.

> Just because you try luminance keying after the fact of shooting doesn't mean you can't be clever in your compositing. If you add a synthetic sky as just described, then you should find matching shots of the sky, with the clouds both in and out of focus. But if all you have is sharp footage, make a copy of the clip and apply a blur filter in post so you have two versions: one sharp, the other blurred. Use the sharp takes to composite with your long shots. Use the blurred-sky shots with your close-ups to effectively reduce the appearance of depth of field, giving the composited scene a more filmic look. You'll also have better luck with luminance keying if you choose clips in which you kept your key light soft during shooting to avoid bright kicks on edges, and if there's no white, such as a shirt collar or even a pocket handkerchief, in the actors' wardrobe.

Using Analog Video and Film Sources

You may occasionally need to upload video footage or analog music clips from tape or LP. If you're working in a fully equipped editing suite, you'll probably be able to use a special deck for this purpose (see Figure 8.7). These decks contain the required A/D (analog to digital) conversion circuitry.

> If you're serious about doing special effects work, get a high-end video capture card for your computer that captures both analog and digital inputs (check out www.pinnaclesys.com and www.matrox.com). The card will give you the ability to edit uncompressed video, allowing the greatest latitude for compositing. The method we describe here (using a DV deck as an A/D converter) yields DV 4:1:1 color space, which is less than ideal for composing rich effects.

Figure 8.7
This Sony DVCAM deck is an editor's handy device for uploading mini DV and DVCAM cassette recordings into the computer. The deck also has an A/D conversion circuit that allows you to input analog video or audio signals from an external player. The deck will digitize those signals and pass them to the computer as a DV data stream.

However, if you're not working in an editing studio, there's a quick, reliable way to do the same trick without a deck.

If you've got an analog clip, you'll need an analog player (such as an audio cassette deck, a turntable, or a VCR) and a DV camcorder with a jack labeled something like "A/V In/Out" (see Figure 8.8). This jack connects to a built-in analog I/O circuit. (If the camcorder or deck gives you the option of S-Video input, use that instead, dub to DV tape, and then capture via FireWire.)

Use a hookup cable with three RCA plugs for connecting the Video, Audio-L, and Audio-R jacks on your analog player to the matching inputs of the camcorder's A/V In/Out jack. Use your regular FireWire cable to connect with the computer's IEEE 1394 port.

Turn on the camcorder and press Play on the source deck. The camcorder will handle the A/D conversion, and the output to FireWire will be a perfectly acceptable DV signal. You can then upload the clip through the Log and Capture window.

24P: Make Your Digital Movies Look Like Hollywood

Figure 8.8
An inexpensive but reliable way to digitize analog video or audio signals is to pass them through the camcorder's AV jack and then output via FireWire cable to the computer. As you play back from the analog VCR, the camcorder digitizes both the video and the audio to create a valid DV data stream.

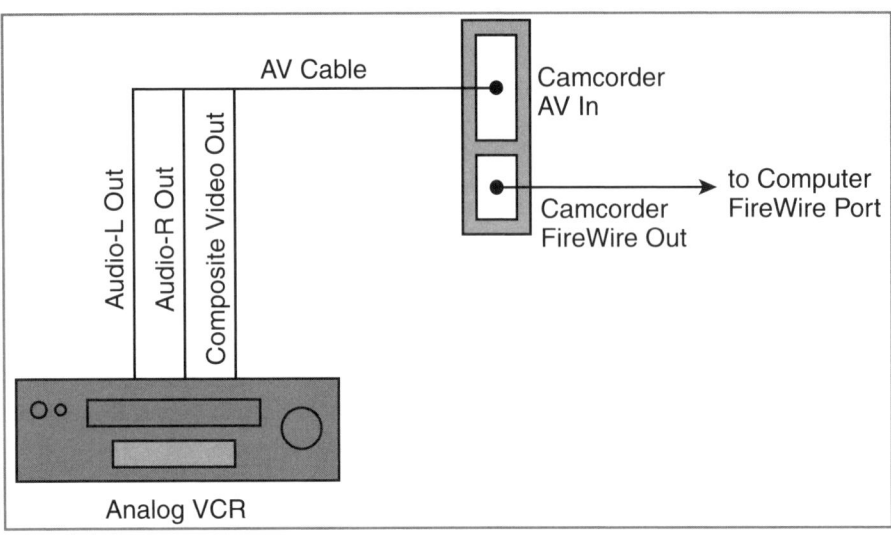

> The technique of passing an analog signal through your camcorder is quick and easy, but it does have a serious drawback: The captured footage will have no timecode. Another approach, which gives better results if you're not in a hurry, is to dub the analog to DV first using the camcorder as the VCR; then capture the recorded DV footage via FireWire as you normally would. This procedure will give you a valid timecode.

If you have neither a camcorder nor a DV deck, you'll need to digitize the signal by feeding it to an analog video card in the computer. (If it's audio only, you can input it to the computer's sound card.) However, here's why we prefer the camcorder method:

◆ The digital output of your analog capture card must match the DV spec; some older models don't.

◆ On input, the device driver for the capture card may prompt you to set encoding options. If you choose the wrong ones, or if the card simply isn't fast enough, you'll get frame dropouts or other technical problems in the DV recording.

If you want to incorporate a film clip into your DV edit, take the clip to a film lab for telecine transfer, which scans the film footage and converts it to video. The usual output of a telecine will be either analog videotape, such as Betacam SP, or studio-quality digital, such as Digibeta tape. It may cost extra to have the lab downconvert the clip to DV.

If you plan to draw extensively on archival sources—older videotapes or film—budget to have it transferred professionally to digital format. Ideally, you'll have these archival sources transferred to uncompressed (broadcast studio quality) digital video, then upload your DV to system that can handle 10-bit video, such as Final Cut Pro or Avid Nitris. There it can all come together.

Color Correction

The topic of digital video color correction is complex because it involves both highly technical processes and experienced, yet subjective, artistic judgment.

The technical issues fall into two main categories, depending on your chosen output medium. (If you're producing for both television and film, you'll have to worry about both.)

Fine-Tuning Color for Broadcast Television

Preparing video for broadcast is particularly difficult because of standards imposed during the early days of analog transmission to keep stations' signals from interfering with one another. Simply put, colors can't be too vibrant. If they are, the signals from adjacent channels in the broadcast spectrum could interfere with one another. That's not possible with digital broadcasting media such as satellite and cable, but remember that these standards were set when the predominant distribution technology was analog radio waves.

The main technical difference between the colors of DV and the NTSC broadcast television standard is color space. Recall from Chapter 1 that DV color space is 4:1:1, and broadcast is 4:2:2. Most NLEs, including Final Cut Pro, will convert from 4:1:1 to 4:2:2 as an option on output. When this is done, the color is technically correct, or broadcast legal. However, the ways color might have shifted in the conversion might be unpredictable. It's not that 4:1:1 color is less rich than 4:2:2. In fact, the result is often quite the opposite. DV colors tend to be less subtle and more primary. This can make greenery greener and red roses rosier than they appear to the eye. But after the conversion to 4:2:2, the shift in color, although technically correct to comply with broadcast standards, might not be aesthetically pleasing. Bright green trees might turn brownish, and the reds might seem downright dull. Human faces could look rosy, bilious, jaundiced, or anything in between.

> Converting DV to broadcast-legal NTSC is not a necessary step when your goal is film transfer. If the colors in the DV output are pleasing to your eye, that's the best indication that they will register properly on film. For more information on film transfers, see Chapter 9.

That's where the aesthetic and creative side of color correction comes into play.

TECH TALK ABOUT COLOR SPACE

In technical terms, the color space notations 4:1:1 and 4:2:2 refer to a three-part color signal encoded on the videotape. This signal is transformed from the RGB picked up by the video camera's chips. For NTSC, the signal's three components are brightness (Y) and chrominance (Cr and Cb). The brightness signal is monochrome, but it also contains much of the green information. The two other components are mixtures of red and blue. The 4:1:1 notation means that Y is sampled at four times the video subcarrier frequency, and Cr and Cb just once each per subcarrier cycle. In 4:2:2, chrominance is sampled twice as often, so the range of tints that can be displayed is greater. However, in terms of picture detail, broadcast video is literally not one bit better than DV because most of the edge information is in the Y signal, which each format samples at the rate of four times subcarrier. (The human eye sees the most detail in the green portion of the spectrum—perhaps because our distant ancestors lived in trees!)

Tweaking Color on Film

Preparing video for transfer to film and theatrical distribution forces you to deal with constraints such as the color reproduction characteristics of various film stocks. Overall, there's a fundamental technical difference between video and film when it comes to color. Video, whether analog or digital, uses the RGB color model (based on primary colors red, green, and blue). Film uses a variation of the CMYK model used in printing, which has four components: cyan, magenta, yellow, and black. In short, the colors in your film-out product might not match those in your projected digital video.

With digital postproduction technology, you might logically assume that adjusting or changing the color of screen images would be simple. Select the image, select the change, push a button, and take a nap while the system renders the result. But, pardon the pun, color choices aren't black and white. You have a lot of latitude, even within the range of what would be considered correct technically. You must make artistic judgments on color adjustment that are far more delicate than they first appear. And your choices will rarely look right the first, second, or even the third time.

Color correction is tricky, and highly skilled technicians called *colorists* in Hollywood work a lot.

Whether the output is intended for television or for film, color correction is always a two-step process:

1. Adjust color for technical correctness, such as broadcast color space (4:2:2) or for the response curve, or color-rendering characteristics, of a specific film stock.
2. When the color is within spec, adjust for pleasing artistic effect. For example, favor a rosy cast on the actors' faces instead of green. Another objective might be to compensate for poor lighting on the set.

The Color Correction Process

Color-correction tools come with NLE systems, such as Avid Symphony and Final Cut Pro (refer to the Color Plates). There are also specialized post-production special-effects tools, such as Boris FX. Also, Red Giant Magic Bullet, which we've recommended mainly for converting 60i footage to 24p, has a fairly reliable broadcast-legal conversion function that requires little more than a click. DaVinci Systems 2K Plus is a bundled system that includes hardware and software for manipulating digital video and film images up to 2K×2K resolution. It's the big-budget tool of choice for manipulating digital intermediates that will be used to make 70mm theatrical film prints.

There are three basic approaches for color correction, which should be available as options within your color-correction application:

- Primary
- Secondary
- Spot

> **TRAVELING MATTES AND ROTOSCOPING**
>
> In the past decade, digital spot-color correction tricks, such as black-and-white subjects on a color background or vice versa, have become commonplace, especially in TV advertising.
>
> The feature film *Schindler's List* was filmed in black-and-white. Among many brilliant sequences is a haunting image of a group of victims being herded down the street. In the midst of the gray figures is a little girl in a bright red coat, the spot of color making her stand out poignantly in the doomed crowd.
>
> Unlike the rest of the movie, this segment was shot in color. A rotoscope, or mask, was created of the little girl's shape, and the color in the background was stripped down to monochrome, leaving the masked shape in its original hue.
>
> In After Effects, changing the color of an object in a color sequence involves first creating the mask of the shape being changed and then adding a hue adjustment layer of the desired color over the masked object.
>
> For a moving shape, a traveling matte is used that takes advantage of the digital video animation process of tweening, or keyframe interpolation.
>
> The selected shape is masked in the first frame and the last frame, and the desired color is laid in. Then every few frames an additional mask is added to cover the changing shape as it moves (every 15 frames is about right). Once masking has been spread out over the sequence and the colors put in, the masked frames are keyframed and then tweened, which generates the subtle changes in motion. After the whole sequence is tweened and the shape's changed color is fixed, more work is usually needed. The designer goes back through the sequence and tightens or cleans up any frames that need additional detailing. (Designers customarily begin with broad strokes in the 15-frame keys and then get progressively more detailed.)
>
> Incidentally, by far the toughest item to work with in a rotoscoping process is human hair—especially if the subject has long, wavy strands of hair. The computer program will have trouble tracking all that detail.

Primary Color Correction

Procedures that you apply to the entire image are termed *primary*. One artistic application of primary color correction is to change the mood of a scene by shifting its overall cast to a color such as blue.

Secondary Color Correction

Secondary color correction applies a certain characteristic to selected pixels within a certain parametric range. For example, you might want to adjust the chroma of all pixels that are above 70 percent saturation. This would give a garish quality to the brightest colors in an image. Obviously, experimentation will give you the best idea of how such a correction would affect your image.

Spot Color Correction

As the term implies, spot color correction changes the color parameters for a selected region of the picture. An excellent example would be a famous shot in *Schindler's List* (1993) in which everything in the frame is black-and-white except for a little girl in a bright red overcoat. (See the sidebar "Traveling Mattes and Rotoscoping," on the previous page, for further information.)

> When you're creating DVD menu graphics, remember that computer-generated colors may be too saturated for video. Also, be aware that computer graphics use square pixels, but digital-video pixels are rectangular. As a result, you may see slight distortion of the menu when it appears on a television screen. To compensate for this, when converting computer graphics to NTSC video in an application such as Photoshop or After Effects, resample the image (permitting distortion) from 720×540 to 720×480 pixels.

Achieving Smooth-Scrolling Titles

Most NLE programs have built-in capabilities for generating titles. But for *really* smooth animation we recommend a plug-in such as Inscriber Technology, TitleMotion Pro, or LiveType, an animation-based titling application included with Final Cut Pro. Most NLE systems permit you to import the still images and animated sequences you create with these programs, adding the graphic files as additional video tracks in your scene.

The most common type of animation for movie credits is called *vertical scrolling*. The trick to achieving a smooth vertical scroll without the type appearing to jump or flicker lies in moving the titles up an even number of scan lines in each video frame—two, four, or eight. If your titling software doesn't have this setting, you'll have to render the title segment and play it back to make sure it's smooth. If it's not, you'll have to adjust the scroll rate by trial and error, rendering and replaying the clip each time, until the jerkiness disappears.

When creating titles and graphics, remember to avoid noisy edges, which are all too easy to create when you're using computer-generated shapes and colors. In general, computer-generated solid colors are often too saturated, or intense, to be broadcast legal.

As to color saturation in your titles, there's an easy way to check whether your computer-generated colors will be legal. The titling or graphics program typically uses an eight-bit color scheme, which means that RGB values can range from 0 to 255. To assure your colors are legal, simply keep the RGB values between 16 and 235.

> If you don't like the look of computer-generated titles, you can shoot backlit typeset sheets called *Kodaliths* (Kodak-brand of lithographic sheet film) with a camcorder and then overlay the title clips on a background in the NLE process. This approach requires dealing with a photo lab to produce the sheets from your typeset printouts, but the distinct advantage is that the camcorder's edge-softening circuitry will eliminate the main problem of CGI titles when doing transfers—video noise at the edges of the typeset characters.

An additional use of titles, especially in documentaries, is to superimpose information (for instance the name and title of the person speaking) on the bottom of the screen. These titles are called *lower thirds* because that's the area of the screen where they're usually supered. Here are some guidelines for preparing lower-third titles:

- Use text large enough for the audience to read easily. The rule of thumb is that text must be readable by an average person sitting at a distance from the screen equal to four times the height of the screen. (This formula works whether they are watching a movie in a theater or on a TV set in their living rooms.)
- White, yellow, or yellow-orange text will super best whatever the background. If the background is busy or light colored, you can add a drop-shadow effect to make the text "pop." *Never assume that dark-colored text will read better over light backgrounds.* That works in print but not in video.
- Don't add animation to lower third titles. It's distracting and makes them harder to read.
- Don't cue the title until a few seconds into the take, giving the audience a chance to settle in. Ideally, cue the title at the speaker's first pause.
- Hold the title on the screen for either five seconds or the time it takes you to read the title aloud twice, whichever is longer. Then fade it off. If you don't have enough time before the next cut, consider finding a way to lengthen the video clip or wait to super the title until you cut back to the person.
- On main titles as well as lower thirds, you must keep your titles within the broadcast-standard safe title area, which leaves a generous border around the image to avoid cutoff by variations in TV picture tubes. All video titling programs include templates for safe title areas.

Cooking Up Some Eye Candy

To create special effects through compositing, you need a sophisticated image-manipulation application such as After Effects. Mastering this application takes some artistic skill and plenty of practice, and designers who are new to this stuff usually feel comfortable only after they've taken some kind of formal coursework or had the benefit of an intense period of on-the-job training.

After Effects can be particularly challenging to use when you're trying to create complex effects, such as compound motion. For example, you might want an object to change size as well as shape and color, while also moving and changing screen direction. Each of these transformations requires you to define a separate pair of keyframes, so timing the effects and coordinating them so that the result looks like a single, continuous action can be quite a task.

More recently, there's been a trend in the software business to simplify such sophisticated effects work and to provide ready-made actions, called *behaviors*, which are nonetheless easy to modify, customize, and combine. For example, Apple Motion is an application that's aimed squarely at ambitious filmmakers who don't have much special-effects experience and yet are eager to try their hands at it . (You'll want a hefty Mac to run it—Apple recommends dual G5 processors.) Motion is designed to simplify the process of animation. Apple also markets Shake, a high-end companion application that's primarily intended for compositing.

The results from using Motion with relatively little training can be pretty amazing. Examples of familiar predefined behaviors that could otherwise be tedious to create are "gravity" and "bounce."

Time Bending

One of the advanced effects you might be tempted to try is time bending, which is done by applying variable video frame rates in postproduction to alter perceptions about the flow of time. Old-fashioned slow motion is an example, and a more recent one is ultra-slow-mo bullet time, described previously in this chapter.

One approach to slow motion is simply to capture all the footage that will be time-bended in post in slow motion to begin with. This can be done by overcranking (increasing the frame rate) in a motion picture camera or by using the Panasonic VariCam camcorder. It's obviously an expensive solution, but it does guarantee smooth results. Whether you speed up time or slow it down, you will always have all the frames you need without requiring the special-effects application to generate any missing frames by interpolation.

There is a variety of ways to achieve time bending more economically entirely in post, even if you shot at a normal frame rate (whether 60i or 24p). In After Effects, the clip to be slowed down is marked by keyframes, the first and the last in the sequence. Then the end keyframe is stretched forward along with the end of the sequence by adding additional frames. The added frames are tweened, which smooths out the action over the added frames to whatever length is desired. Within the sequence, the designer can vary the speed at will, accelerating, decelerating, freezing, or stepping through the action, warping the flow of time in complex ways.

Keyframing to produce time bending is a relatively quick process, which you can view in real time as you play back your editing decisions. When time is speeded up, frames are simply dropped. When time is slowed down, frames are duplicated.

However, duplicating frames can create erratic slow motion. You can smooth it out in a subsequent step called *frame blending*, in which the application generates new intermediate frames by interpolation. Plug-ins RE:Visions Twixtor and Retimer SD can help you generate smoother time and frame blending in post. Be aware that frame blending takes time because the computer must render each new frame.

If They Asked Us, Could We Write the Book?

There are whole volumes—not to mention college-level courses—aimed at teaching you how to use special-effects software tools to conceptualize and then generate imagery that no one has ever seen. If you want to get serious, we highly recommend *After Effects Hands-On Training* by Craig Newman and Lynda Weinman.

Not to make any excuses, but consider this chapter just the barest introduction. If we've given you even an inkling of the ways you can experiment, we can guiltlessly proceed to the topic of preparing to show your finished movie to the world.

> Movies are make-believe, and special effects take full advantage of that fact. Let's be real—no matter how skillfully you shoot a battle scene, the moviegoers don't leave the comfortable safety of their seats. Granted, the opening sequence of *Saving Private Ryan* comes close to making us forget we're watching a movie. Spielberg uses some expert special effects (in combination with the shutter-speed tricks discussed previously) to re-create the disorientation and panic of a soldier charging through nonstop shelling and machine-gun fire.
>
> However, B-movie action director Sam Fuller quipped that the only way to make a truly realistic war movie would be to fire live ammunition at the audience from the screen.

chapter 9
Thinking Like a Distributor

The ultimate test is whether people will pay to see it.

The respect of your peers, academic achievement, and festival awards can be well-deserved indications of craftsmanship and artistic merit. But if you want to be in the game—and stay in the game—you must find a way to get your movie distributed commercially.

The livelihoods (and personal fortunes) of movie distributors depend on making big financial bets about what the general public will pay to see. Someday, and perhaps someday soon, the economies of digital distribution will provide independent producers ready access to mass markets for movies. Until that day comes, a handful of theatrical distribution companies will remain the gatekeepers to your paying audiences.

So, you'd better learn how they think, what they want, and how to deliver it to them.

We Ask Once More: Do You Really Need Film Output?

Maybe. Maybe not.

Sorry that we can't give a more definitive answer, but remember, this is show business, and there's no business on Earth less businesslike than show business. Oh, the money is serious enough. But there are no rules, and just when you think you've figured out the rules, they change.

Movie distributors want a product that audiences will accept. We've tried to make a convincing argument that film-look digital video, a product with a polished Hollywood look, is your best chance of success in a highly competitive marketplace.

Time was, and it was not so long ago, that you couldn't even think about approaching movie distributors without literally having a film negative in the can.

Now, film festivals will accept submissions on digital videotape or disc. At film markets, the annual conventions where film buyers congregate, deals are done over video monitors after sampling a tape or disc version of your movie. In either situation, theaters used for public and private screenings typically have digital projectors.

If your movie is the top jury-prize winner or the buzz of the town, a distributor may be willing to pick up the cost of film transfer. If, however, you have neither a negative nor any strong interest in your project, making a negative at your own expense *might* improve your chances of closing a sale. But there's no guarantee, and it's an expensive gamble.

How expensive? Tape-to-film transfers for a feature-length movie range from about $20,000 to $80,000, depending on recording technology, output resolution, and finishing options (we'll explain the differences).

Still want to play?

We'll discuss all your lower-cost options first. Then, if you're feeling lucky, you can venture with us into the realm of getting film out from digital video.

But first, let's see how the commercial movie marketplace works from the distributor's point of view.

The Economics of Commercial Theatrical Distribution

The main reason that digital distribution and exhibition methods will eventually replace film distribution is not aesthetic. It's all about money, and the distributors will drive the change because they stand to save billions.

A movie distributor is a wholesaler of films licensed from studios and independent producers to the owner-operators of theaters (mostly theater chains). The theatrical market is divided between domestic and foreign. In the domestic market, the major studios control distribution because they own distribution companies.

It's difficult for new companies to enter this game because it takes big, big bucks.

A two-hour movie ships in six large cans, each containing one 20-minute projector reel. Each 35mm print costs about $3,000 (more for 70mm). Besides the lab costs of manufacturing the print, the costs of shipping are huge. To assure reliable delivery on an opening weekend, it's standard practice for a major movie distribution company to pay for private couriers to accompany prints as checked baggage on commercial air carriers. When you consider that these days a big movie will open in at least 1,000 theaters on the first weekend, that's about $4 million for prints and shipping, just to *begin* the run.

As costly as shipping cans of film can be, this is a modest sum in comparison to the advertising costs required to pack the theaters on opening weekend. Ads in newspapers, magazines, television, and radio will cost tens of millions of dollars. Again, that's just to get started.

In terms a distributor would use, launching a movie in 1,000 theaters nationwide on the same day is called *going wide*. A distributor will normally spend half again what the picture cost to make to buy prints and ads (P&A). That is, they will spend another $50 million on top of a $100 million blockbuster production budget.

The rest of the math in the distribution game is also bewildering. Box-office gross receipts, the revenue that theater operators collect from ticket sales, are split about 50-50 with the distributor. Unless the movie is a blockbuster, the theater owner breaks even on the ticket sales, just covering expenses. The profit comes from selling drinks and snacks.

> The $3 soft drink you buy at the concession stand is almost all profit. The paper cup costs a few cents, and the soda costs even less. There are unsubstantiated reports of theaters collecting paper cups from the trash, rinsing them out, and reusing them to further increase profits.

From his half of the take, the distributor reimburses himself for P&A, then deducts a nice profit, and returns the rest to the movie owner, usually a studio, as the producer's gross.

Here's the discouraging news: Most movies lose money. To turn a profit, a movie's box-office gross must make *triple* its production budget. Studios have a rule of thumb (which, like all their rules, don't always apply) that eight out of 10 movies will lose money. One will break even, and one will make a profit. Problem is, even the savviest producer in town doesn't know which one it will be out of the 10, and so they have to make them all.

The studios have found a way to improve those odds. A slightly higher percentage of movies in the $100 million range end up making money. Why? Mostly because the stakes are so high that they keep throwing media hype and ever-increasing amounts of P&A at it until people end up going just to find out what all the buzz is about.

The studios also now know something they might have suspected but hadn't proven as recently as 10 years ago: DVD sales will equal or exceed box-office grosses.

And that's where the real profit is for the producers and studios.

> The studios' biggest fear is illegal downloading over the Internet, which appears justifiable based on the experience in the music business. As we'll mention again in this chapter, the evolution of audio technology and its impact on the music business may be a fair predictor of what's to come in the digital video marketplace.

Given the implications of all this high-stakes math, marginally profitable theatrical exhibition today exists for one reason only—to stimulate public interest and create a strong aftermarket of home video sales and rentals.

See where all this is going? What do you think will happen when theatrical-quality digital distribution directly into the home isn't just for the well-heeled folks who can afford to drop a few thousand bucks on a plasma HDTV?

Everyone in show business knows what's coming. It's just that the vested interests, the companies in the film manufacturing industry and the major studios, would like the transition to be slooooooooow enough for them to wring every last cent out of the old way of doing things.

In the end, economics will change the rules. It won't be long before the costs of film-based distribution can no longer be justified.

Meanwhile, we all have to live in the here and now.

Using a Sales Agent to Approach Distributors

Assuming you're an independent producer and not affiliated with any studio, your best access to distributors is to retain the services of a sales agent. A motion-picture sales agent will offer your completed (or partially completed) movie to domestic and foreign distributors for licensing. The agent may sell to television, as well as to domestic and foreign theatrical distributors. Since sales agents tend to specialize, it's possible for multiple agents to represent the same movie in different markets.

One of the keys to foreign sales is having a star who is recognized in that market. If you have such a bankable star or some prior recognition in the domestic market, you'll more easily gain the attention of foreign distributors. If you have such a hook, a common strategy is to go after foreign theatrical distributors first, before approaching the majors about the domestic rights. For the sales agent, selling foreign rights usually requires attending one or all of three annual trade shows:

◆ American Film Market (AFM) in Santa Monica, California (February)

◆ Cannes Marché du Film on the French Riviera (May)

◆ MIFED in Milan, Italy (October)

Where can you find a sales agent?
Start your search with the Independent Film and Television Alliance (IFTA), an industry trade organization. You'll find a directory of member companies at www.afma.com.

If you can only attend one, make it AFM, where more foreign sales are done than at either of the two other markets.

The distribution arms of the major studios control domestic theatrical distribution. The best way to get them interested is to win attention at one of the top film festivals—Toronto, Sundance, Berlin, or Cannes.

Television syndication deals are made at the National Association of Television Program Executives (NATPE) in Las Vegas, which takes place every year in January. However, contracts for producing TV movies are done directly with the networks or with major studios affiliated with those networks. With a few exceptions, networks and cable companies buy TV rights to movies that have already run in theaters, or they contract for made-for-television projects and supervise the production. Unless it's a "festival channel," they don't buy movies from independents that haven't yet run in theaters.

Another possible sales strategy is for the agent to seek finishing money, or postproduction financing for a partially completed project. If foreign distributors like the project, it may be possible to convince investors to put up finishing money.

A practice often used in made-for-television movie deals is called *negative financing*. The fees networks pay producers are not large by studio standards, typically $1 to $3 million. That might be just enough to cover your production costs (although you'll certainly stand a better chance if you shoot digital). Your biggest expense will probably be the salary for a star with TV-Q (a popular, recognizable face). You would need $300,000 to $1 million just to hire the star.

The television movie deal will usually (but not always) let you keep the income from foreign sales. Your sales agent can then go after foreign distributors. If you're successful at getting those commitments, the foreign revenues will constitute the bulk of your profits.

In another type of deal, called a *negative pickup*, the network or studio commits no cash. They simply guarantee to pick up (reimburse your costs and distribute) a movie you have yet to make—provided that you're successful in delivering them the negative. Your sales agent then raises the production money by selling the back end (foreign and video-store distribution). In the interim, you may need to take out a bank loan to cover expenses while you're shooting.

What Deliverables Do Distributors Require?

To better understand how a movie distributor thinks, put yourself in the place of the buyer of a house. You're committing big bucks, and one of the things you want to be very sure of is that, at the completion of the sale, you will have clear title to the property.

It's no different when you buy or sell the rights to distribute a movie. The seller must be able to prove to the buyer through written evidence that he is the owner of the property and has the right to sell it without infringing the rights of any third parties.

In practice, this means that producers must have a paper trail of all production agreements, payroll records, rights clearances, and so on.

Along with the master recording or negative of the movie itself, these papers constitute a set of deliverables, or contractually required submission items, to the distributor as a condition of completing the sale.

Unfortunately for the sake of independent movies, many first-time producers aren't fully aware of these obligations, and they fail to keep adequate records before and during production. Very often, they can't produce actors' releases or music clearances, or they don't prepare duplication masters to the distributor's specification.

> **Where can you find an entertainment lawyer?** Search the directory of the American Bar Association, www.abanet.org, using the Lawyer Locator to find attorneys whose area of practice is "entertainment and sports." Another good search tool for both directories of attorneys and legal citations is FindLaw, www.findlaw.com. Another good resource for referrals is Independent Feature Project, www.ifp.org.

The best way to avoid problems with documentation is to retain the services of an experienced attorney who specializes in entertainment law. This is a highly technical field, and your friendly family lawyer won't have the background for it. Find one of these experts early in the project and keep her on board as a closely consulted member of your production team. Your entertainment attorney might also be able to refer you to reputable sales agents, talent and literary agents, casting directors, and other professionals and representatives who otherwise might not return your calls.

Sample List of Deliverables

The deliverables that a distributor requires will be spelled out in your distribution contract, which you should read carefully, understand fully, and follow to the letter. But before you sign, realize that deliverables are negotiable. A sample list of deliverables is presented in Table 9.1. (Deliverables for television won't include film, but most of the other requirements will be the same.)

> A key deliverable is the film negative. At the beginning of negotiations, it's quite common for a distributor to demand custody of the film negative. However, try to revise the agreement to specify that the distributor will have access to the negative instead. The usual practice is for a film lab to hold your negative in its vault, and you simply grant the distributors access rights when they want to order release prints from that lab. The discussion may then shift to which lab the distributor prefers.

Table 9.1 Distribution Contract Deliverables

Film Items	Comments
Access to 35mm negative or internegative	Soundtrack and titles may have to be on separate reels
35mm print	Answer print for purposes of judging quality
NTSC master videotape	D5, Digibeta, or DVCPRO-50 format, PAL or SECAM for foreign markets
Dialogue list	Dialogue-only version of the script (in English)
Music cue sheet	List of selections, rights holders, and clearances
Foreign-language dialogue tracks	Optional, as separate DA88 DAT with split tracks (M&E on Audio 3 and 4)

Table 9.1 Continued

Film Items	Comments
Documentation	
Employment list	Names and contact information for everyone on the movie payroll at any time: cast, crew, production, administration
Dubbing restrictions	Actors' contracts might require approvals or additional payments for foreign-language versions, including subtitled versions
Prior distribution history	Including festivals and foreign markets
Distribution obligations and restrictions	Specified in talent contracts, including back-end participation
Contracts	Music rights, literary rights, service agreements for production resources; evidence of production liability insurance and Errors and Omissions (E&O) rider to protect against claims of infringement
Notarized Certificate of Origin	Formally establishes country of copyright
Certificate of Authorship	Formally establishes author of the work for purposes of copyright, includes underlying rights to script, novel, life story, etc.
Short Form Assignment of Chain of Title	Listing any prior sales or licenses of the work
Registered Certificate of Copyright	If U.S., Library of Congress Form PA, with raised seal
Publicity and Ad Materials	
Promotional still photos	Scenes from the movie
Production still photos	Behind-the-scenes and making-of shots
Subject releases for stills	

Table 9.1 Continued

Film Items	Comments
Biographies of cast and crew	Especially for principal actors: Height, weight, color of hair, color of eyes, and clothing sizes
Synopsis of screen story	Approximately 250–500 words
Advertising materials	Art for print ads and posters
Screen credits	Often specified in talent contracts and union agreements
Cast list	
Technical crew list	
Movie trailer	35mm negative, print, and videotape master

Copyright: A Crucial Issue

Much of the documentary material you must provide the distributor is for the purposes of establishing and enforcing copyright. Your movie is private intellectual property, and it has commercial value only to the extent that your property rights will be honored.

As the recent history of the music business has shown, issues of copyright and copyright enforcement have been complicated greatly with the advent of digital copying and distribution technologies. In an effort to clarify these issues, the United States Congress passed the Digital Millennium Copyright Act (DMCA) of 1998. Unfortunately, but perhaps not surprisingly, the new law begs more questions than it answers.

For more information on the law, as well as for downloadable copyright forms, go to this Library of Congress Web page: www.copyright.gov. Original screenplays for unproduced movies for which there is one author can use Short Form PA (Performing Arts). Any collaborative dramatic work, such as adapted screenplays, motion pictures, and videos *must* use the Long Form PA. Line-by-line instructions are provided with each form.

As with all other legal aspects of movie production, rely on your entertainment lawyer for advice on protecting your copyright and making sure you don't infringe on the rights of others. And that's not only for ethical reasons—it's also good business practice to avoid complications that could prevent you from enjoying any profits you eventually see from your hard work.

Preparing Video Output for Different Distribution Media

With the negotiations behind you, it's time to consider the practical aspects of actually delivering content to distributors and exhibition venues.

OUTPUTTING 24FPS DV TO VIDEO

If you've edited your movie at 24fps, you'll have to output 60i NTSC from the NLE for use in any of the conventional video formats. This means, for example, shooting 24pa (Advanced Method) and then recovering the frames in the NLE by selecting 2:3:3:2 pulldown. The footage will then be converted yet again using 3:2 pulldown on output to 60i.

There are some exceptions, however. When you output to any of the streaming Internet formats using QuickTime, Windows Media Player, or RealPlayer, advanced options permit you to specify frame rates other than 30fps. Also, some DVD authoring applications give you the option of creating 24fps encoded MPEG-2. This avoids conversion to 60i before burning the disc and lets you fit a longer movie on a disc. The DVD player handles the conversion from 24fps to 60i for display. (For more information, see "Authoring a DVD," later in this chapter.")

Each release format has a different standard of quality, and each its own particular use. Your options are the following:

◆ Printing to tape
◆ Burning a CD
◆ Creating video files for the Internet
◆ Authoring and burning a DVD
◆ Tape-to-film transfer

Printing to Tape

In the days of analog video, most editing was done on tape, and making a copy was called *dubbing* (not to be confused with the same term used for ADR). Nowadays, outputting to tape from digital editing software is called *printing*. (Computer technicians call it *exporting*.)

> Use of the term *printing* for digital video copying implies that the result is another original, not a copy. However, analog *dubbing* implies a loss of quality. When you copy from one analog tape to another, signal strength diminishes slightly, and noise increases. A copy is therefore of lower quality than the original, and a copy of a copy is lower still. In the analog world, there's great emphasis on using first- or second-generation copies as masters. In the digital world, it's a pointless distinction.

Printing to tape from an NLE such as Final Cut Pro will take at least as long as the actual running time of your movie, possibly longer (see Figure 9.1). In general, the more special effects you've included in your movie, the longer it will take the computer to render the imagery before tape recording actually starts.

> If your movie is longer than the total running time (TRT) of the cassette format you're using, you'll have to create it as separate, shorter projects. (Don't use the long-play (LP) camcorder mode. You could lose data.) End each segment at an act break or intermission. Similarly, movies for television are typically divided into act breaks, where commercials are inserted. The ideal act break for TV is at a cliffhanger moment in the plot, which leaves the audience wanting to know what happens next—so they won't switch channels during the commercials. (Specs for act breaks will be included in the deliverables portion of your production contract. Ordinarily, there must be a 5sec slug between breaks, but they don't necessarily have to be on separate tapes.)

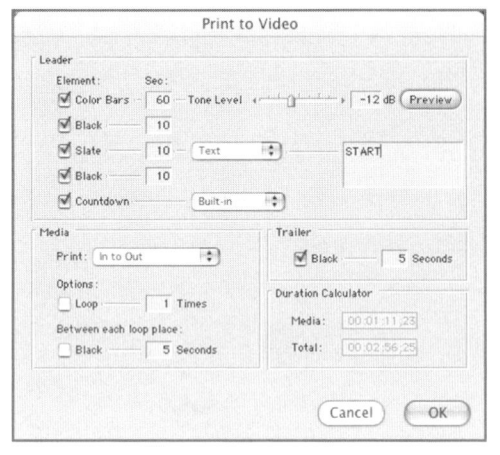

Figure 9.1
When you initiate the command File→Print to Video in Final Cut Pro to print your DV project to tape, you can select options for adding professional-spec head and tail leaders, including Color Bars and Tone (with adjustable level), Black frames, Slate (from typed text or from an external clip file), another sequence of Black, and a Countdown sequence (built-in or from an external file). In general, TV broadcasters and tape duplicators will want the color bars and tone, and film-out transfers will require the black-to-countdown sequence. (When preparing your final masters, use the FCP Edit to Tape command instead. The Avid command is Digital Cut, and other systems have different names for it.)

Copying a DV Cassette to VHS Tape

If your computer has a video output card, you may be able print your movie directly to analog videotape. For professional-quality results, rent a Betacam SP deck for this purpose. But even if your goal is just to create a VHS tape for your own reference, always print a DV cassette version first. Unless something goes weirdly wrong with the computer or the camcorder, or unless the tape itself is defective, the digital videotape will be an exact and error-free copy of your movie project. You can then use it as a duplicating master for making analog dubs. No matter how good your recording equipment, analog videotapes will always be poorer in quality than your digital masters.

> Among your print output options from the NLE, anything less than Full Quality DV format won't be suitable for broadcast, videotape duplication, or creating high-quality DVDs. It's also possible to dub from a DV cassette in the camcorder directly into a VHS tape machine, connecting the camcorder's composite video and audio outputs to the inputs of the recorder (see Figure 9.2).

Although VHS tapes seem to be disappearing from the video stores and so from our daily lives, an analog VCR makes a handy movie-duplication machine. A VHS dub is quick and inexpensive to make. If your prospect has an NTSC player, VHS tape is still an easy thing to provide.

> NLEs can output PAL or SECAM, as well. However, to create a tape, you'll need to rent a tape machine that will record in the format. Be warned that the conversion requires special plug-ins and a lot of rendering time. The alternative is to output NTSC and take it to a dub house for conversion, but that's an expensive solution.

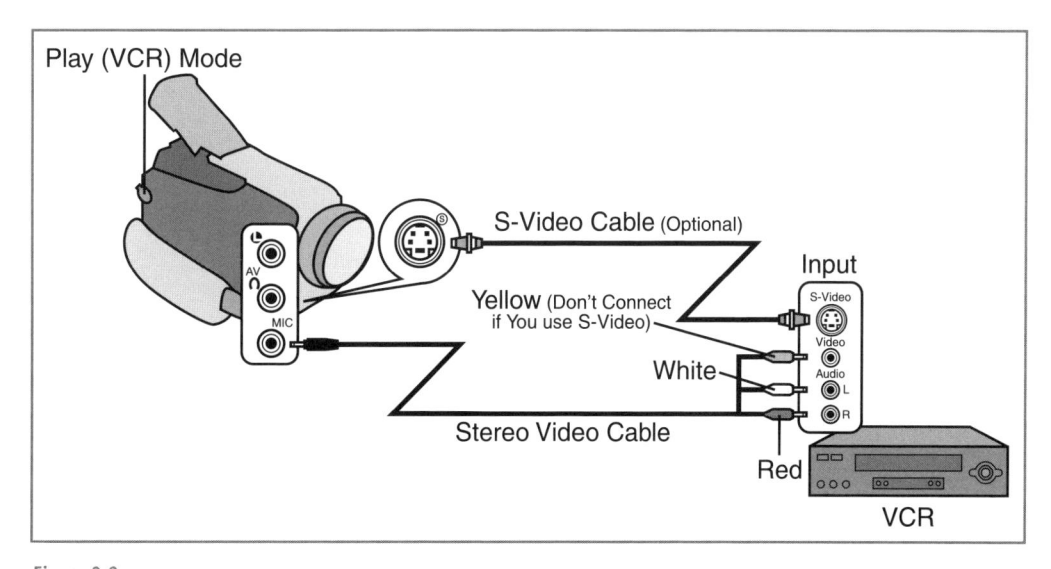

Figure 9.2
You don't have to use a high-end camcorder to make VHS dubs. A consumer-level model or a DV deck will do just as well. For example, the Canon ZR series has an AV cable with a three-contact mini plug on one end for insertion into the camcorder's AV jack, and three RCA plugs on the other for insertion into the VCR input jacks. If both the camcorder and the VCR are equipped with S-Video jacks, use that video connection instead and leave the yellow RCA plug disconnected at the VCR. You'll still need to connect the red and white audio plugs. (S-Video, also referred to as Y/C, gives a higher quality signal than composite video.)

Videotape Mastering for Duplication

To make more than a few VHS copies, you will need to retain the services of a video duplication facility, or dub house. These vendors can handle both mastering and copying.

A standard submission format for dubbing is a Sony Digibeta cassette, but if you have your show on some other format, they will charge you for the conversion. The maximum Digibeta cassette size is 120 minutes, so if your show is longer than 124 minutes you'll have to find a good break point to fit it onto two or more cassettes.

At the dub house, copying is master-to-slave. A master player controls a rack full of slave recorders, copying your movie onto tens or even hundreds of videocassettes at a time.

> You can create a Digibeta master yourself by renting a Sony deck for a day, but they are pricey. DVCPRO-50 is a less expensive format for both equipment and tape. See if your vendor will accept this format. To create an analog master for dubbing, it's also possible to submit your show on analog Sony Betacam SP.

These days, dubbing prices are highly competitive. Get several bids on your job, but don't necessarily choose the lowest price. The low bidder may be using cheap cassettes with substandard magnetic tape or plastic housings that break easily.

If you order thousands of tapes, allow several days for your order to be completed under normal turnaround. Rush charges will apply if you need them quicker, and at some point turnaround, even at premium rates, will be limited by the vendor's production capacity.

Burning a CD

If you've produced a short or a TV commercial, an alternative for making a quick copy that will play back on computers is to burn a CD-ROM. You start by outputting the movie project from the NLE to the hard drive as an Apple QuickTime Full Quality DV movie file. (Technically, Full Quality DV is defined as 30fps, 720×480 resolution, and high-quality 48kHz stereo sound.) You can then load a blank disc into the computer and simply drag and drop the file in the Finder to the CD icon on the desktop. (That's the Mac procedure. You can do it much the same way in Windows Explorer.) This will create a full-resolution video that can be played back on any computer with a QuickTime player, but the disc won't work in most DVD players and may be unreadable by some Windows PCs.

> For historical reasons nobody understands or cares about, a magnetic computer storage device, such as a hard drive, is spelled d-i-s-k, and the optical variety, such as a CD or a DVD, is a d-i-s-c. This distinction is so pointless that perhaps a decade from now there will be a single, standard spelling.

A typical CD can hold about 700MB—less than four minutes of full-quality DV, whereas a DVD can hold about 4GB. So if your computer can burn CDs but not DVDs, either your movie must be very short or you'll have to choose one of the video compression options, which reduces the quality of the movie and also the amount of storage required. "CD-ROM," one of the lower-quality QuickTime options, creates a file that's 20–30 times smaller than full-quality DV. However, it does this by printing every other frame (15fps), providing ¼ the screen resolution (320×240), and thankfully, leaving the stereo sound at CD quality (44.1kHz). This type of file will play back only on a computer that has QuickTime player installed.

So you could conceivably burn one reference-quality CD of compressed QuickTime for each reel of your movie.

> As an alternative to applying QuickTime compression, PC users can try Canopus ProCoder or Microsoft Windows Media Player Encoder.

> Most DVD drives are fast enough to play back a video directly from a CD. However, many CD drives aren't. If you load a CD into your computer and try to read it, the playback may be erratic. You'll see the video play for while, stop for a moment while the drive catches up, and then play will resume. To avoid this problem, copy the entire video file to your hard drive first; then play back the file you created.

Creating a VCD

A special CD format called *Video CD* (VCD) can hold a little more than an hour of movie, which it achieves using MPEG-1 compression. The resolution is about the same as QuickTime for CD-ROM—and so it's much less than full DV quality—but the VCD format has the advantage of being compatible with many DVD players, as well as most computers. This is another reference-quality alternative.

To create a VCD, you will need an application such as Roxio Toast Titanium. It has a plug-in for the NLE that permits you to output your movie directly to a disc in a conventional CD burner.

Creating Video Files for the Internet

As yet, there is no commercially viable distribution of movies over the Internet, but that situation will change eventually, perhaps sooner than later. (Pornography is a notable exception, but apparently lack of high video quality never prevented anyone from making money in that market.)

In the meanwhile, the Internet can be a kind of showcase, much as the festivals are. You can submit your short movie for exhibition on Atomfilms (http://atomfilms.shockwave.com/af/home), but you don't stand to gain financially except indirectly, by drawing attention to your talents.

There are three main video playback applications: Apple QuickTime, Windows Media Player, and RealNetworks RealPlayer. We'll discuss QuickTime because it's a fit with Final Cut Pro, but you have similar options with the other two.

Among the QuickTime formats, Full Quality DV is useful for archiving and mastering. CD-ROM is intended mainly for postcard-sized displays when playing back from a computer's local hard drive or over a high-speed network.

> A handy use of streaming video for filmmakers is as a compact file format for exchanging clips and dailies via the Internet and e-mail to facilitate your collaboration with members of your production team who may be at different locations.

Even more compressed QuickTime options are

- E-mail
- Web
- Web Streaming

E-mail. Of all the options, this one creates the smallest, lowest-quality files. The goal is compactness for sending as an e-mail attachment that will play back as a matchbox-sized display. The frame rate is a rather jerky 10fps, the resolution is 160×120, and the audio is reduced to a single track (mono). However, by this scheme, a three-minute movie can be squeezed into less than 2MB.

Web. Designed for posting on Web sites, this option can produce 12fps, 240×180 movies with medium-quality stereo sound. With this option, a three-minute movie compresses to about 4MB. (This is just one of several available data rates.) However, if you post a video file to a Web site in this format, the user may have to download the entire file before it starts to play. Generally, people aren't that patient. The alternative is to use the Web streaming option.

Web streaming. This option uses constant bit rate (CBR) encoding to deliver somewhat less quality than the Web option, but it adds compatibility with Internet servers that are specially designed to deliver video over lower-speed connections. Technically, the output process embeds hints in the QuickTime file that the QuickTime Streaming Server application can read. The hints are markers for starting and stopping the file transmission, doling it out in a series of data bursts, rather than as a continuous feed. If your Web hosting company supports streaming video (and many don't because it can overload their servers), they will probably require you to upload it in streaming format.

There are actually quite a few more flavors of streaming Web files you can create with QuickTime. You've undoubtedly noticed streaming sites that offer three separate versions of videos—each optimized for a different network speed. If you select Expert Settings for QuickTime compression, the options include optimized compressions for Modem–Audio Only, Modem, DSL/Cable (Low, Medium, or High speed), or LAN (such as a T1 corporate network). Of particular interest to 24fps filmmakers, you can further fine-tune the compression settings for frame rate, resolution, audio quality, and output file format—all of which give you alternatives, some better and some worse, than 60i. By manipulating the Expert Settings, you can even increase 60i output quality for a professional broadcast submission standard, such as DVCPRO-50.

Authoring a DVD

If you've tried your hand at DV production at all, you probably know that a DVD isn't like tape or like a CD-ROM—it's a complex and unique multimedia device. You can't just take a DV tape or movie file and copy it to DVD, as you can with a CD. (Actually, you can, but the result will be a data DVD, which will be playable only on a computer.)

The DVD format was designed about a decade ago as a kind of multimedia replacement for books. A DVD can store not only video, but also still pictures, digital music, and all kinds of audio files, as well as computer-generated documents and data files. What's more, a DVD can hold software programs that tell computerized players what to do with its content and how to react to choices users make. A computer-based DVD can even update its own content by accessing the Internet automatically, based on hyperlinks embedded in its programs.

Levels of DVD Players

A lesser-known feature of the DVD recording standard is player level, which describes the computerized capabilities of the playback device. Player level isn't crucial when you're creating feature-film DVDs for a mass audience, but if you want to innovate in the medium of interactive multimedia, the possibilities are endless.

DVD authors can specify player level to assure that players at multiple locations will respond to programming in the same way. The higher the level is, the more capable the player is of sophisticated, automated interactions with the user.

Consumer DVD players are Level 1 and allow the user to control playback of clips by selecting menu items with a keypad or remote control. Any disc intended for a mass audience should be targeted at Level 1 so that it will be compatible with as many players as possible. Levels 2–4 are computer based and permit complex interactions, including fetching programs automatically from Web locations, running different programs and displaying other complex behaviors based on user selections, storing results and user inputs and forwarding those files over the network, and so on.

Certainly, the full potential of the DVD medium hasn't been realized yet—and future generations of these devices are already being designed. There's no question—DVDs and their successor formats will play a major role in our daily lives. But futuristic speculation aside, as a media producer, you have to follow a special procedure to create a DVD that will play back reliably in both computers and set-top players.

DVD Structure

A major difference between DVDs and tapes or CDs becomes apparent as soon as you insert one in a player. The movie doesn't necessarily start when you press Play. You may see an on-screen menu instead. Each item on the menu represents a separate chapter on the DVD—and the term itself tells you that the designers of the DVD were thinking about the way books are organized.

> DVDs typically use compressed video files in the MPEG-2 variable bit rate (VBR) format. Although the compression causes some loss of quality over the original DV recordings, it's usually not apparent to viewers. Prior to authoring, you must convert your DV footage to MPEG-2. The Compressor application that comes with Final Cut Pro can do this, or you can use other third-party applications, either Mac or PC. In later versions of authoring applications such as iDVD or DVD Studio Pro, the conversion to MPEG-2 is done automatically.

In effect, each chapter is a separate movie. This book's companion DVD is organized that way—each chapter is a different short subject.

However, when all you want on your DVD is your lone movie project, the disc must still be divided into chapters. If you don't take pains to insert chapter markers in your movie, you'll end up with a one-chapter DVD.

> Some commercial DVDs will play an entire movie just as soon as you insert them in the player. Achieving this behavior is actually somewhat more complicated technically than creating a menu with chapters. The disc must contain a program that's set to play automatically, to suppress the menu display, and to ignore any chapter markers that might exist in the movie.

Even the term for building a DVD—*authoring*—harks back to its similarity to book organization. Although the authoring process can be quite complex, DVD authoring applications such as Apple DVD Studio Pro and Sony Digital DVD Architect give you the ability to create commercial-quality discs without much technical hassle.

If your movie is no longer than 10 minutes or so, dividing it into chapters is probably unnecessary. The movie itself will be one chapter and one DVD menu item. But for longer movies, and especially for documentaries and instructional videos, chapter organization can be very helpful to the user.

So your first step in authoring a DVD should be to embed chapter markers in your movie. You do this while you're still working in the NLE. Ideally, chapter markers should come at act breaks. If you're also preparing for film-out, the act breaks could coincide with reel changes.

It will rarely make sense to embed a chapter marker in the middle of a scene—unless you've deliberately created a pause in the action for this purpose. To find act breaks, think about how television movies are interrupted for commercials. A perfect act break completes a scene but leaves the audience eager to find out what happens next.

We're not going to cover all the details of authoring a DVD here. Suffice it to say that DVD Studio Pro and comparable applications include a wide variety of ready-made menus and behaviors (see Figure 9.3), which greatly simplifies the task. As is the case with NLE plug-ins, if you want to further customize the results, you can, but a lot more technical training and skill will be required.

Drop zones

Figure 9.3
If you're burning DVDs you'll use to show potential distributors, you don't need to build complicated menus. You can use an entry-level application like iDVD, which comes bundled with all recent-model Macs. Like the more sophisticated options in DVD Studio Pro, iDVD includes a set of prebuilt templates so that you don't have to build menus from scratch. You can drag media stills, video clips, and sound files onto the menu to create buttons or drop zones. A button is simply a menu selection that contains a link to the media clip that will be played when the user selects the button. A drop zone is a "hot spot" within the menu. If you drop a clip in a drop zone, it will play within that window when the menu is presented to the user. A drop zone is one way to create motion effects and other complex behaviors without much fuss.

As a final step in DVD authoring, you can set some restrictions on the distribution of the material. Your distributor may require one or more of these controls, which are intended to help preserve the commercial value of the movie and to discourage piracy.

Region code. The disc's region code defines its authorized geographic area of distribution. It specifies the default language and restricts playback to players that are preset by their manufacturers to a particular region code. The player will reject and won't play back a DVD that doesn't match its region-code setting.

And here's something that matters very much to distributors but is little known to the public: The region code helps them restrict home viewing of movies until after theatrical runs in the region. The region code also sets the default language track automatically, possibly also activating different trailers and ads.

Digital scrambling. You also have the option of scrambling, or encrypting, the disc data, thereby restricting playback to players with licensed decoding circuits. You can even be selective about which sectors of the disc will be encrypted, permitting some public copying, if you wish, of just those portions. Copying discs is also made difficult by encryption. This Contents Scrambling System (CSS) is a joint effort by the Motion Picture Association of America (MPAA, www.mpaa.org) and the DVD Copy Control Association (DVDCCA, www.dvdcca.org). Even though you set this option prior to burning a disc, the encryption isn't applied at that time. It's activated and applied by the disc duplication service, which operates under a CSS license.

Analog copy protection. An option that helps prevent copying from DVD to analog videotape is called the *Analog Protection System* (APS). To use it when you author your disc, you must buy a license from Macrovision (www.macrovision.com). Applying APS causes the DVD player to add electronic noise to its analog video output. The frequency is such that TV sets don't pick up the noise. VCRs have a circuit that detects it and generates interference with recording.

Disc Manufacturing Considerations

You can choose to replicate your discs either by burning or pressing. Here are the main considerations.

Blank discs sold for use in computer-based burners are generally ss/sl (single-side/single-layer), although dual-layered burners are beginning to appear on the market. DVDs with a capacity for feature-length movies, which can hold about 2.4 hours of video, are designated DVD-9 and are ss/dl (single-side/dual-layer). With the exception of a few high-priced burners, the plastic layers must be bonded together in a DVD pressing plant. Sandwiching the two layers doubles the disc's capacity. One side of a single-sided disc faces the laser head of the player, and a label can be printed on the unused side.

To get dual-sided disc copies, which further increases capacity, you must retain the services of a disc duplicator. The DVD-10 discs designated ds/sl (dual-side/single-layer) hold about 2.6 hours of video, and ds/dl (dual-side/dual-layer), or DVD-18, holds 4.7 hours. Double-sided discs can't have large labels because the laser must be able to read both sides. The duplicator can print a small amount of text on the blank inner ring of the disc, just enough for a title and no more.

As this book goes to press, there is no generally accepted optical disc standard for HDTV. Proposed technologies include the Sony Blue Laser (see Figure 9.4), part of a proposed consortium standard labeled Blu-rayDisc. Toshiba, NEC, and a group of other manufacturers have announced a competing standard, HD DVD, that bears a closer resemblance to conventional DVDs and might be a more economical retrofit to existing equipment at pressing plants.

Figure 9.4
Intended for use as an HD distribution medium, the Sony Blue Laser is a 5.25-inch optical disc housed in an airtight cassette to prevent dust contamination. The recorder/player uses a gallium nitride laser operating in the blue-violet end of the light spectrum. The laser creates ultra-thin tracks, yielding a storage capacity of about 25GB per single-layer disc, or 50GB for dual-layer. (Photo courtesy Sony Electronics, Inc.)

If you need thousands of copies, you'll be dealing with a pressing plant, and as with videotape duplication, you should get several bids. As a rule of thumb, preparing the glass master from which the plastic discs are pressed is fairly expensive, costing several thousands of dollars, which means that each disc costs at least a few bucks.

Need to find a disc duplicator? Do a Web search for "dvd pressing" or "dvd replication." You also might want to consider low-volume on-demand duplication. The service holds your video master and burns DVDs only when you or your customers order them, even if the quantity is just a few. For further information, see CustomFlix, www.customflix.com.

Some duplication services can handle relatively short runs of DVDs because they use a burning process that doesn't require preparation of a glass master. They use a master-to-slave process, much like videotape duplication, and jukebox-style burners. These industrial burners can burn CDs as well as DVDs and can even intermix different shows in the same batch. (For further information, see the Rimage burners at www.rimage.com.)

When you finish the authoring process in DVD Studio Pro, the final step is called a *build*. Even with a fast computer, the process is much like DV rendering: The build can take a long time, perhaps a very long time. Remember also that, if you're dealing with a pressing plant, the submission format is not necessarily a finished DVD, which you might not be able to burn yourself, anyway. The common requirement is to prepare a Digital Linear Tape (DLT), which might require you to rent one of those tape drives, or it might be possible to ship a FireWire drive to the vendor.

> When you burn discs yourself, just as with videocassettes, don't buy the cheapest stock you can find. Ultra low-priced discs may be unreliable.

Archiving Your Project

Once you've output your movie to tape or disc, don't blow your project files off the hard drive just yet. While the recording or file you create by printing to tape or saving to disk might be full-quality DV, it will serve you well as a duplication master, but it's not an editable version of your project. If you want to make changes later—adjusting scene in and out points or incorporating ADR, for example—you'll have to load the original project files back into the editing program.

To ensure that you can return to edit your project at some future date, you must archive the project and all its supporting files. An excellent and inexpensive storage medium is an external FireWire drive.

> In the NLE, we recommend backing up the entire project folder in a single operation to a data storage area that's large enough to hold it. If your movie is short, a single data DVD (4GB capacity) might work. But backing up files in groups to a series of CDs, while it's possible, might well cause unnecessary headaches later when you try to reopen the project and import the files into your NLE. If you don't have sufficient storage space, be sure to at least save the project file, which is essentially an EDL. This file contains pointers to all the original camcorder timecodes and can be used to recapture the clips later, as long as you keep the cassettes. (You'll be more successful rebuilding your edit from a project file if you saved all your clips in the same project folder initially.)

Submitting to Broadcast Television Networks

Preparing digital videotape for submission to a network is every bit as complex as dealing with a motion-picture distributor, but there are some important differences. If the network retained you under a production contract, the network's current Programming department, which is less concerned about content than with receiving your show in good order by a specific airdate, will administer it. Another influential department is Standards and Practices, which will make sure that your documentation, including copyrights, releases, and clearances, is adequate.

24P: Make Your Digital Movies Look Like Hollywood

From a technical standpoint, your key customer is the Broadcast Engineering department. They want your tapes delivered just so. Typical specs are

- Video: 4:2:2 color space, not more than 80 percent saturated, no noisy edges, lower-third and safe-title areas correct with readable text, and aspect ratio (4:3 or 16:9 letterbox)
- Color bars, slate, tone, and countdown at the head of each tape (they will give you specs for this)
- Titles and credits with correct name spellings and following contract requirements
- Split audio tracks: dialogue on 1 and 2, music and effects on 3 and 4
- Act breaks as the network specifies, with slates
- Preferred digital media: Digibeta or DVCPRO-50 tape cassette (Betacam SP if analog)

Producing for a Corporation

If you are producing for a corporation, the Marketing and Communications, or "marcom," department will contract for your work. They are responsible for creation and approval of all media materials produced for customers, stockholders, and the general public. The department employs lawyers, marketing executives, and public relations experts. Advertising and public relations may be separate departments, and they may subcontract to outside agencies. The actual purchase of broadcast airtime for commercials is usually done by an advertising agency. The agency performs the extensive accounting required to verify viewership and airtimes and also pays royalties to actors and spokespersons.

In any case, legal and technical requirements will be specified in your contract. However, as a professional producer, you will be expected to know and adhere to industry standards, such as following broadcast-legal specs for videotapes. These specs might or might not be spelled out in the contract.

Working with a Film Recording Service

If your goal is film out, the ideal approach is to select your transfer service before you shoot. Digital tape-to-film transfer is a very specialized process. There aren't that many vendors to choose from, and each of them has its own proprietary methods. For this reason, there isn't any single set of technical specifications to follow.

> We see little point in making a 16mm transfer, although some vendors provide this service. No commercial distributors release in this format anymore, and blowing 16mm up to 35mm at a film lab will be just as expensive as doing a DV-to-35mm transfer in the first place, with a poorer-quality result. If your purpose in making a 16mm print is to prove how your product will look on film, making a film-look video or paying for a few short 35mm test prints of selected shots will serve the same purpose at much less expense.

These vendors will all give advice on which camcorders and settings you should use, how you should light, and how you should prepare your edited videotape masters. They will also quote rates for processing test footage so you can see results in advance and plan your shooting accordingly. You'll also find some preliminary technical information (including Frequently Asked Questions) on their Web sites. Some of the vendors who have experience with DV conversion include:

- Deluxe Efilm (www.efilm.com)
- DuArt (www.duart.com)
- DVFilm (www.dvfilm.com)
- FotoKem (www.fotokem.com)
- Swiss Effects (www.swisseffects.ch)

Some of these Web sites include movie credits, and studying how other filmmakers did it, particularly viewing the finished product in a theater, is as good a place as any to begin.

But aside from your impressions of the aesthetic result, your selection of a film recording service ultimately will have to weigh trade-offs of cost and quality. In those matters, we can give you some specific advice.

Transferring a two-hour movie from DV tape to 35mm film will cost from $10,000–$80,000. The main cost factor is the film recording hardware itself. The more expensive the recording equipment, the more the service has to charge to recover its investment and make a profit. There are three basic categories of cost and sophistication in film transfer technology. In order of increasing cost and quality, these are the following:

- Kinescope
- Flying spot
- Laser

Kinescope

With its origins in the early days of television before the advent of videotape recording, the kinescope process uses a motion-picture camera to photograph a movie as it plays on a television screen. These days, the television screen is a hi-def plasma or LCD panel.

Recording is done in real time, as the taped version of the movie rolls on a video deck. However, the actual service will take longer, due to time needed for setup, reel changes, loading of film magazines, and film processing. The camera must use a wide lens opening and fast film stock, which can cause some optical distortion at the edges of the picture and undesirable graininess in the image.

The plasma TV monitor may perform frame doubling, which helps fill in scan lines. But other than that, the process has no way of enhancing the quality of the image over what you'd see when playing back a tape on the average big-screen TV. Since theatrical movie screens are so much larger, the result simply won't have the required spatial resolution, and either scan lines will be visible or the image will simply look too soft.

For a two-hour movie, a kinescope will cost about $10,000 to $15,000 and will take a few days.

Because of its relatively low quality, movie distributors generally will not regard kinescope transfers as commercial-quality output.

Flying Spot

The scanning beam of a high-resolution cathode ray tube (CRT), much like a conventional TV picture tube, is called a *flying spot*. In this process (see Figure 9.5), the glowing spot paints each frame very slowly on the face of the tube, in three scanning passes—once for each primary color (red, green, and blue). Every frame is a photographic triple exposure. Scanning options are 1,024 (1K), 2K, and 4K horizontal scanning lines per frame. The lowest resolution (1K) is somewhat less than that of the 35mm film grain, so it's theoretically possible for scan lines to be visible. A resolution of 2K is a good match for the resolution of film, and 4K more nearly matches the resolution of 70mm film.

A manufacturer of flying spot film recorders is Celco (www.celco.com).

In practice, 1K resolution on 35mm is pretty good and much better with today's technologies than it was just a decade ago. The transfer service may be able to use frame-doubling software to enhance the resolution and eliminate scan lines. Also, the glowing, soft edge of the spot actually helps to blur the boundaries between scan lines. Since the recording process is relatively slow compared to kinescope, standard motion-picture film stocks can be used, giving excellent sharpness and detail.

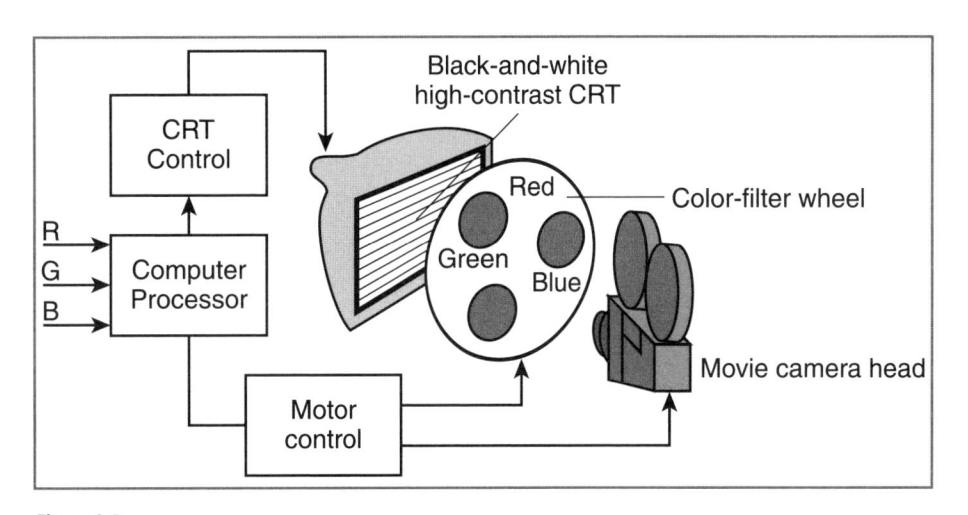

Figure 9.5
A computer film recorder builds up a film image in three progressive scans on a high-contrast black-and-white CRT. Different primary color filters rotate into position on each pass to record red, green, and blue. Laser film recorders operate on the same principle, except there's no screen, and the laser etches the image directly onto the surface of the film in the camera.

Older flying-spot recorders took about a minute to record each film frame. Transfers took a minimum of a couple of weeks, with the recorders cranking night and day. Today's CRT recorders operate at 1 sec/frame at 1K. Transfers at 1K and 2K can cost about $350 per minute of running time, or about $40,000 for a feature. The 4K option is typically used for 65mm IMAX or 70mm transfers from HD masters and costs about twice as much, or about $80,000.

Laser

There's a heated debate in the industry as to whether laser is superior to flying spot. For transferring DV to 35mm, we think it's a toss-up. The laser process is similar in concept, painting each frame three times, once for each primary color, except the laser beam etches the image directly on the film. Laser film recorders operate at 2K or 4K resolutions. You can read more about this technology at the Web sites of the laser-recorder manufacturers:

- Arri (www.arri.com)
- Cineon (www.cineon.com)

At equivalent resolutions of 1K, 2K, or 4K, flying spot and laser transfers are comparable as to cost, quality, and turnaround time. As a broad generalization, we suspect your critical eye will favor flying spot at 1K, laser at 4K. In between, at the 2K resolution used for most commercial-quality 35mm transfers, perhaps the quoted price will be the deciding factor.

Even though newer film recorders are relatively fast, you should allow two to four weeks for the film transfer, not because of the speed of recording but because the transfer service will be juggling other jobs.

Summary of Film-Out Technical Requirements

Here are some generalizations about shooting 24p and submitting to a film transfer service. At minimum, this summary will put you on the right track and give you an appreciation of what's involved. But don't use it as a bible. Work closely with the vendor to tailor your shooting and editing to their proprietary process.

Since you have so much control over output quality in editing and postproduction, use that to your advantage. If you're intending distribution on both film and video, make two DV masters: one for the film transfer service and the other for the broadcast engineers.

Aspect ratio. Shoot in the aspect ratio that's native to the camcorder chipset. Since you're going for wide-screen film release, shoot in 16:9 if that's the format of the camcorder's CCDs. If you must shoot in 4:3, the next best thing is to shoot with an anamorphic lens. If you don't do that, shoot 4:3 and leave some air top and bottom in your framing; then apply letterbox format in postproduction.

Focus. This is the perhaps the most visibly critical factor. Any slight softness you see on the monitor on the set or in the editing suite will become decidedly blurred on the wide screen. Your tools for assuring sharpness when you're shooting are a camcorder with a B&W viewfinder, a camcorder monitor with good resolution and contrast, and never relying on autofocus (except perhaps to engage it briefly when you're zoomed in all the way, but don't trust it blindly).

Frame rate. Shoot in 24p Advanced (24pa) if the camcorder has that mode, with the Vertical Detail set to Thin. Recover the 24fps imagery in the NLE before you assemble your clips, using the 2:3:3:2 scheme to remove pulldown and deinterlace. Convert to 60i as a last step on output. If you shoot in 60i, edit in 60i and apply Magic Bullet as a finishing step in After Effects. If you apply Magic Bullet to convert frame rate, don't convert back to 60i; submit the .AEP (rendered at 24fps) uncompressed animation file with square pixels to the transfer service. And don't ever shoot in 30p (called *Movie Mode* on some camcorders) and expect a transfer service to convert it to film. Other permissible non-DV file formats for submission to transfer services include QuickTime 5 and Windows Media 9 at 24fps. (Normal DV pixels are rectangular. The postproduction application should be able to convert them to squares.)

Camcorder settings. For 60i footage, $\frac{1}{60}$ sec shutter speed should capture frames cleanly so that the shutter isn't opening or closing in mid-frame. For 24p shooting, use a shutter speed of $\frac{1}{48}$ if available, otherwise $\frac{1}{50}$. (On some camcorders, a shutter speed that matches the frame rate is the same as Shutter=Off.) Don't use the semi-automatic Aperture Priority mode, which will let the camcorder vary the shutter speed to suit your manual f-stop setting and could auto-select shutter speeds that will cause noticeable flickering.

Color space. If the DV camcorder shoots 4:1:1, there's no need to convert to 4:2:2 in postproduction as long as your goal is getting film out rather than broadcast video. Since film can render more colors than video CCDs can capture, you don't have to restrict the video color space in any way. In general, the best color correction for film will be the way the shots look to your eye. In doing DV color correction in post, your priorities should be people's faces first, foliage second, sky third. If you're shooting a commercial that features someone's product, it moves to the top of the list. (Glamour shots of food are particularly troublesome.) Be aware that contrast will increase, and colors may shift toward the primaries. In particular, be cautious about reds getting redder on film. Flesh tones may look rosier, but that might not be the effect you intend.

Film-look effects. Save these for your video output you want to look *like* film. For example, there's no point in adding film grain effect, since the film product will have its own grain, and you don't want to compound the effect unpredictably. Adding jitter would also be a bad idea. Exceptions would be video clips for which you deliberately want to exaggerate the effects so that they look like an old kinescope or aged film. The motion blur of shooting (or finishing) at 24p and your Hollywood-style craftsmanship will make it onto the film.

Titles. This requirement varies a lot from one transfer house to another. Some want your titles incorporated into the video master. Others want them on separate reels. Some will offer to do optical or CGI titles for you and therefore don't want to see them on your video track. If the service adds the titles optically, you might submit them typeset on high-contrast Kodalith sheets. If they create CGI titles, they will probably want a computer graphics file, such as an Adobe Photoshop file, that contains the entire scroll as a single tall image, rather than as a succession of frames.

Reels. Divide the show into reels, each no longer than 20min, although they can be shorter—not much shorter, though, or you will unnecessarily increase the cost of creating an optical soundtrack. As we've said, choose the act breaks as dramatic cliffhangers. Avoid spanning the break with dialogue, music, sound effects, or visual transition effects such as fades. Otherwise, there could be a noticeable interruption at the break.

Soundtracks. At the end of each reel, you must provide about 2sec of the beginning of the audio track for the next reel. (The actual requirement is 0.8sec, but add some extra.) This segment is called *audio pull-up*, and it's needed because, in a movie projector, the sound pickup head is located 20 frames behind the projector gate, which causes the cutover point between picture and sound to be out of sync during reel change. The transfer service may permit the soundtrack to be on your DV master recording (rather than on separate reels). A standard audio format would be four tracks: 1 (dialogue stereo Left), 2, (dialogue stereo Right), 3 (mixed music and effects, stereo Left), and 4 (mixed music and effects, stereo Right). The DV will only hold four tracks, so if you're producing for Surround Sound, the soundtracks will have to be on separate reels. For example, a 12-track ProTools file could contain the six tracks of dialogue and six tracks of mixed music and effects required for Surround Sound 5.1. Submit separate soundtrack reels on CD or on a FireWire drive. The transfer service shouldn't put an optical soundtrack on the master negative. Even at the film stage, a good reason to keep picture and sound on separate reels is that soundtrack requirements for theatrical release prints vary by type of projection system. For example, Dolby SR encodes stereo on an optical track of the release print. Another format, DTS (Digital Theater Systems), is used primarily for 70mm distribution and puts the audio on separate optical discs. If necessary, the film lab will combine the master negative and the soundtrack on the internegative they create prior to release printing.

Speed changes. If you shoot and edit at 60i and then apply frame-rate acceleration or deceleration in digital post, you will almost certainly see some tearing in the 24fps film transfer. If your movie relies on speed changes, a better approach would be to shoot and edit in 24p, apply the speed changes in After Effects and don't convert back to 60i, but submit the .AEP file to the transfer service. This way, if you do interpolation or frame blending in After Effects, you'll be able to inspect the frames for tearing before you output the file, and since the frame-to-frame transfer is 1-to-1, no tearing should occur.

Head and tail leaders. Each DV reel must be preceded and followed by a specified sequence of black video frames, sound beep, and slates. The exact specifications will probably be unique to each transfer service.

An overview of the basic steps in the digital tape-to-film transfer process is shown in Figure 9.6.

Several of the film transfer services are divisions of film laboratories, which can simplify the process of coordinating their efforts. Eventually, the lab must combine picture negative, soundtrack, and titles in an optical printing process to create a color master positive. For release printing, the lab will then make several color duplicating negatives, each of which will wear out eventually from the process of striking prints (refer again to the bottom portion of Figure 9.6).

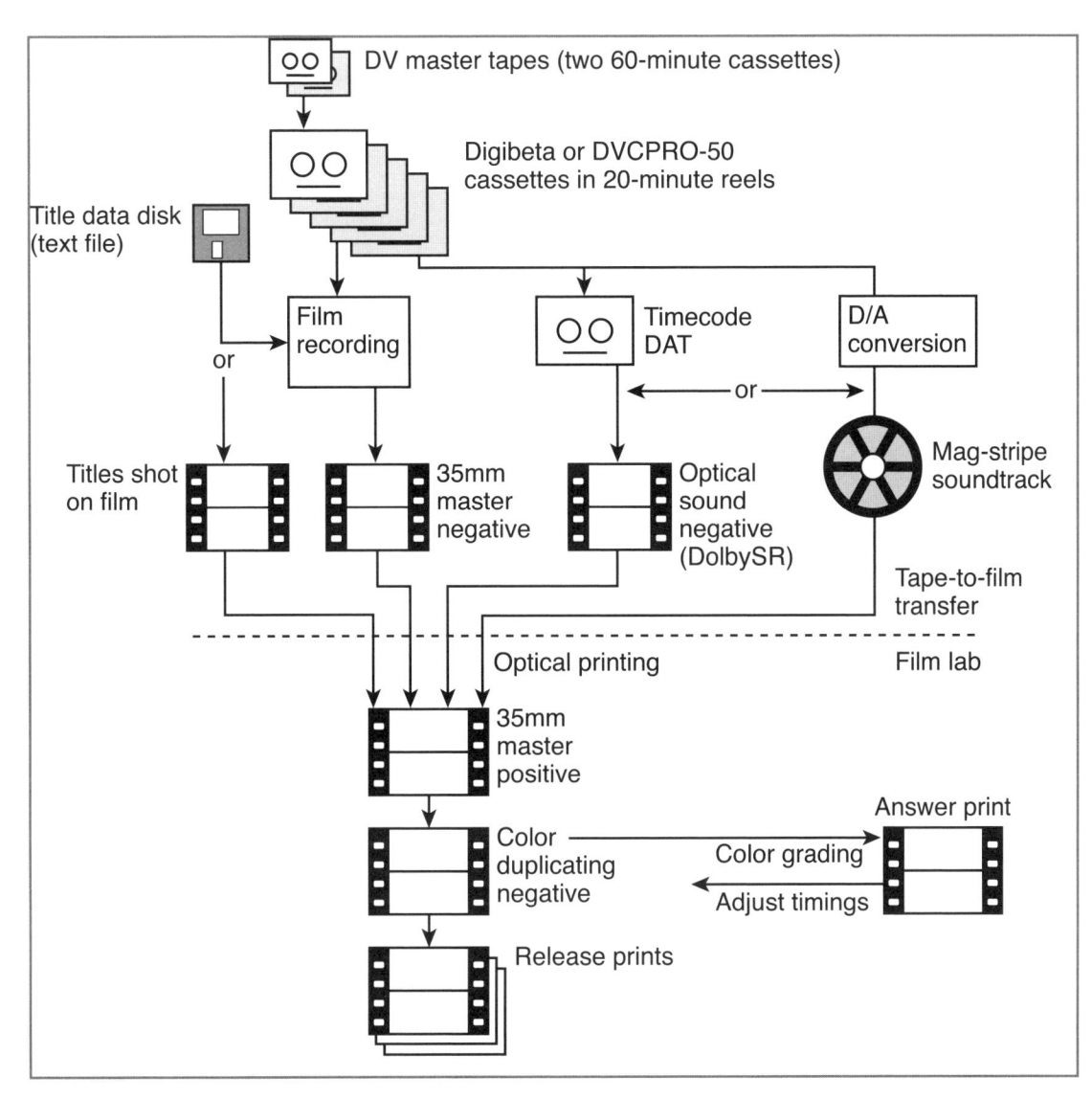

24P: Make Your Digital Movies Look Like Hollywood

Figure 9.6
In this diagram, the division line separates the workflows in the film transfer process and at the lab. Branched lines in the flow indicate some of your options, such as providing titles as computer files or as film positives, as well as outputting an optical soundtrack on film or a mag-stripe master. Your life will be a lot less complicated if the film transfer service is a division of a film laboratory or, at least, if they have a solid track record of working closely with one another.

9. Thinking Like a Distributor

193

Before you (or the distributor) authorize the making of release prints, the lab will send you one or more answer prints. You may want to do some final color correction at this point. The lab can perform color grading, in which the color cast, or overall tint, can be adjusted from scene to scene. The lab can also control the timing of prints, which varies the intensity of light used for printing each scene.

Welcome to Showbiz

When your distribution deal is signed and your negative is in the can, you will have traversed the boundary between aspiring filmmaker and cinema hotshot. Especially if you've managed to use the distributor's money to make the negative, you should be feeling pretty good about yourself.

One thing that's in short supply in Hollywood is humility. Yes, you absolutely deserve to be proud of successfully navigating the technical maze that connects the New World of digital video to the mysterious regions of the Celluloid Masters.

Just remember, those kids down the block who are shooting their skateboard movie with a borrowed camcorder have a huge advantage you didn't. By the time they're ready to shoot their break-in commercial movies, film distribution will almost certainly be a thing of the past.

They will never spend a penny for film transfer, and they will never be frustrated by the idiosyncrasies of this hybrid process. (Read more about their future, and yours, in the next chapter.)

Oh, and we started this chapter by promising we'd acquaint you with how a movie distributor thinks. That mindset isn't complete unless you know the showman's creed, a core belief they've held about ticket takers for centuries:

"You'll never get an honest count."

> Director John Huston experimented with film-based color correction in at least three of his features. In *Moulin Rouge* (1952), he attempted to mimic the garish colors used by painter Henri de Toulouse-Lautrec and gave the film a sensual, rosy tint. *Moby Dick* (1956) was dismal in color, faded almost to monochrome, having the vintage look of Currier & Ives prints of the nineteenth century, many of which depicted whale-hunting scenes. *Reflections in a Golden Eye* (1967) was adapted from novelist Flannery O'Connor's murky venture into the subconscious of forbidden impulses and overheated libidos. Huston gave that film a golden sepia dreaminess. The result was so odd that audiences hated it, many demanding their money back, thinking they'd seen a damaged print. However, *Reflections* and *Moby Dick* are being re-released on DVD with cinematographer Oswald Morris's camera-original colors. Interestingly, it was the release prints that were colored in the lab. Both negatives were left unchanged, making possible new full-color releases that might cause Huston's ghost to look down with the trademark scowl he wore so often in life!

chapter 10
Thinking Ahead

If you want to start a riot in Hollywood, shout from the rooftops:

"Film is dead! Long live film look!"

Seven Predictions About the Future of Digital Filmmaking

We might be wrong about some of these, but we're more than happy to offer them as further thought-provokers, discussion-starters, and career-planning hints:

Digital projection in theaters will eliminate the need for distribution of film release prints.

It's just a matter of when. There are at least three technologies competing for the retrofit of every commercial theater in the world (and for the construction of new ones): Digital Light Processing (DLP) developed by Texas Instruments, Digital Direct Drive Image Light Amplifier (D-ILA) from JVC, and Silicon X-tal Reflective Display (SXRD) from Sony.

DLP uses an array of microscopically small mirrors on a proprietary chip to vary the pixel values of a bright, reflected beam of light. Theatrical DLP projectors capable of illuminating giant screens are available in 1K and 2K resolutions and include the Barco DP100 (see Figure 10.1) and the Christie CP2000 (see Figure 10.2). These projectors are priced between $80,000 and $100,000, so a multiplex that needs a dozen of them will make quite an investment, but not necessarily more than buying and maintaining film projectors.

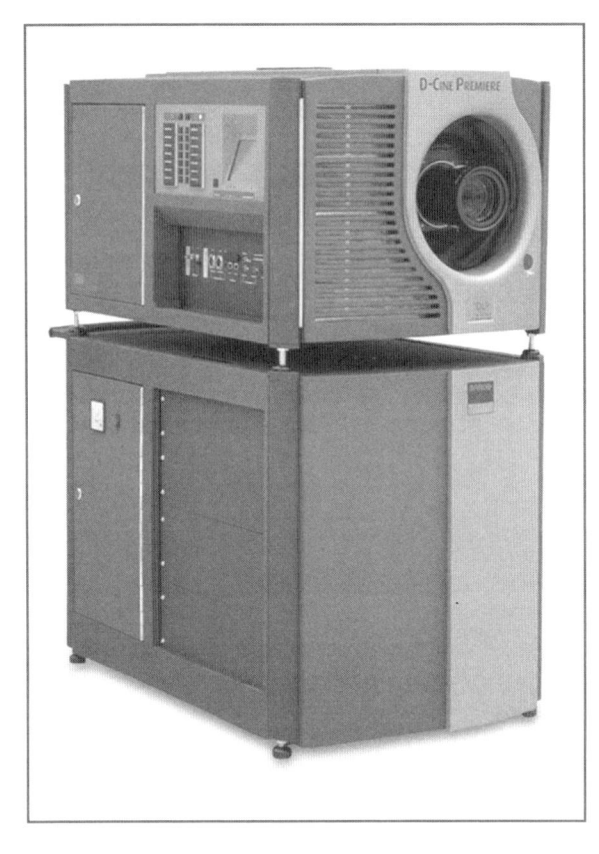

Figure 10.1
The Barco DP100 is a DLP theatrical projector with 2K resolution that is already installed in many commercial venues. (Photo courtesy Barco N.V.)

Figure 10.2
Christie Digital Systems also sells film projectors and control systems and claims it has more experience in the exhibition business than other manufacturers. Its CP2000 DLP theatrical projector offers 2K resolution and compatibility with the company's computer-based theatrical control networks. (Photo courtesy Christie Digital Systems, Inc.)

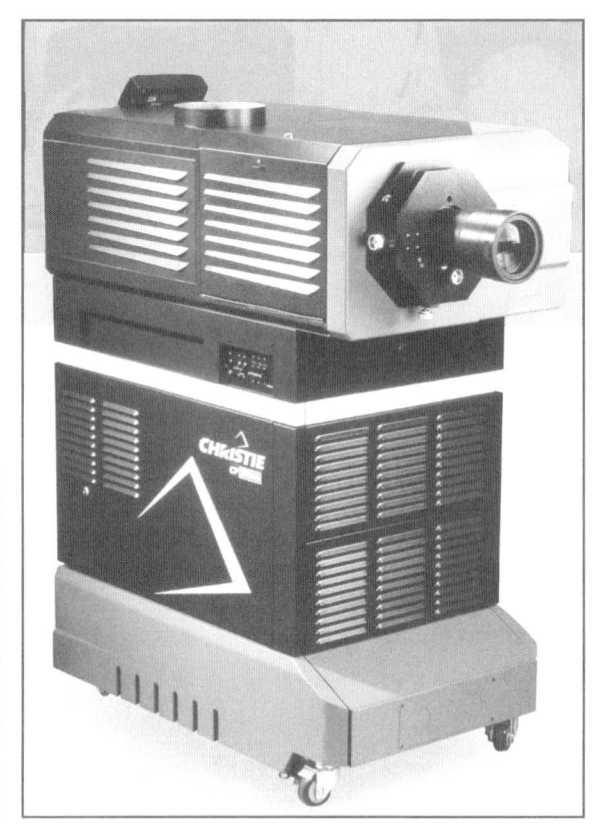

D-ILA and SXRD are both LCOS (liquid crystal on silicon) chip technologies, which essentially do the same thing DLP does—control the reflection of an intense light beam pixel-by-pixel. Kodak has endorsed D-ILA as its favored technology, and the same company that supplies most of the release prints to theaters worldwide is bidding actively to replace motion-picture projectors with D-ILA units.

D-ILA resolution is about 2K currently, and it's competitive with DLP. However, an industry consortium of movie studios and manufacturers has set the bar somewhat higher. This group, Digital Cinema Initiatives, LLC (DCI), has announced that the resolution required to meet or exceed audience expectations is 4096×2160 pixels. So far, only Sony claims to have reached this level and demonstrated it by introducing the SRX-R110 projector with 4K resolution (see Figure 10.3).

We've already described how the huge expense and difficult logistics of shipping film reels to theaters will eventually cost-justify the retrofitting of theaters. However, there's another huge financial consideration, one not discussed as openly with the public—the cost of employing highly skilled projectionists to operate and maintain motion-picture projectors, which are complex electromechanical systems. The all-digital theater will be networked, linking not only all the projectors and program schedules under software control, but also incorporating point-of-sale (POS) booking and ticketing systems and even driving flat-panel displays in the lobby that replace paper movie posters with rotating publicity stills and video clips.

All-digital theaters of the future are already designed, and much of the gear is on the market, if any theater owner-operator is ready to take the plunge. Here's how Kodak proposes for the theater of the future to be controlled by an integrated digital network (see Figure 10.4).

Figure 10.3
The Sony SRX-R110 digital projector is the first to offer 4K image resolution. This model is designed for corporate boardrooms and private theaters. (Photo courtesy Sony Electronics, Inc.)

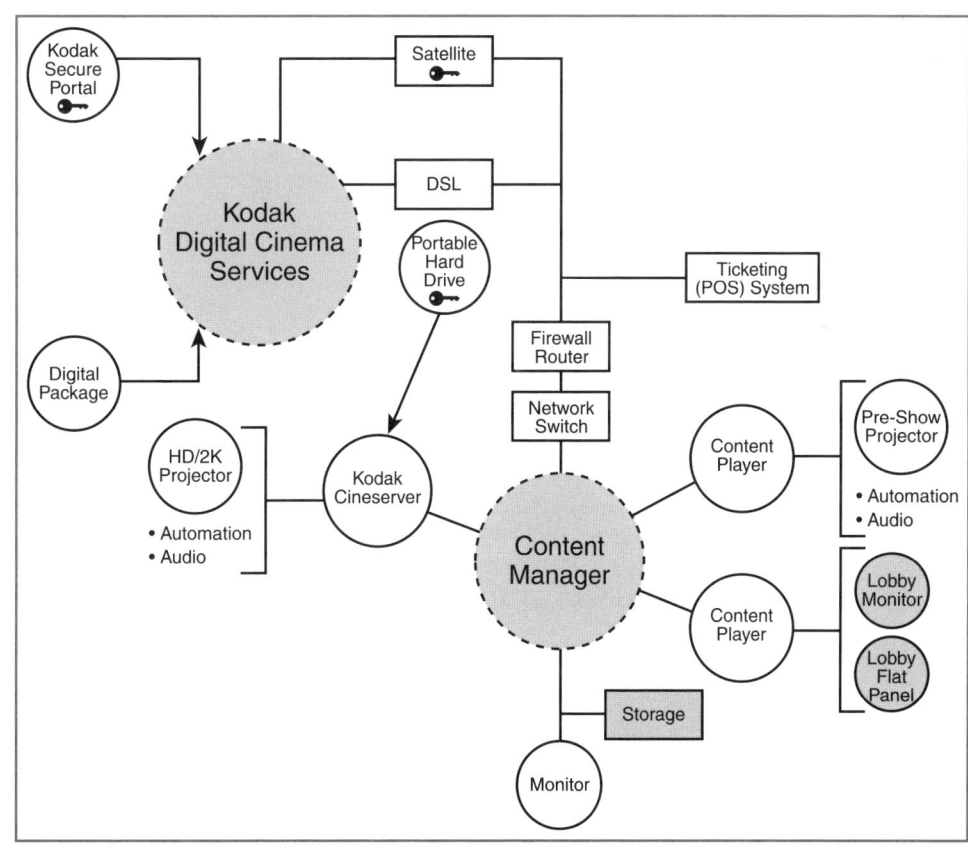

Figure 10.4
Kodak's vision for networked theater operations integrates satellite or broadband distribution, multiple software-controlled digital projection and show scheduling, automated point-of-sale (POS) systems, and even electronic posters in the lobby. (Courtesy Eastman Kodak Company)

Shooting on film will be around longer than film projectors.

Although some industry observers speculate that audiences and theater owners will decide that 2K digital resolution is "good enough," we don't think that's likely. With both the DCI and the Society of Motion Picture and Television Engineers (SMPTE) endorsing 4K as the Holy Grail, that's where we're headed. As we discussed in Chapter 9 in our description of the film-out process, the software that drives computer film recorders is already capable of converting DV and HD originated video to 1K, 2K, or even 4K resolution. Granted, DV to 4K is a stretch, but we're talking about the future here.

For the high-end product, equivalent to 70mm film, the acquisition technology may be film for some years to come. When digital video reaches the threshold of 4K (or even 2K) in the camera, you'll know the end is near. And until the contrast range of CCDs improves, some film artisans will simply refuse to make the switch (but they will have to argue harder to justify their funding).

An emerging chip technology to watch closely is the Foveon X3 direct image sensor, a camera chip that its developers claim captures light more nearly the way film does (see Figure 10.5). Technically, it's not a charge-coupled device (CCD) but a complementary metal oxide semiconductor (CMOS). The chip's thin sandwich of layers uses the principle that the three primary colors penetrate and can be sensed by the chip at different depths. The result is a single-chip design with high resolution. The 10.2 megapixel model of the X3 has a resolution of 2268×1512, much sharper than the sharpest HD picture. So far, the chip can be found only in still cameras. (For more information, see www.foveon.com.)

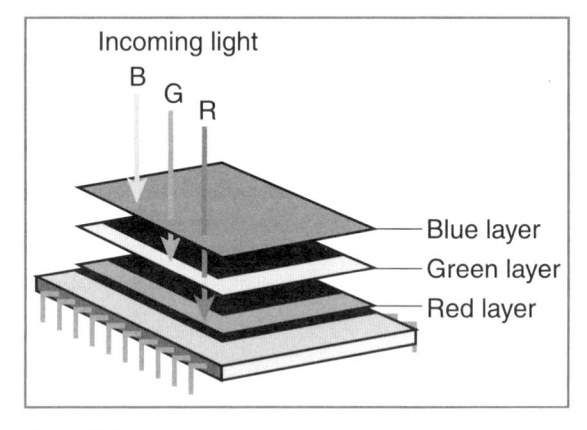

Figure 10.5
The Foveon X3 CMOS camera sensor uses a multilayered light-capturing scheme that resembles the layering of the photosensitive grain on film emulsion.

Camcorder and NLE technology will follow Moore's Law.

Now that moviemaking technology centers on the silicon chip, it's joined the same rocketship ride that turned the IBM 360 (a computer that filled a room in the 1960s) to the Mac G5, the first personal computer to have a 64-bit processor (same size as the 360 had).

Back in 1965, when those 360s were still humming, Intel executive Gordon Moore made the prediction that the number of transistors on a silicon chip would double every 18 months or so. Trade journalists dubbed his speculation "Moore's Law." It has held true for decades, and this growth shows no signs of relenting (see Figure 10.6).

Moore's Law is particularly applicable to the future of moviemaking technology for several reasons. The main challenge facing camcorder manufacturers today is not the resolution of the chips (witness the Foveon), but the processing power and recording bandwidth of camcorder circuitry. For example, the Thomson Grass Valley Viper camera with its 4:4:4 HD color space puts out a gush of data that can only be captured on an array of hard drives. In the years ahead, that capability must be shrunk to briefcase size and smaller so it will all fit inside the camcorder housing.

The further evolution of microcircuits will also greatly improve the "smarts" of digital camcorders. Yes, we've advised you to turn off those automatic camcorder controls. That's because, at this point, they can't begin to match the accuracy of skilled manual operation. But that will change. Autofocus and automatic image stabilization, in particular, will get better—much better.

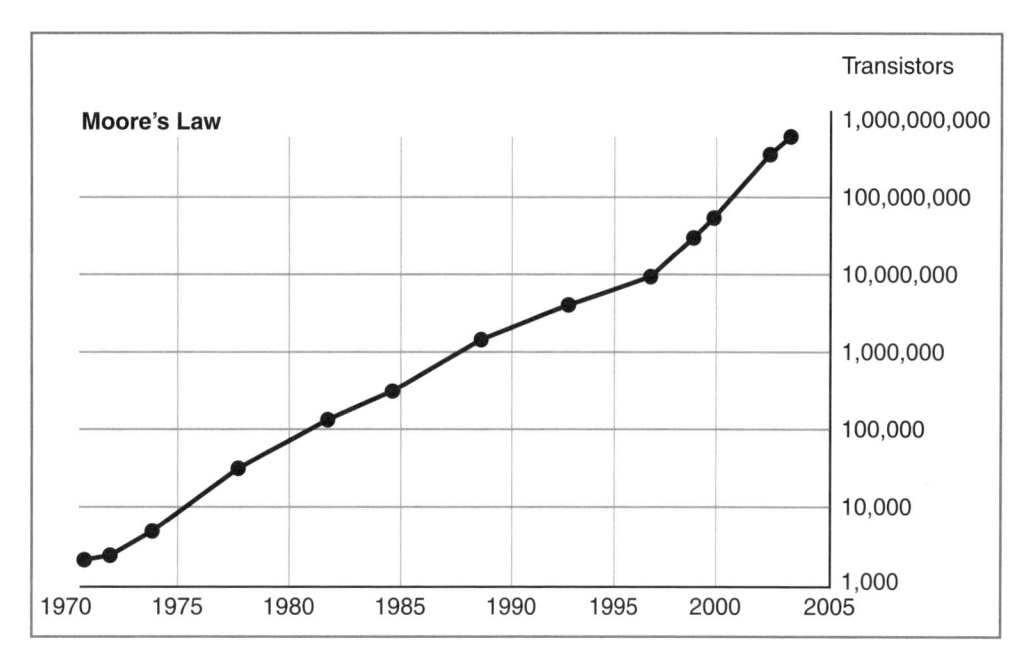

Figure 10.6
Intel executive Gordon Moore's prediction about the density of transistors doubling on chips about every 18 months has held true, and there's no reason to expect it won't apply to camcorder sensors and circuits.

And beyond simply improving existing features, camcorder designers are already thinking about how to make them superior to film cameras in many ways. For example, Sony has demonstrated camera technology that performs spot exposure and spot color correction in real time. For example, when you shoot at night, the camcorder will turn down its sensitivity to the pixels in the sky, so that they stay black, not noisy. But any lit subjects in the foreground will be exposed correctly. To achieve this, the camera's processing circuits must examine the image much the way the human brain does, filtering the incoming data to feature some objects and ignore others.

When some precise requirements are met, controversy will end.

When asked about the future of video imagery, computer graphics engineer John Cool smiled like a Cheshire cat and quipped, "Well, there's no such thing as crummy audio."

He meant that digital audio technology has already progressed to the point where you can't buy equipment that produces noticeable distortion at any price. The limits of human perception have been reached when it comes to the quality of the music playing on your iPod.

Some day, perhaps not so far away, the sophistication of digital video will reach the limits of perception. For example, when it comes to resolution, the precise point of achievement is easy to define if you know two facts (see Figure 10.7):

1. According to the SMPTE, the optimal viewing distance, whether for a television in a small room or the screen in a large theater, is four times the height of the screen.

2. The human eye cannot detect details that are separated by less than 2min of arc (a very tiny, but measurable, angle).

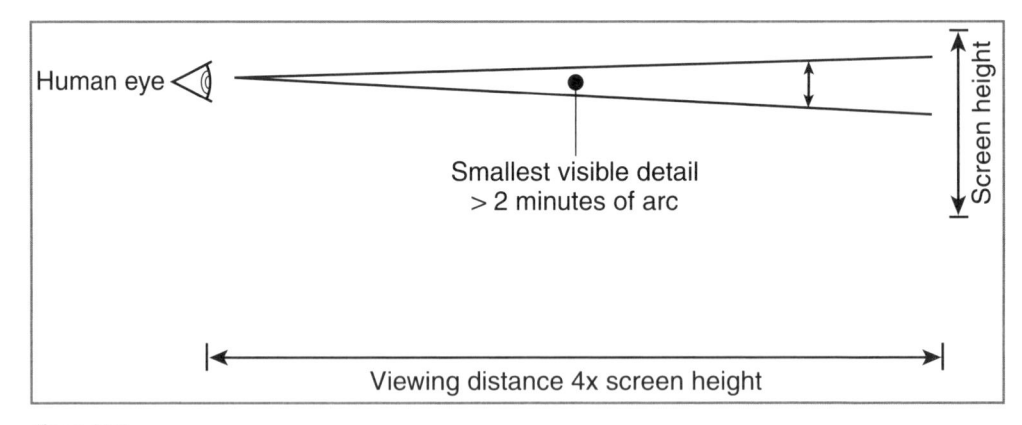

Figure 10.7
When digital video exceeds the limits of human visual perception, all debates about how much resolution is enough will end. At that point, further innovation is less necessary, and video gear will start to become a commodity product, like audio players.

When you do the math, you find that the ideal size television screen for a typical living room is about three feet high (just the size of today's HDTV panels), the comfortable viewing distance in a theater with a 10-foot-high screen is about 40 feet, and the limit of human visual perception on either TV or movie screen *at that distance* is about 2,000 horizontal lines.

Humans see in stereo, so perhaps video development will veer off in that direction.

The theatrical experience will be the same, yet different.

Just a few years back, sales and rentals of movies on tape and DVD surpassed box-office receipts. Not even counting movies shown on broadcast television, the numbers show that more people watch first-run movies at home than at a neighborhood theater (see Figure 10.8).

Pundits in the media business point to the timeless need of people to get out and mingle with their neighbors, even if most of them are strangers. Editor Walter Murch is a great believer in the group experience of watching a film in a crowded theater, and other filmmakers wax philosophical about how we're not much different from the cave people who needed to huddle around a fire and spin yarns about demons, monsters, and the thrill of the hunt.

No matter how slick the home viewing experience gets, movie going as a social experience is probably here to stay. Evidence of this is the fact that, while video stores were booming and DVDs became the fastest growing electronic product introduction in history, new commercial theaters were being built at a brisk pace. At the end of the twentieth century, another cultural phenomenon—shopping—changed dramatically. As price became all important, discount and big-lot stores threatened the very existence of mainline department stores. Back at the shopping mall, the only village experience many people have these days, department stores were not renewing their leases, and they certainly weren't stepping up to serve as the anchors (featured tenants) of new malls.

Mall developers are savvy investors, and they are betting on this future: Cineplexes are the new anchors. The real estate tycoons think people will come to the mall to see the movie, stay to shop, mingle, and dine.

Our brief journey into geometry leads us to suspect that the folks who are planning 4K resolution for theaters are thinking big screens and relatively close viewing distances, an experience like IMAX.

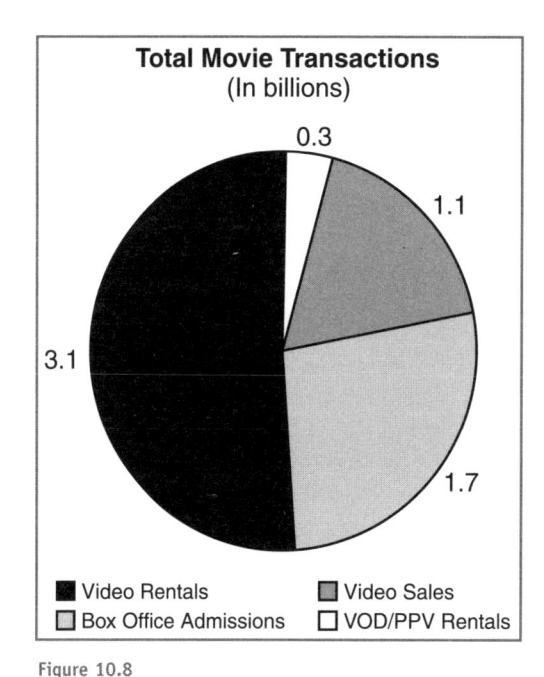

Total Movie Transactions
(In billions)

- Video Rentals: 3.1
- Box Office Admissions: 1.7
- Video Sales: 1.1
- VOD/PPV Rentals: 0.3

Figure 10.8
In a recent survey, video sales and rentals from all sources except broadcast television amounted to almost three-quarters of box-office receipts. (Source: Adams Media Research)

The effect on theater operators favors the multiplex. A new theater complex with perhaps 20 screens doesn't have that many because it needs to show 20 different movies. It's all about offering staggered start times. To snag walk-in customers who may have had no intention of seeing a movie when they left home, the theaters will start the same popular movie every half hour. And, as people grow accustomed to the luxuries of video on demand (VOD) provided at home by cable and satellite broadcasters, they may be less and less inclined to wait around for a movie to start.

Big studios and big networks will continue to exist.

Broadband Internet distribution will make it easy and economical for filmmakers to gain access to a world market. Returning to the analogy with the music business, consider how garage bands sell CDs they burn themselves and downloadable MP3 singles from their own Web sites. Independent channels of movie distribution may follow much the same business model.

> Communications bandwidth will *not* be a barrier to in-home delivery of video entertainment. Over the last decade, the big telecom carriers have invested heavily in laying fiber optic cable. (And having to make big cash outlays without seeing a rapid increase in demand sank some of them.) The theoretical information-carrying capacity of a single strand of glass fiber no thicker than a human hair is mind boggling, enough to download the entire Library of Congress in less time than you'd take to read just one of the pages. That's *theoretical,* mind you. But the future capacity is already there, lurking in those cables in the ground. The main reason it isn't fully utilized is that the industry can't afford for current narrow-band communication services to be so cheap that they're virtually free.

But advertising in the mass media will always be expensive. Yes, a clever Internet strategy can drive people to your Web page and create a buzz about your movie, as the makers of *The Blair Witch Project* (1999) demonstrated so successfully. But advertising cost isn't just about the cost of placing ads in the media. Strategy to build brands, product development, top-notch creative and art direction, and consistent, long-term effort—that kind of investment in advertising and promotion will be impossible for an individual filmmaker to match.

Because they can afford to advertise in the mass media, studios and networks will remain the gatekeepers to the marketplace, no matter how inexpensive the cost of production becomes.

But no one has the faintest idea how the democratization of video will change the world.

None of what we've said about the big players should be discouraging. We set out to show you how to compete with them, make the moguls sit up and take notice, and paint your name in foot-high letters on the silver screen.

What's different today from just a few years ago is that for the first time in history, storytellers of modest means can manufacture dreams for millions of people all over the planet. And, as long as they tell great stories, many of those creations will be as compelling as anything Hollywood can produce.

Of all our predictions, we have the least to say about this one.

That's because filmmakers like *you* will write the answers.

So, please get that movie made. We want to take credit for sending you on your way!

Index

Numbers
2D effects, 150–151
2½D effects, 151–152
3D effects, 153
24p
   archiving, 5
   cameras, 2–4, 43
   defined, 2
   DVDs, 5
   editing
      60i, 140–141
      accelerator cards, 139
      converting, 137–141
      deinterlacing, 138–139
      interlacing, 138–139
      overview, 135–136
      postproduction, 140–141
      prerendering, 139–140
      pulldown, 137–139
      rendering, 139–140
      tearing, 138–139
      temporal displacement, 138
      timecodes, 136
   film look, 19
   film out, 4, 19
   frame rate, 2
   marketing, 4–5
   movies
      35mm comparison, 6–7
      advantages, 4–5
      DV comparison, 6–7
      first 24p movie, 4
      mindset, 6–7, 21
   progressive scanning, 2
   resolution, 200–201
24pa, 43
30fps, 11
30p, 20
35mm movies, 24p comparison, 6–7
50i (PAL), 4, 20–21
60i
   cameras, 11
   editing 24p, 140–141
   film look, 19–20
   film out, 19–20

A
accelerator cards, 139
action scenes
   directors, 102–103
   microphones, 82
actors
   budgets, 101–102
   casting, 120–121
   closeups, 107–108
   dialogue. *See* dialogue
   rehearsals, 120–124
   schedules, 105
ADR (automated dialogue replacement), 87
   background, 92
   backtiming, 95
   bins, 95
   cueing, 91, 95
   effects, 92–93, 95–98
   foley artists, 95–96
   interlock stages, 91
   licenses, 94
   looping, 91

Index

mixdown, 96–97
music, 92–95
overview, 87
realism, 97–98
recording, 90–98
split tracks, 96
spotting tables, 92–93
streamer tracks, 91
subwoofers, 97
SurroundSound, 96–97
Synchro Arts VocALign Project, 92
two-pops, 91
walla sounds, 92
advantages (24p), 4–5
advertising future, 202
AE (auto exposure). *See* **automatic controls**
AF (autofocus). *See* **automatic controls**
AFMA Web site, 170
After Effects, 163–165
AG-DVX100, 3
air (microphones), 75
AJ-HDC27F, 3
ambience (audio effects), 74
American Bar Association Web site, 171
American Society of Composers, Authors, and Publishers (ASCAP) Web site, 94
anamorphic lenses, 15–16
angles, cameras, 109
aperture priority, 56
archiving
24p, 5
distribution, 186
Arri Web site, 190

ASCAP (American Society of Composers, Authors, and Publishers) Web site, 94
aspect ratio
distribution, 190
film look, 15–16
film out, 190
letterbox format, 15
producers, 31
wide-screen format, 15–16
atmosphere (microphones), 81–82
Atom Films Web site, 179
attackers (producers), 40
attorneys, distribution, 171
attractors (producers), 40
audience (DPs), 68–69
audio
ADR (automated dialogue replacement), 87
background, 92
backtiming, 95
bins, 95
cueing, 91, 95
effects, 92–93, 95–98
foley artists, 95–96
interlock stages, 91
licenses, 94
looping, 91
mixdown, 96–97
music, 92–95
overview, 87
realism, 97–98
recording, 90–98
split tracks, 96
spotting tables, 92–93
streamer tracks, 91
subwoofers, 97

Surround Sound, 96–97
Synchro Arts VocALign Project, 92
two-pops, 91
walla sounds, 92
audio recordists, 37
bit rates, 77
budgets, 38
camera and sound log, 85–86
cameras, 84–85
DATs, 37
dialogue
ADR. *See* ADR
producers, 36–37
directors, 82
distortion, 85, 90
DME. *See* dialogue; music; effects
dual-system, 37, 84–85
editing, 82
effects
ambience, 74
off-screen, 74
on-screen, 74
producers, 37–38
film out, 192
jam sync, 85
microphones. *See* microphones
mixers, 36–37
multichannel audio, 84
music
continuity, 73
effects, 157–158
emotions, 73
overview, 72–74
producers, 37–38
time, 73
transitions, 73

noise
  editing, 85–87
  reducing, 85–87
  troubleshooting, 90
 overview, 71–72
 postproduction
  checkerboarding, 89
  converting, 77
  editing background noise, 90
  editing dialogue, 89–90
  editing software, 88
  process, 87–90
  producers, 37–38
  tracks, 87–90
 pumping, 85
 realism, 72–74
 recording modes, 77
 schedules, 38
 silence, 82
 timecodes, synchronizing, 85
 tracks, stacking, 90
audio gain, 56–57, 85
audio recordists, 37
auto exposure (AE). *See* **automatic controls**
auto white balance (AWB). *See* **automatic controls**
autofocus (AF). *See* **automatic controls**
automated dialogue replacement. *See* **ADR**
automatic controls (cameras)
 DPs, 47–49, 57
 producers, 34
 semiautomatic controls, 56
AWB (auto white balance). *See* **automatic controls**

B

backlight, 59–60
background
 ADR, 92
 light, 66
 noise, 90
backtiming (ADR), 95
batteries, 83
battery testers, 83
"being there," 12
bias (cameras), 56–57
bins (ADR), 95
bit rates (audio), 77
blimps (boom microphones), 76–77
blocking shooting, 112
blown out (contrast range), 13
BMI (Broadcast Music, Inc.) Web site, 94
boom microphones
 blimps, 76–77
 overview, 76
 rigging, 76–81
 shock mounts, 76
brain waves, frame rates relationship, 12
breakdown sheets (scripts), 104
broadcast legal colors (color space), 30
Broadcast Music, Inc. (BMI) Web site, 94
broadcasting. *See* **television**
browser window (NLE), 130–131
budgets
 actors, 101–102
 audio, 38
 directors, 101–102
 locations, 101–102
 movies, 24
 producers, 31, 38
bullet time effects, 153, 164–165

C

cable movies, 24
cables (microphones), 80
call sheets (directors), 122–124
camera and sound log, 85–86
cameras. *See also* **shooting**
 24p, 2–4, 43
 24pa, 43
 30 fps, 11
 60i, 11
 angles, 109
 aperture priority, 56
 aspect ratio
  distribution, 190
  film look, 15–16
  film out, 190
  letterbox format, 15
  producers, 31
  wide-screen format, 15–16
 audio, 84–85
 audio gain, 85
 automatic controls 34, 47–49, 57
 bias, 56–57
 camera and sound log, 85–86
 Canon XL1, 3
 chips, 198
 controls, 48
 cranes, 32–33, 35, 109–110
 dollies, 32–33, 35, 109–110
 dolly grips, 32–33
 doorway dollies, 32–33
 DPs, 42–43, 53–54
 effects, 57
 ergonomics, 49

Index

eye cups, 46
fields, frames relationship, 11
film look. *See* film look
film out, 191
focus, 51
formats. *See* formats
frame rates, 11
frames, fields relationship, 11
future
    film, 198
    Moore's Law, 199–200
gain, 56–57, 85
Glidecam, 35
hand-held, 35
image stabilization, 56
interlacing, 11–12
JVC JY-HD10U, 3
LCDs, 46–47
lenses, 44–45
    anamorphic, 15–16
    long, 14–15
    telephoto, 14–15
    wide-angle, 14–15
live events, 57
low-light mode, 56–57
monitors, 51
motion blur, 11–13, 26
moving
    directors, 109–110
    producers, 32–33, 35
    time, 106
noise, 56–57
oscilloscopes, 51
overscanning, 46

painting with light, 35
Panasonic AG-DVX100, 3
Panasonic AJ-HDC27F, 3
panning, 109–110
playing takes, 55
plugs, microphones, 78–80
recording. *See* recording
resolution. *See* resolution
sand-and-snow mode, 57
scanning modes, 11
semiautomatic controls, 56
sepia tone, 57
shooting
    film-style, 5–6, 33–34
    future, 198
    news-style, 5, 33–34
shutter angle
    DPs, 54–55
    motion blur, 26
    producers, 26
    shutter speed relationship, 54
shutter priority (DPs), 56
shutter speed
    DPs, 54–55, 57
    distribution, 191
    film out, 191
    frame rate relationship, 54
    motion blur, 26
    producers, 26
    shutter angle relationship, 54
Sony CineAlta, 3
Sony HVR-Z1U, 3
sports mode, 57
spotlights, 57, 67–68
support, 35

tapes
    loading, 49
    speed, 57
tilting, 109–110
timecodes
    audio, synchronizing, 85
    directors, 124–125
    DPs, 55
    editing (24p), 136
transitions, 57
tripods, 35, 49, 54
trucks, 109–110
video gain, 56–57
viewfinders, 46–47, 51
waveforms, 51
zebra stripes, 49–50
Canon XL1, 3
canvas window (NLE), 132
capturing clips (NLE), 132
cardioid microphones. *See* **shortie microphones**
casting actors, 120–121
CDs, distribution, 178–180
Celco Web site, 189
checkerboarding postproduction audio, 89
checklist, producers, 33–39
chips (cameras), 198
chroma keying
    directors, 125–127
    effects, 155–156
chromatic resolution. *See* **color space**
CineAlta, 3
cinematographers. *See* **DPs**

Cineon Web site, 190
clarity. *See* **noise**
clips (NLE)
    capturing, 132
    folders, 133
    inserting, 134
    managing, 133
    transferring, 132
    trimming, 132–133
close mic'd microphones, 75
closeups, shooting, 107–108
color
    color balance. *See* white balance
    color correction (effects)
        film, 160
        overview, 159–160
        process, 160–162
        rotoscoping, 161
        spot color, 161–162
        television, 159
        travel mattes, 161
    color space
        broadcast-legal colors, 30
        distribution, 191
        effects, 159
        film look, 14
        film out, 191
        oversaturation, 30
        producers, 30
    DPs, 69
    temperature. *See* white balance
color balance. *See* **white balance**
color correction (effects)
    film, 160
    overview, 159–160
    process, 160–162
    rotoscoping, 161

    spot color, 161–162
    television, 159
    travel mattes, 161
color space
    broadcast-legal colors, 30
    distribution, 191
    effects, 159
    film look, 14
    film out, 191
    oversaturation, 30
    producers, 30
communication, 70
composite effects, 155–156, 163–165
continuity
    jump cutting, 143
    music, 73
    overview, 115–116
    screen directions, 117–118
    shock video, 143
    stage lines, 116–117
    time dependencies, 118–119
contracts
    copyrights, 174–175
    overview, 171–174
contrast
    contrast range. *See* contrast range
    film noir, 42
contrast range (exposure latitude), 13
    DPs, 49–50, 57, 61
        diffusion, 62
        filters, 64–65
        gels, 64–65
        reducing, 62–63
        shiny boards, 62
        silks, 62
        white balance, 52, 63–65
    film look, 13

    blown out, 13
    saturation, 13
    stop downs, 13
    whites, 13
    producers, 26–29
        diffusion, 27–29
        exterior light, 28
        filters, 27–28
        flags, 28
        gels, 27–28
        interior light, 27–28
        masks, 27
        PAs, 28
        reflectors, 28
        shiny boards, 28
        silks, 28
        white balance, 27–28
controlling sets, 122–124
controls. *See* **automatic controls**
converting
    audio (postproduction), 77
    editing (24p), 137–141
copy protection (distribution), 184
copyrights (distribution), 174–175
corporations (distribution), 187
cranes (cameras)
    directors, 109–110
    producers, 32–33, 35
creating negatives, 52
crews
    audio recordists, 37
    directors, 100
    producers, 33–34
cueing ADR, 91, 95
cutaways, shooting, 111

D

DATs (audio), 37
DCCA (DVD Copy Control Association) Web site, 184
deinterlacing editing, 138–139
deliverables
    copyrights, 174–175
    overview, 171–174
Deluxe Efilm Web site, 188
depth of field. *See also* focus
    DPs, 45, 53–54
    film look, 14–15
    producers, 30–31
detail. *See* resolution
dialogue
    ADR (automated dialogue replacement), 87
        background, 92
        backtiming, 95
        bins, 95
        cueing, 91, 95
        effects, 92–93, 95–98
        foley artists, 95–96
        interlock stages, 91
        licenses, 94
        looping, 91
        mixdown, 96–97
        music, 92–95
        overview, 87
        realism, 97–98
        recording, 90–98
        split tracks, 96
        spotting tables, 92–93
        streamer tracks, 91
        subwoofers, 97
        Surround Sound, 96–97
        Synchro Arts VocALign Project, 92
        two-pops, 91
        walla sounds, 92
    audio, editing, 89–90
    directors, 102–103
    producers, 36–37
diffusion (contrast range), 27–29, 62
Digital Direct Drive Image Light Amplifier (D-DILA), 195–196
digital intermediates (DIs), 52
Digital Light Processing (DLP), 195–196
digital video, DV relationship, 2
D-ILA (Digital Direct Drive Image Light Amplifier), 195–196
director of photography. *See* DPs
directors
    action scenes, 102–103
    actors
        budgets, 101–102
        casting, 120–121
        rehearsals, 120–124
        schedules, 105
    audio, 82
    budgets, 101
        actors, 101–102
        locations, 101–102
    call sheets, 122–124
    cameras
        cranes, 109–110
        dollies, 109–110
        moving, time, 106
        panning, 109–110
        tilting, 109–110
        trucks, 109–110
    chroma keying, 125–127
    communication, 70
    continuity
        overview, 115–116
        screen directions, 117–118
        stage lines, 116–117
        time dependencies, 118–119
    crews, 100
    dialogue, 102–103
    effects, 125–127
    international movies, 103
    keying, 125–127
    locations, 101–102, 122
    logistics, 122
    luminance keying, 125
    master scenes, 103, 107, 115
    overview, 99–100
    producers, 101
    production
        planning, 103–106
    schedules, 103–106
    screenwriters, 101
    scripts, 101
        breakdown sheets, 104
        master scene script, 103
    sets, controlling, 122–124
    setup, 122
    shooting
        blocking, 112
        camera angle, 109
        closeups, 107–108
        cutaways, 111
        establishing shots, 111
        framing, 109

improvisation, 112–113, 119–121
inserts, 111
lenses, 109
master scenes, 103, 107, 115
moving cameras, 109–110
night, 106
over the shoulder shots, 111
planning, 106–108
point of view, 111
pushing in, 108
ratio, 119
shot design, 109–111
structure, 112–113, 119–121
terminology, 111
zooming, 108–109
shot lists, 114–115
shot plan drawings, 114
slating, 124–125
storyboards, 113–114
takes, 124–125
timecodes, 124–125
transportation, 122
travel mattes, 126
troubleshooting, 127–128
DIs (digital intermediates), 52
distortion (audio), 85, 90
distribution
archiving, 186
attorneys, 171
CDs, 178–180
copy protection, 184
corporations, 187
deliverables
copyrights, 174–175
overview, 171–174
DVDs, 38–39, 179–180, 182–186

film festivals, 170
film out. *See* film out
future, 202
IFTA, 170
negative financing, 171
negative pickup deals, 24
negative pickups, 171
overview, 167
producers, 38–39
sales agents, 170–171
security, 184
studios, 168–170
television, 38–39, 186–187
theaters, 168–170
trade shows, 170
VCDs, 180
video, 175–178
Web, 180–182
DLP (Digital Light Processing), 195–196
DME. *See* **dialogue; music; effects**
DOGMA 95, 10, 25
dollies
directors, 109–110
dolly grips, 32–33
doorway dollies, 32–33
producers, 32–33, 35
dolly grips, 32–33
doorway dollies, 32–33
double-tracking microphones, 84
DPs (director of photography), 41
audience, 68–69
cameras, 53–54
24p, 43
24pa, 43
aperture priority, 56
audio gain, 85

automatic controls, 47–49, 57
bias, 56–57
controls, 48
effects, 57
ergonomics, 49
eye cups, 46
focus, 51
gain, 56–57, 85
image stabilization, 56
LCDs, 46–47
lenses, 44–45
live events, 57
loading tapes, 49
low-light mode, 56–57
monitors, 51
noise, 56–57
oscilloscopes, 51
overscanning, 46
overview, 42–43
playing takes, 55
resolution, 56
sand-and-snow mode, 57
semiautomatic controls, 56
sepia tone, 57
shutter angle, 54–55
shutter priority, 56
shutter speed, 54–55, 57
sports mode, 57
spotlights, 57, 67–68
tape speed, 57
timecodes. *See* timecodes
transitions, 57
tripods, 49, 54
video gain, 56–57
viewfinders, 46–47, 51
waveforms, 51
zebra stripes, 49–50

color, 69
communication, 70
depth of field, 45, 53–54
digital intermediates (DIs), 52
focus, 45, 53–54
leading the eye, 68–69
light
    backlight, 59–60
    background, 66
    contrast range, 49–50, 57, 61
    contrast range, diffusion, 27–29, 62
    contrast range, filters, 64–65
    contrast range, gels, 64–65
    contrast range, reducing, 62–63
    contrast range, shiny boards, 62
    contrast range, silks, 62
    contrast range, white balance, 52, 63–65
    effects, 66–68
    eyelight, 68
    fill light, 58–60
    film look, 58, 61–68
    key light, 58–60
    kickers, 68
    mood, 61
    motivating, 60
    moving objects, 66
    overhead fluorescents, 65
    reducing, 66
    reflections, 65
    reflectors, 62
    rim lights, 67
    spotlights, 57, 67–68
    three-point light, 58–60
objects, moving, 69
overview, 41–42, 69–70
techniques, 68–69
wardrobe, 69
zooming, 53–54
dual-system audio, 37, 84–85
DuArt Web site, 188
dubbing (postproduction ADR), 87
    background, 92
    backtiming, 95
    bins, 95
    cueing, 91, 95
    effects, 92–93, 95–98
    foley artists, 95–96
    interlock stages, 91
    licenses, 94
    looping, 91
    mixdown, 96–97
    music, 92–95
    overview, 87
    realism, 97–98
    recording, 90–98
    split tracks, 96
    spotting tables, 92–93
    streamer tracks, 91
    subwoofers, 97
    Surround Sound, 96–97
    Synchro Arts VocALign Project, 92
    two-pops, 91
    walla sounds, 92
dust. *See* **noise**
DV
    24p comparison, 6–7
    digital video relationship, 2
    format, 2–4

DVD Copy Control Association (DCCA) Web site, 184
DVDs
    24p, 5
    distribution, 38–39, 179–180, 182–186
    DVD Copy Control Association (DCCA) Web site, 184
DVFilm Web site, 188

E

easing in/out effects, 154–155
edge detection (effects), 149, 154
edit decision list (EDL), 141
editing
    24p
        60i, 140–141
        accelerator cards, 139
        converting, 137–141
        deinterlacing, 138–139
        interlacing, 138–139
        overview, 135–136
        postproduction, 140–141
        prerendering, 139–140
        pulldown, 137–139
        rendering, 139–140
        tearing, 138–139
        temporal displacement, 138
        timecodes, 136
    audio, 82
        background noise, 90
        dialogue, 89–90
        noise, 85–87
        software, 88

communication, 70
continuity, 143
EDL (edit decision list), 141
final cuts, 144–145
jump cutting, 143
match cutting, 144
negative cutters, 141
NLE. *See* NLE
overview, 129–130
shock video, 143
speed ramping, 144
split edits, 142–143
editors. *See* **editing**
EDL (edit decision list), 141
effects
    ADR, 92–93, 95–98
    After Effects, 163–165
    audio
        ambience, 74
        off-screen, 74
        on-screen, 74
        producers, 37–38
    cameras, 57
    chroma keying, 155–156
    color correction
        film, 160
        overview, 159–160
        process, 160–162
        rotoscoping, 161
        spot color, 161–162
        television, 159
        travel mattes, 161
    color space, 159
    composites, 155–156, 163–165

directors, 125–127
edge detection, 149
film out, 191
filters, 148–149
frames, 164–165
keyframes, 164–165
keying, 155–156
light, 66–68
luminance keying, 156
motion blur, 26
music, 157–158
NLE, 148–149
overview, 147–148
planning, 155
producers, 38
scrolling titles, 162–163
space/time
    2D, 150–151
    2½D, 151–152
    3D, 153
    bullet time, 153, 164–165
    easing in/out, 154–155
    edge detection, 154
    farings, 154–155
    frames, 154–155
    interpolatimg, 154–155
    keyframes, 154–155
    layers, 152–153
    morphing, 155
    overview, 149–150
    slow motion, 164–165
    time bending, 164–165
    transitions, 154–155
    tweening, 154–155
video, 157–158

emotions (music), 73
ergonomics, 49
establishing shots, 111
exposure
    auto exposure. *See* automatic controls
    exposure latitude. *See* contrast range
exterior light (contrast range), 28
extreme closeups, 107–108
eye candy. *See* **effects**
eye cups (cameras), 46
eyelight, 68
eyes (resolution), 200–201

F

farings, 154–155
features. *See* **movies**
fields, frames relationship, 11
fill light, 58–60
film
    color correction effects, 160
    film festivals (distribution), 170
    film look. *See* film look
    film noir, 42
    film out. *See* film out
    film-style shooting, 5–6, 33–34
    films. *See* movies
    future, 198
film festivals (distribution), 170
film look
    aspect ratio, 15–16
    audio. *See* audio
    "being there," 12
    color space, 14

depth of field, 14–15
directors. *See* directors
distribution. *See* distribution
DPs. *See* DPs
editors. *See* editing
effects. *See* effects
film out, 191
focus, 14–15
formats
    24p, 19
    30p, 20
    60i, 19–20
    overview, 19
    PAL, 4, 20–21
frame rates, brain waves relationship, 12
interlacing, 11–12
letterbox format, 15
light
    contrast range, 13
    DPs, 58, 61–68
marketing, 4–5
motion blur, 11–13
noise, 18
overview, 2, 9–10
producers. *See* producers
resolution, 17
rules, 21
Vow of Chastity, 10, 25
wide-screen format, 15–16
film noir, 42
film out
    24p, 4
    distribution, 167–168
        aspect ratio, 190
        audio, 192

        cameras, 191
        color space, 191
        effects, 191
        film look, 191
        flying spot, 189–190
        focus, 191
        frame rates, 191
        kinescope, 188–189
        lasers, 190
        leaders, 192
        overview, 175
        prints, 192–194
        process, 192–194
        recording services, 187–190
        reels, 192
        shutter speed, 191
        speed, 192
        tearing, 192
        titles, 191
    formats
        24p, 19
        30p, 20
        60i, 19–20
        PAL, 4, 20–21
    producers, 24–25
film-style shooting, 5–6, 33–34
films. *See* **movies**
filters
    contrast range, 27–28, 64–65
    effects (NLE), 148–149
    linoleum, 64
Final Cut Pro. *See* **NLE**
final cuts, 144–145
FindLaw Web site, 171

flags (contrast range), 28
fluorescent lights, 65
flying spot (film out), 189–190
focus. *See also* **depth of field**
    autofocus. *See* automatic controls
    distribution, 191
    DPs, 45, 51, 53–54
    film look, 14–15
    film out, 191
    focus pull, 15
    target size, 15
focus pull, 15
folders (clips), 133
foley artists (ADR), 95–96
formats
    aspect ratio, 15–16
    cameras. *See* cameras
    DV, 2–4
    film look/film out
        24p, 19
        30p, 20
        60i, 19–20
        overview, 19
        PAL, 4, 20–21
    HD, 2–4
    HDV, 2–4
    letterbox, 15
    PAL, 4, 20–21
    recording. *See* recording
    shooting, 39
    wide-screen, 15–16
FotoKem Web site, 188
Foveon X3 direct image sensor chips, 198
fps (30 fps), 11

frame rates
  24p, 2
  cameras, 11
  film look, brain waves relationship, 12
  film out (distribution), 191
  shutter speed relationship, 54

frames
  effects, 154–155, 164–165
  fields relationship, 11
  fps, 11
  frame rates
    24p, 2
    cameras, 11
    film look, brain waves relationship, 12
    film out, 191
    shutter speed relationship, 54
  size (aspect ratio)
    distribution, 190
    film look, 15–16
    film out, 190
    letterbox format, 15
    producers, 31
    wide-screen format, 15–16
  timecodes
    audio, synchronizing, 85
    directors, 124–125
    DPs, 55
    editing (24p), 136

framing shooting, 109

future
  advertising, 202
  cameras, 198–200
  distribution, 202
  film, 198

Moore's Law, 199–200
movies, 199–201
NLE, 199–200
projectors, 195–197
promotion, 202
resolution, 198, 200–201
shooting, 198
studios, 202
television, 202
theaters, 195–197, 201–202

G

gain (cameras), 56–57, 85
gels (contrast range), 27–28, 64–65
Glidecam Web site, 35
grain
  film look, 18
  producers, 32
grips (dolly grips), 32–33

H

hand-held cameras, 35
HD format, 2–4
HDV format, 2–4
human eye, resolution, 200–201
HVR-Z1U, 3
hypercardioid microphones. *See* **boom microphones**
hyperrealism
  ADR, 97–98
  audio, 72–74

I

IFTA (Independent Film and Television Alliance), 170
image stabilization (cameras), 56
improvisation, shooting, 112–113, 119–121
Independent Feature Project Web site, 24
Independent Film and Television Alliance (IFTA), 170
independent movies, 25
inserting clips (NLE), 134
inserts, shooting, 111
interior light (contrast range), 27–28
interlacing
  cameras, 11–12
  editing, 138–139
  film look, 11–12
interlock stages (ADR), 91
international movies, 103
interpolatimg effects, 154–155
interviews, microphones, 81–82

J

jam sync (audio), 85
jitter (producers), 32
jump cutting, 143
JVC JY-HD10U, 3
JY-HD10U, 3

K

key light (DPs), 58–60
keyframes (effects), 154–155, 164–165

keying
　directors, 125–127
　effects, 155–156
kickers (light), 68
kinescope (film out), 188–189

L

lapel microphones. *See* **lav microphones**
lasers (film out), 190
latitude, exposure. *See* **contrast range**
lav microphones
　overview, 76
　rigging, 82–83
lavaliere microphones. *See* **lav microphones**
layers (effects), 152–153
LCDs (cameras), 46–47
leaders (film out), 192
leading the eye, 68–69
lenses
　anamorphic, 15–16
　cameras, 44–45
　long, 14–15
　shooting, 109
　telephoto, 14–15
　wide-angle, 14–15
letterbox format, 15
Library of Congress Web site, 174
licenses (ADR), 94
light
　backlight, 59–60
　background, 66

contrast range, 26–29, 49–50, 57, 61
　blown out, 13
　diffusion, 27–29, 62
　exterior light, 28
　film look, 13
　filters, 27–28, 64–65
　flags, 28
　gels, 27–28, 64–65
　interior light, 27–28
　masks, 27
　PAs, 28
　reducing, 62–63
　reflectors, 28
　saturation, 13
　shiny boards, 28, 62
　silks, 28, 62
　stop downs, 13
　white balance, 13, 27–28, 52, 63–65
effects, 66–68
eyelight, 68
fill light, 58–60
film look, 58, 61–68
film noir, 42
key light, 58–60
kickers, 68
light kits, 27
low-light mode, 56–57
mood, 61
motivating, 60
moving objects, 66
overhead fluorescents, 65
painting with light, 35
reducing, 66
reflections, 65

reflectors, 62
rim lights, 67
spotlights, 57, 67–68
three-point light, 58–60
light kits, 27
line producers, 23
linoleum filters, 64
live events (DPs), 57
loading tapes, 49
locations, 101–102, 122
logistics (directors), 122
long lenses, 14–15
looping ADR, 91
low-light mode (cameras), 56–57
luminance keying
　directors, 125
　effects, 156

M

Macrovision Web site, 184
managing clips (NLE), 133
manufacturing. *See* **distribution**
marketing, 4–5
masks (contrast range), 27
master scenes, 103, 107, 115
match cutting, 144
Matrox Web site, 157
microphones
　action scenes, 82
　air, 75
　atmosphere, 81–82
　audio, producers, 36–37

batteries, 83
battery testers, 83
boom
   blimps, 76–77
   overview, 76
   rigging, 76–81
   shock mounts, 76
cables, strain relief, 80
cardioid. *See* shortie
close mic'd, 75
double-tracking, 84
hypercardioid. *See* boom
interviews, 81–82
lapel. *See* lav
lav
   overview, 76
   rigging, 82–83
lavaliere. *See* lav
mixers, 80–81
overview, 75–76
parabolic, 75
phantom power, 80–81
pin. *See* lav
plants, 82
plugs, cameras, 78–80
shortie
   overview, 76
   rigging, 81–82
shotgun. *See* boom
singers, 81
talkback circuits, 81
tracks, 84
types, 76

wireless
   multichannel audio, 84
   rigging, 83–84
mindset
   24p, 6–7, 21
   film-style, 5–6
   news-style, 5
mixdown (ADR), 96–97
mixers
   audio, 36–37
   microphones, 80–81
monitors (cameras), 51
mood (light), 61
Moore's Law, 199–200
morphing effects, 155
motion blur
   film look, 11–13
   producers, 26
Motion Picture Association of America (MPAA) Web site, 184
motivating light, 60
movies
   24p
      35mm comparison, 6–7
      advantages, 4–5
      DV comparison, 6–7
      first 24p movie, 4
      mindset, 6–7, 21
   aspect ratio
      distribution, 190
      film look, 15–16
      film out, 190
      letterbox format, 15
      producers, 31
      wide-screen format, 15–16

budgets, 24
cable, 24
cameras. *See* cameras
editing. *See* editing
film look. *See* film look
film noir, 42
future
   advertising, 202
   distribution, 202
   Moore's Law, 199–200
   projectors, 195–197
   promotion, 202
   studios, 202
   television, 202
   theaters, 195–197, 201–202
independent, 25
Nicolas:, 4
NLE, 24
process, 6
resolution. *See* resolution
schedules, 24
television, 24
Vow of Chastity, 10, 25
moving
   cameras
      directors, 109–110
      producers, 32–33, 35
      time, 106
   objects
      DPs, 69
      light, 66
   screen directions, 117–118
   speed ramping, 144
MPAA (Motion Picture Association of America) Web site, 184

multichannel audio wireless microphones, 84
music
    ADR, 92–95
    audio (producers), 37–38
    continuity, 73
    effects, 157–158
    emotions, 73
    overview, 72–74
    time, 73
    transitions, 73

N

negative cutters, 141
negative financing, 171
negative pickup deals, 24, 171
negatives, creating, 52
networks. *See* **television**
news-style shooting, 5, 33–34
Nicolas, 4
night, shooting, 106
NLE (non-linear editing), 24
    browser window, 130–131
    canvas window, 132
    capturing clips, 132
    edge detection, 149
    effects, 148–149
    filters, 148–149
    folders, 133
    inserting clips, 134
    managing clips, 133
    Moore's Law, 199–200
    movies, 24
    overview, 130–135
    playback, 135
    timeline window, 131
    transferring clips, 132
    transitions, 134–135
    trimming clips, 132–133
    viewer window, 131
noise
    audio, 85–87, 90
    background, 90
    cameras, 56–57
    film look, 18
    producers, 32
non-linear editing. *See* **NLE**
NTSC (60i)
    cameras, 11
    editing 24p, 140–141
    film look, 19–20
    film out, 19–20
    60i

O

objects, moving
    DPs, 69
    light, 66
off-screen audio effects, 74
on-screen audio effects, 74
oscilloscopes (cameras), 51
over the shoulder shots, 111
overhead fluorescents, 65
oversaturation (color space), 30
overscanning (cameras), 46

P

painting with light, 35
PAL (Phase Alternating Line), 4, 20–21
Panasonic AG-DVX100, 3
Panasonic AJ-HDC27F, 3
panning cameras, 109–110
parabolic microphones, 75
PAs (production assistants), 28
PGA (Producers Guild of America), 24
phantom power, 80–81
Phase Alternating Line (PAL), 4, 20–21
pickup deals (negative), 24
pin microphones. *See* **lav microphones**
Pinnacle Systems Web site, 157
planning
    effects, 155
    production, 103–106
    shooting, 106–108
plants (microphones), 82
playback (NLE), 135
playing takes, 55
plugs, microphones, 78–80
point of view, shooting, 111
postproduction
    ADR (automated dialogue replacement), 87
        background, 92
        backtiming, 95
        bins, 95
        cueing, 91, 95
        effects, 92–93, 95–98
        foley artists, 95–96
        interlock stages, 91
        licenses, 94

looping, 91
mixdown, 96–97
music, 92–95
overview, 87
realism, 97–98
recording, 90–98
split tracks, 96
spotting tables, 92–93
streamer tracks, 91
subwoofers, 97
SurroundSound, 96–97
Synchro Arts VocALign Project, 92
two-pops, 91
walla sounds, 92
audio
    checkerboarding, 89
    converting, 77
    editing background noise, 90
    editing dialogue, 89–90
    editing software, 88
    process, 87–90
    producers, 37–38
    tracks, 87–90
dubbing. *See* ADR
editing (24p), 140–141
preproduction, shooting test rolls, 39–40
prerendering (24p), 139–140
prints (distribution), 192–194
process
    color correction effects, 160–162
    film out (distribution), 192–194
    movies, 6
    postproduction audio, 87–90

producers
aspect ratio, 31
attackers, 40
attractors, 40
audio
    audio recordists, 37
    budgets, 38
    DATs, 37
    dialogue, 36–37
    dual-system, 37
    effects, 37–38
    microphones, 36–37
    mixers, 36–37
    music, 37–38
    postproduction, 37–38
    schedules, 38
broadcast-legal colors, 30
budgets, 31, 38
cameras
    automatic controls, 34
    cranes, 32–33, 35
    dollies, 32–33, 35
    dolly grips, 32–33
    doorway dollies, 32–33
    Glidecam, 35
    hand-held, 35
    moving, 32–33, 35
    painting with light, 35
    support, 35
    tripods, 35
checklist, 33–39
color space, 30
crews, 33–34

depth of field, 30–31
directors, 101
distribution, 38–39
    DVDs, 38–39
    television, 38–39
effects, 38
film look overview, 24–26
film out overview, 24–25
jitter, 32
light, 26–29
line producers, 23
motion blur, 26
noise, 32
oversaturation, 30
overview, 23–24
PGA, 24
radials, 38
resolution, 31–32
shooting
    film-style, 33–34
    formats, 39
    news-style, 33–34
    test rolls, 39–40
transitions, 38
wipes, 38
Producers Guild of America (PGA), 24
production, planning, 103–106
production assistants (PAs), 28
productions. *See* **cameras; movies**
progressive scanning, 2
projectors
    D-ILA (Digital Direct Drive Image Light
        Amplifier), 195–196
    DLP (Digital Light Processing), 195–196

future, 195–197
SXRD (Silicon X-dal Reflective Display), 195–197
promotion (future), 202
pulldown (editing), 137–139
pumping (audio distortion), 85
pushing in (shooting), 108

Q–R

quality. *See* **resolution**
quiet on the set, 82
radials, 38
ratio, shooting, 119
realism
    ADR, 97–98
    audio, 72–74
recording
    ADR, 90–98
        background, 92
        backtiming, 95
        cueing, 91, 95
        effects, 92–93, 95–98
        interlock stages, 91
        licenses, 94
        looping, 91
        music, 92–95
        realism, 97–98
        spotting tables, 92–93
        streamer tracks, 91
        Synchro Arts VocALign Project, 92
        two-pops, 91
        walla sounds, 92
    formats. *See* formats

recording modes (audio), 77
recording services (film out), 187–190
recording modes (audio), 77
recording services (film out), 187–190
Red Giant Bullet Suite, 140
reducing
    audio noise, 85–87
    contrast range, 62–63
    light (DPs), 66
reels (film out), 192
reflections (light), 65
reflectors
    contrast range, 28
    light (DPs), 62
rehearsals, 120–124
relieving strain (microphone cables), 80
rendering, 139–140
resolution
    cameras (DPs), 56
    chromatic. *See* color space
    color space
        broadcast-legal colors, 30
        distribution, 191
        effects, 159
        film look, 14
        film out, 191
        oversaturation, 30
        producers, 30
    film look, 17
    future, 198
    human eye, 200–201
    producers, 31–32
    quality, 200–201
retrofitting theaters, 195–197

rigging microphones
    boom, 76–81
    lav, 82–83
    shortie, 81–82
    wireless, 83–84
rim lights (DPs), 67
rotoscoping (color correction), 161
rules, film look, 21
running and gunning, 5, 33–34

S

sales agents, 170–171
sand-and-snow mode (cameras), 57
saturation (contrast)range, 13
scanning
    progressive scanning, 2
    scanning modes (cameras), 11
scenes (master scenes), 103, 107, 115
schedules
    actors, 105
    audio, 38
    cameras, moving, 106
    directors, 103–106
    movies, 24
    producers, 38
scratches. *See* **noise**
screen directions, 117–118
screenwriters, 101
scripts (directors), 101
    breakdown sheets, 104
    master scene scripts, 103
scrolling titles, 162–163
security, distribution, 184

semiautomatic camera controls, 56
sepia tone, 57
sets, controlling, 122–124
setup, directors, 122
Shaner, Pete, 4
sharpness. *See* **resolution**
shiny boards (contrast range), 28, 62
shock mounts (boom microphones), 76
shock video, 143
shooting. *See also* **cameras**
    directors
        blocking, 112
        camera angle, 109
        closeups, 107–108
        cutaways, 111
        establishing shots, 111
        framing, 109
        improvisation, 112–113, 119–121
        inserts, 111
        lenses, 109
        master scenes, 103, 107, 115
        moving cameras, 109–110
        night, 106
        over the shoulder shots, 111
        planning, 106–108
        point of view, 111
        pushing in, 108
        ratio, 119
        shot design, 109–111
        structure, 112–113, 119–121
        terminology, 111
        zooming, 108–109
    film-style, 5–6, 33–34
    formats. *See* formats

future, 198
news-style, 5, 33–34
producers, 33–34, 39–40
test rolls, 39–40
shortie microphones
    overview, 76
    rigging, 81–82
shot design, 109–111
shot lists, 114–115
shot plan drawings, 114
shotgun microphones. *See* **boom microphones**
shutter angle
    DPs, 54–55
    motion blur, 26
    producers, 26
    shutter speed relationship, 54
shutter priority (DPs), 56
shutter speed
    DPs, 54–55, 57
    distribution, 191
    film out, 191
    frame rate relationship, 54
    motion blur, 26
    producers, 26
    shutter angle relationship, 54
silence (audio), 82
Silicon X-dal Reflective Display (SXRD), 195–197
silks (contrast range), 28, 62
singers, 81
singles, 107–108
size, frames (aspect ratio)
    distribution, 190
    film look, 15–16

film out, 190
letterbox format, 15
producers, 31
wide-screen format, 15–16
slating, 124–125
slow motion effects, 164–165
soft light (contrast range), 27–29, 62
software
    After Effects, 163–165
    audio editing, 88
    NLE. *See* NLE
    Red Giant Bullet Suite, 140
Sony CineAlta, 3
Sony HVR-Z1U, 3
sound. *See* **audio**
Sound Hunter Web site, 95
source, light, 60
space effects
    2D, 150–151
    2½D, 151–152
    3D, 153
    bullet time, 153, 164–165
    easing in/out, 154–155
    edge detection, 154
    farings, 154–155
    frames, 154–155
    interpolatimg, 154–155
    keyframes, 154–155
    layers, 152–153
    morphing, 155
    overview, 149–150
    slow motion, 164–165
    time bending, 164–165
    transitions, 154–155
    tweening, 154–155

special effects. *See* effects
speed
    film out, 192
    speed ramping, 144
    tapes, 57
speed ramping, 144
split edits, 142–143
split tracks, 96
sports mode (cameras), 57
spot color (color correction), 161–162
spotlights, 57, 67–68
spotting tables (ADR), 92–93
stacking audio tracks, 90
stage lines (continuity), 116–117
stop downs (contrast range), 13
storyboards, 113–114
strain relief (microphone cables), 80
streamer tracks (ADR), 91
streaming. *See* distribution, Web
structure, shooting, 112–113, 119–121
studios
    distribution, 168–170
    future, 202
    negative pickup deals, 24
subwoofers, 97
support (cameras), 35
Surround Sound, 96–97
Swiss Effects Web site, 188
SXRD (Silicon X-dal Reflective Display), 195–197
Synchro Arts VocALign Project Web site, 92
synchronizing audio timecodes, 85

T

takes
    directors, 124–125
    playing (DPs), 55
talkback circuits (microphones), 81
tapes
    loading, 49
    speed, 57
    transferring to film, 52
target size (film look), 15
tearing
    editing, 138–139
    film out, 192
techniques (DPs), 68–69
telephoto lenses, 14–15
television
    color correction, 159
    distribution, 38–39, 186–187
    future, 202
    movies, 24
    producers, 38–39
temperature (white balance)
    AWB. *See* automatic controls
    contrast range, 13, 27–28, 52, 63–65
temporal displacement (editing), 138
terminology (shooting), 111
test rolls (shooting), 39–40
texture. *See* noise
theaters
    distribution, 168–170
    future, 195–197, 201–202
    retrofitting, 195–197
three-point light (DPs), 58–60
tilting cameras, 109–110

time
    cameras, moving, 106
    effects
        2D, 150–151
        2½D, 151–152
        3D, 153
        bullet time, 153, 164–165
        easing in/out, 154–155
        edge detection, 154
        farings, 154–155
        frames, 154–155
        interpolatimg, 154–155
        keyframes, 154–155
        layers, 152–153
        morphing, 155
        overview, 149–150
        slow motion, 164–165
        time bending, 164–165
        transitions, 154–155
        tweening, 154–155
    music, 73
    time bending
        effects, 164–165
        motion blur, 26
    time dependencies, 118–119
    timecodes
        audio, synchronizing, 85
        directors, 124–125
        DPs, 55
        editing (24p), 136
    timeline window (NLE), 131
time bending
    effects, 164–165
    motion blur, 26

time dependencies, 118–119
timecodes
    audio, synchronizing, 85
    directors, 124–125
    DPs, 55
    editing (24p), 136
timeline window (NLE), 131
titles
    film out, 191
    scrolling, 162–163
tracks
    ADR
        split tracks, 96
        streamer tracks, 91
    audio
        postproduction, 87–90
        stacking, 90
    microphones, 84
trade shows (distribution), 170
transferring
    clips (NLE), 132
    tapes to film, 52
transitions
    cameras (DPs), 57
    editing (NLE), 134–135
    effects, 154–155
    music, 73
    producers, 38
transportation (directors), 122
travel mattes
    color correction, 161
    directors, 126
trimming clips (NLE), 132–133

tripods
    DPs, 49, 54
    producers, 35
troubleshooting
    audio noise, 90
    directors, 127–128
trucks (cameras), 109–110
tweening effects, 154–155
two-pops (ADR), 91
types (microphones), 76

U–V

VCDs distribution, 180
vertically scrolling titles, 162–163
video
    distribution, 175–178
    effects, 157–158
    gain (cameras), 56–57
viewer window (NLE), 131
viewfinders (cameras), 46–47, 51
Vinterburg, Thomas, 10
Vow of Chastity, 10, 25

W

walla sounds (ADR), 92
wardrobe (DPs), 69
waveforms (cameras), 51
Web
    distribution, 180–182
    sites
        AFMA, 170
        American Bar Association, 171
        American Society of Composers, Authors, and Publishers (ASCAP), 94
        Arri, 190
        Atom Films, 179
        Broadcast Music, Inc. (BMI), 94
        Celco, 189
        Cineon, 190
        Deluxe Efilm, 188
        DuArt, 188
        DVD Copy Control Association (DCCA), 184
        DVFilm, 188
        FindLaw, 171
        FotoKem, 188
        Foveon, 198
        Glidecam, 35
        Independent Feature Project, 24
        Library of Congress, 174
        Macrovision, 184
        Matrox, 157
        Motion Picture Association of America (MPAA), 184
        PGA, 24
        Pinnacle Systems, 157
        Sound Hunter, 95
        Swiss Effects, 188
        Synchro Arts VocALign Project, 92
white balance
    AWB. *See* automatic controls
    contrast range, 13, 27–28, 52, 63–65
wide-angle lenses, 14–15
wide-screen format (aspect ratio), 15–16
windows (NLE)
    browser window, 130–131
    canvas window, 132
    timeline window, 131
    viewer window, 131

wipes (producers), 38
wireless microphones, 83–84

X–Z
XL1, 3
zebra stripes, cameras, 49–50
zooming
    DPs, 53–54
        shooting, 108–109

THOMSON ™
COURSE TECHNOLOGY

Professional ■ Trade ■ Reference

Write, direct, produce, shoot, edit, distribute, tour with, and sell your own no-budget DIGITAL movie!

"Read this excellent book and learn how to produce profitable independent films whilst sticking your finger in the eyes of the devil-worshipping media conglomerates who are sucking us dry of our spiritual and economic capital."
—LLOYD KAUFMAN, President of Troma Entertainment, and creator of *The Toxic Avenger*.

Write,
Finance,
Direct,
Produce,
Shoot,
Edit,
Distribute,
Tour With,
and Sell
Your Own
No-Budget
DIGITAL
Movie

MUSKA/LIPMAN Publishing

$30 FILM SCHOOL
Michael W. Dean

We're entering a new era. Mini-DV filmmaking is the new folk, the new punk rock, the new medium where anyone can tell his story. *$30 Film School* is an alternative to spending four years and a hundred thousand dollars to learn the trade. It is influenced by punk rock's Do-It-Yourself spirit of just learning the basics and then jumping up on a stage and making a point, and by the American work ethic back when it was pure, before it became all about corporations crushing the little guy. Throw in the hacker idea that information wants to be free (or at least very cheap) and you've got our deal. Inside you'll find many interviews from insightful independent filmmakers and artists, as well as a host of practical advice, knowledge, and resources.

$30 Film School
ISBN: 1-59200-067-3 ■ $30.00

THOMSON
COURSE TECHNOLOGY
Professional ■ Trade ■ Reference

Call 1.800.354.9706 to order
Order online at www.courseptr.com

Bring your ideas to life!

THOMSON COURSE TECHNOLOGY
Professional ■ Trade ■ Reference

Today's animation audience expects more than a nice picture to believe in a character. Now you can develop the skills and techniques you need to create characters that will draw your audience into the world you've created.

Maya 6 Revealed
ISBN: 1-59200-365-6 ■ $24.99

Get ready to explore all that Maya 6 has to offer! Giving you a firm foundation, *Maya® 6 Revealed* allows you to master concepts on both a technical and artistic level. Begin by examining the concept behind each task—the goal and the necessary features that are involved. Then go in-depth with the objective of your task as you study examples and learn the steps necessary to complete it. Working your way through comprehensive, step-by-step lessons, you'll develop the confidence you need to create amazing graphics using Maya 6.

Thomson Course Technology is proud to be the official publisher for Softimage Co.

Experience XSI 4
ISBN: 1-59200-210-2 ■ $49.99

Take an exclusive look into how the design process of characters for motion pictures has changed through the application of XSI. Develop the skills you need to create a detailed animated character that can then be composited into a live action scene using the XSI compositor. Author Aaron Sims includes his own incredible characters to demonstrate the techniques applied in their creation and co-author Michael Isner of Softimage discusses the groundbreaking technology and powerful tool set that XSI delivers.

LightWave 3D 8 Revealed
ISBN: 1-59200-582-9 ■ $24.99

Digital 3D Design
ISBN: 1-59200-391-5 ■ $24.99

Hollywood 2D Digital Animation:
The New Flash Production Revolution
ISBN: 1-59200-170-X ■ $39.99

Adobe Photoshop for VFX Artists
ISBN: 1-59200-487-3 ■ $39.99

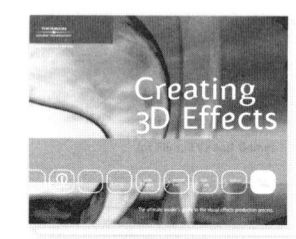

Creating 3D Effects for Film, TV, and Games
ISBN: 1-59200-589-6 ■ $49.99

Call 1.800.354.9706 to order
Order online at www.courseptr.com

THOMSON COURSE TECHNOLOGY

Professional ■ Trade ■ Reference

STEP INTO THE 3D WORLD OF ANIMATION WITH THE *INSPIRED* SERIES!

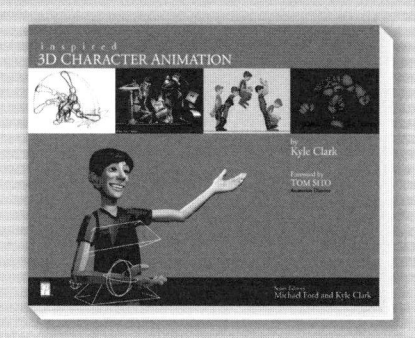

Inspired 3D Character Animation
1-931841-48-9

Inspired 3D Character Setup
1-931841-51-9

Inspired 3D Lighting and Compositing
1-931841-49-7

Inspired 3D Modeling and Texture Mapping
1-931841-50-0

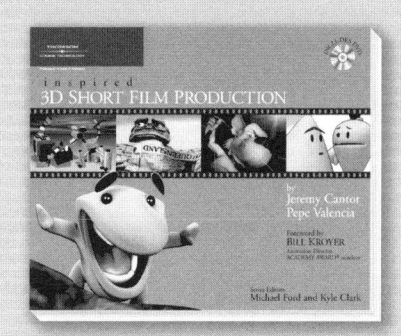

Inspired 3D Short Film Production
1-59200-117-3

Filled with tips, tricks, and techniques compiled by the animators of blockbuster films at Hollywood's biggest studios, these four-color books are a must-have for anyone interested in character creation.

Series Editor Kyle Clark is a lead animator at Microsoft's Digital Anvil Studios. His film credits include *Star Wars Episode I—The Phantom Menace*, *Sleepy Hollow*, *Deep Blue Sea*, *The Adventures of Rocky and Bullwinkle*, *Harry Potter and the Sorcerer's Stone*, and *Brute Force* video game for the Xbox.

Series Editor Michael Ford is a senior technical animator at Sony Pictures Imageworks. He is a certified Level 2 Softimage instructor whose film credits include *Stuart Little*, *Stuart Little 2*, *The Perfect Storm*, *The Mummy*, *Godzilla*, *Species II*, *Mortal Kombat II*, and *The Faculty*.

THOMSON COURSE TECHNOLOGY
Professional ■ Trade ■ Reference

Call 1.800.354.9706 to order
Order online at www.courseptr.com

License Agreement/Notice of Limited Warranty

By opening the sealed disc container in this book, you agree to the following terms and conditions. If, upon reading the following license agreement and notice of limited warranty, you cannot agree to the terms and conditions set forth, return the unused book with unopened disc to the place where you purchased it for a refund.

License:
The enclosed software is copyrighted by the copyright holder(s) indicated on the software disc. You are licensed to copy the software onto a single computer for use by a single user and to a backup disc. You may not reproduce, make copies, or distribute copies or rent or lease the software in whole or in part, except with written permission of the copyright holder(s). You may transfer the enclosed disc only together with this license, and only if you destroy all other copies of the software and the transferee agrees to the terms of the license. You may not decompile, reverse assemble, or reverse engineer the software.

Notice of Limited Warranty:
THE ENCLOSED DISC IS WARRANTED BY THOMSON COURSE TECHNOLOGY PTR TO BE FREE OF PHYSICAL DEFECTS IN MATERIALS AND WORKMANSHIP FOR A PERIOD OF SIXTY (60) DAYS FROM END USER'S PURCHASE OF THE BOOK/DISC COMBINATION. DURING THE SIXTY-DAY TERM OF THE LIMITED WARRANTY, THOMSON COURSE TECHNOLOGY PTR WILL PROVIDE A REPLACEMENT DISC UPON THE RETURN OF A DEFECTIVE DISC.

Limited Liability:
THE SOLE REMEDY FOR BREACH OF THIS LIMITED WARRANTY SHALL CONSIST ENTIRELY OF REPLACEMENT OF THE DEFECTIVE DISC. IN NO EVENT SHALL THOMSON COURSE TECHNOLOGY PTR OR THE AUTHOR BE LIABLE FOR ANY OTHER DAMAGES, INCLUDING LOSS OR CORRUPTION OF DATA, CHANGES IN THE FUNCTIONAL CHARACTERISTICS OF THE HARDWARE OR OPERATING SYSTEM, DELETERIOUS INTERACTION WITH OTHER SOFTWARE, OR ANY OTHER SPECIAL, INCIDENTAL, OR CONSEQUENTIAL DAMAGES THAT MAY ARISE, EVEN IF THOMSON COURSE TECHNOLOGY PTR AND/OR THE AUTHOR HAS PREVIOUSLY BEEN NOTIFIED THAT THE POSSIBILITY OF SUCH DAMAGES EXISTS.

Disclaimer of Warranties:
THOMSON COURSE TECHNOLOGY PTR and the author specifically disclaim any and all other warranties, either express or implied, including warranties of merchantability, suitability to a particular task or purpose, or freedom from errors. Some states do not allow for EXCLUSION of implied warranties or limitation of incidental or consequential damages, so these limitations mIGHT not apply to you.

Other:
This Agreement is governed by the laws of the State of Massachusetts without regard to choice of law principles. The United Convention of Contracts for the International Sale of Goods is specifically disclaimed. This Agreement constitutes the entire agreement between you and Thomson Course Technology PTR regarding use of the software.